What's Left to Eat?

What's Left to Eat?

Sue Gebo, M.P.H., R.D.
Consulting Nutritionist

McGraw-Hill, Inc.

New York St. Louis San Francisco Auckland Bogotá
Caracas Lisbon London Madrid Mexico
Milan Montreal New Delhi Paris San Juan São Paulo
Singapore Sydney Tokyo Toronto

Library of Congress Cataloging-in-Publication Data

Gebo, Sue
    What's left to eat? / Sue Gebo.
        p.   cm.
    Includes bibliographical references and index.
    ISBN 0-07-023476-0 : — ISBN 0-07-023534-1 (pbk.)
    1. Food 2. Diet. 3. Nutrition. I. Title.
TX353.G35 1992   91-31308
641.3—dc20

1 2 3 4 5 6 7 8 9 0 DOC/DOC 9 6 5 4 3 2 1

ISBN   0-07-023476-0 {HC}
ISBN   0-07-023534-1 {PBK}

The sponsoring editor for this book was Sybil Parker, the editing supervisor was Kimberly A. Goff, the designer was Sue Maksuta, and the production supervisor was Pamela A. Pelton. This book was set in Palatino by McGraw-Hill's Professional Book Group composition unit.

Printed and bound by R. R. Donnelley & Sons.

Illustrations by Cynthia Y. Cooper.

To my parents—
and to the late Joe Lynch,
whose innocent question inspired
this book.

Contents

Part IV. Safe and Healthy Menus and Recipes   197

Chapter 1. Magnificent Menus

Chapter 2. Rave-Review Recipes

Part V. The Resource Corner

Preface

At one of my recent lectures, I waxed eloquent on th topic of sodium and high blood pressure. During the lecture, gasps could be heard throughout the audience when the sodium contents of various common foods were revealed. After the presentation, an elderly gentleman came up to chat with me. He related his story of a recent surgical operation for an aneurysm, and his problems with high blood pressure. Finally, in genuine perplexity, he asked, "What's left to eat?"

Whether we're healthy or ill, young or old, that question hits a familiar chord. "What can I eat that's safe, pesticide-free, and guaranteed not to cause or aggravate high blood pressure, heart disease, or cancer? What can I eat to keep my cholesterol down, my prostate healthy, my breasts cancer-free, and still enjoy eating?" The answer, happily, is *not* "Nothing!"

In the eighties, Alar, aflatoxin, and oat bran made their public debut on TV news. Outbreaks of *Listeria,* a milk-borne bacterial infection, *Salmonella,* and other food-borne illnesses made headlines. Our president developed colon cancer, and bran cereals became linked with cancer prevention. Fat and cholesterol achieved notoriety, and food labels began to reflect the cholesterol-phobia which had grabbed the public consciousness.

Yet, heart disease and cancer still claim over one million US lives annually, and the fear of food-induced illnesses remains high. What's left to eat?

The public is screaming for answers.

Here are the answers.

Sue Gebo, M.P.H., R.D.

Advice to the Reader

We fear things in proportion to our ignorance of them.
Titus Livius, 1st century A.D.

The purpose of this book is to educate you about food-related risks. Some of these risks may be familiar to you; some will be new. All of them are part of our world, as inescapable as breathing. As a consumer, you have the right to know about risks, and you have the opportunity to decide which ones you want to control.

As the book progresses, you may feel alarmed, frustrated, or confused. In the interest of being complete, the book may at times seem overwhelming. But keep reading. In each chapter you will find rays of sunshine, guidance through the fearsome facts presented. And, if you stay the course, the skies will clear in Parts III and IV, where specific action steps are presented in greater detail.

How to Read This Book

Begin at the beginning...and go on till you come to the end...
Lewis Carroll,
Alice's Adventures in Wonderland, 1865

This volume is laid out so that each chapter builds upon previous chapters, making it difficult to really "get" the meaning of a chapter or topic if snatched out of context. While each chapter covers a distinct topic and may appear to be self-contained, you'd best resist the urge to flip to the "juicy" parts. The book is most effective if the chapters are read sequentially, following the natural progression of the central themes.

Acknowledgments

Many thanks to:

Bruce Riefe for planting the seeds of this project; Sybil Parker for her competence, insight, good nature, and unswerving fortitude in ushering it through its many phases; Anita Owen and Reva Frankle for their respective "thumbs-up" reviews of my initial proposal; Cindi Cooper for her brilliant art work and sisterly support; Nancy Crevier for her creative cuisine; the American Heart Association for their gracious permission to include four of their innovative recipes; Martha Mapes and Susan Male Smith for their respective thoughtful and thorough reviews of the manuscript; Kim Goff, Sue Maksuta, Rachel Handler, and others at McGraw-Hill for their critical roles in shaping and promoting this project; Joe Vasile, my dear husband, for his loving patience and support while I was lost to the manuscript; Ernie Gebo, my loving father, for being my best cheerleader; and my family, friends, and colleagues, whose support means so much.

What's Left to Eat?

PART I

FOOD SAFETY
DANGER
OR
DRAMA

*... a man seldom thinks with more earnestness of
anything than he does his dinner.*   MARK TWAIN

Never before have we Americans been so preoccupied with what
we're putting into our mouths. A recent survey shows that a
whopping 83 percent of American adults are concerned about
the health effects of what they eat.[1]

And no wonder! Nearly weekly, some food problem or other
splashes across the front page or stuns us from the news.
Major media blitzes on issues like Alar underscore our
concerns. As for those well-publicized food product recalls for
bacterial contamination—aren't they further testimony to the
failings of the food industry and the government?

Since Ralph Nader's consciousness-raising report on food
protection in 1970,[2] a generation has emerged, harboring a
profound distrust for the food industry—and the government.
Ralph Nader asserts in his 1970 report: "Food is the most
intimate consumer product."[2] We Americans are more than a
little concerned about the havoc we perceive being wrought
with this "most intimate consumer product."

So—*is* anything safe to eat?

Let's find out.

References

1. The Gallup Organization, Inc., *Gallup Survey of Public Opinion
   Regarding Diet and Health,* The Gallup Organization, Princeton, New
   Jersey, 1990.

2. Turner, James S., *The Chemical Feast—The Ralph Nader Study Group
   Report on Food Protection and the Food and Drug Administration,*
   Grossman Publishers, New York, 1970.

CHAPTER 1

PESTICIDES

He who considers thoroughly each step spends most of life on one foot.

Chinese Proverb

Fear is a poor policy-maker.

JACK PARNELL, DEPUTY SECRETARY,
U.S. DEPARTMENT OF AGRICULTURE.[1]

Awash on a sea of suspicion that we're enduring daily assaults by life-threatening pesticide residues, many Americans have lost a sense of perspective. At times, profound concern for ourselves and our children has gotten a choke-hold on our emotions—and we've ceased to think rationally. We've been known to boycott apples, flush apple juice down the drain, and snub Chilean produce, thereby self-righteously crippling entire economies.

Given the unhappy state of food supplies in other parts of the world, we Americans must be a bizarre sight to less-fortunate nations. In the face of abundant, available food, we prefer to let piles of produce rot, or forgo other "poisoned" foods of the moment, rather than challenge each new media tidbit or famous face proclaiming pesticide-induced doom.

Recent consumer concern about pesticides climbed to an all-time high in 1989 when 82 percent of those surveyed by the Food Marketing Institute rated pesticide residues as a *serious hazard*.[2] By 1990, the percentage had dropped slightly, to 80 percent.[2]

Americans enjoy nearly limitless choices. If we demand a product, and the market is large enough, suppliers appear. Hence, the ranks of "organic" food producers have swelled. If there is strong enough public sentiment, there are legislators to trot out laws and regulations that turn our wishes into the new rules of the game. Witness California's "Big Green," a sweeping initiative that, if passed (voted down November 7, 1990), would have phased out most pesticides in California.

Yet, there is danger in a system so easily molded by public outcry.

Most disturbing is the simple truth that, when public outrage about pesticide use is raised, *facts* are often in short supply. Those who formulate laws and initiatives (like California's Proposition 65, to be discussed later) are generally *not* experts in toxicology, food science, nutrition, or agriculture. They often know little more than the average consumer about true human risk from pesticides. The resulting legislation or referenda, if passed, *can* place needlessly impossible limits on those who grow our food—to the ultimate detriment of us all.

For most Americans, assessing one's *own* risk from chemical residues in food is an impossible task. Most of us simply do not have the resources, or the skills, to wade through the reams of relevant information, sort out the fact from the fiction, and formulate a useful, practical approach. As a result, many of us randomly avoid products, or forsake regular markets in favor of organic food suppliers, without really knowing why.

What follows is a rational, carefully considered review. We'll explore the realm of substances used by food growers to keep fungi, weeds, and insects at bay and to regulate growth. We'll examine some recent figures on the extent of pesticide residues in our food. And we'll see what's being done to protect our food—and us—from toxic chemicals.

Pesticides—A History

Pesticides are far from new. Hundreds of years ago, farmers employed such compounds as arsenic, lead, and copper sulfate to control insects. Until the late nineteenth century, no one questioned their use. Then, in 1891, the New York City Health Department issued an order that all grapes coated with a greenish powder be taken off market shelves.[3] Testing had shown that the greenish powder was copper sulfate mixed to potentially toxic proportions.

When news of this crisis spread, eastern cities threatened a ban on the sale of grapes. In a bold move to avoid bankruptcy, grape growers pleaded with the U.S. Department of Agriculture (USDA) for help. The USDA responded with a public statement attesting to the safety of the residue, criticizing the attention-grabbing *New York Times* article.

What followed were five decades of dancing around the issue, with some farmers abandoning pesticides, some farmers defending their use, and the USDA pressuring states to pass laws that would make it illegal *not* to use insecticides (a measure designed to prevent unsprayed fields from infesting neighboring farms).[4]

By the early 1900s, evidence had accumulated that fruit and vegetable pesticide residues were harming, even killing, consumers. Following an outpouring of heart-rending pleas for pesticide reform published in magazines, books, and newspapers, in 1947 the U.S. government passed its first law to regulate pesticide use.[4]

At the time of this new law's inception, DDT had taken over as the miracle pesticide, wiping out more insects and working more quickly than arsenic, copper sulfate, and other old standbys. On the heels of DDT came a whole new arsenal of more powerful pesticides. Farmers expanded their farms and began to specialize in one or two crops, fine-tuning their pesticide use to specific crop pests.[4]

Then came the 1960s. The 1962 publication of *Silent Spring*[5] cast a long shadow on the pesticide boom. Rachel Carson, the biologist who authored the book, painted a stark picture of a future world gutted by pesticides. She also presented evidence of the buildup of DDT and other pesticides in the food chain, even tainting breast milk. (The title *Silent Spring* referred to the image of a spring without birds, extinct because of the effects of pesticides.)

Silent Spring inspired and crystallized concern among scientists about pesticide safety. By 1972, DDT was banned, and the U.S. government had toughened its pesticide regulations. Nevertheless, DDT used years ago is still detected in foods; it has remained in the environment due to its lengthy breakdown process.[4]

Despite new regulations and the banning of DDT, pesticide use continued to grow until its peak in 1982. That year marked nearly 40 years of synthetic pesticide use, and that same period had seen a *doubling* of agricultural production. There's no question—pesticides helped make these mammoth farming endeavors possible.

The number of pounds of pesticides used annually has continued to drop since 1982, as a growing number of farmers have learned that some of their previously routine applications were unnecessary.[4] We'll explore this trend later in this chapter.

Alar—A Portrait

Until the Alar crisis, recent public concern about pesticides had been confined largely to health enthusiasts who frequented natural food stores. But then sounded the alarm.

"Our nation's children are being harmed by the very fruits and vegetables we tell them will make them grow up healthy and strong."[6] So began the pivotal 1989 report from the Natural Resources Defense Council (NRDC). The report fixed particular focus on the pesticide daminozide, produced by Uniroyal Chemical under the trade name Alar. Alar, used on apples, was portrayed as a killer with particular fondness for preschoolers who, in the first six years of life, were estimated to consume enough Alar to result in one death per 4200 preschoolers exposed.[6]

A day before the official publication date of the NRDC report, the TV program *60 Minutes* fanned the flames by featuring the report and its focus on Alar. Apples, the major crop on which Alar was used, suddenly became linked in the public consciousness to cancer in children.

Alar, used as a growth regulator, prevented apples from falling off the tree prematurely and helped retain apple crispness between harvest and consumer purchase. Because of the NRDC report, and the media attention it inspired, Uniroyal took Alar off the market.

Should they have done so? Did Alar really present a threat to young children?

That depends on whom you believe. The NRDC scientists, using reports generated by the Environmental Protection Agency (EPA) and other government agencies, came to one set of conclusions, the upshot of which placed children at higher risk than adults due to their proportionally greater consumption of apple products (apple juice, applesauce, fresh apples).

The EPA, in response to the NRDC's charges, issued a joint statement with the Food and Drug Administration (FDA) and the USDA, which revealed that data used by the NRDC's scientists had been rejected as unreliable by an independent scientific advisory board in 1985.[7] The statement also reassured consumers that apples were safe and that extensive testing had shown minimal risk to all consumers from Alar.

Uniroyal, in its own defense, responded with a mass mailing to professional nutritionists which cited the research used to confirm that Alar was neither carcinogenic (cancer-causing) nor mutagenic (capable of inducing genetic damage).[8] This research suggested that a 25-pound child would have to drink 19,000 quarts of apple juice per day for life to get the exposure level which caused increased blood vessel tumors in mice.[8]

The chemical with alleged cancer-causing properties was actually not Alar, but a breakdown product of Alar called UDMH (*unsym-dimethylhydrazine*). At exceedingly high levels, UDMH caused the above-mentioned blood vessel tumors in mice. But research had previously shown that UDMH was only formed when Alar-treated apples were exposed to heat, such as in the making of apple juice and applesauce. So, *fresh* apples were *never* a threat, and estimates suggested that only between 10 and 20 percent of all apples were treated with Alar, making the actual potential exposure from apple juice and applesauce much lower than the NRDC had alleged. And where is the child who drinks 19,000 quarts of apple juice a day?

Despite the efforts of scientists to quell the fury, public sentiment, fueled by media fanfare, forced the demise of Alar. What will happen the next time?

Toxicity versus Hazard

The larger issue in these matters is consumer understanding—or mis-understanding—of what actually constitutes a threat to health. Stars like Meryl Streep appeal to our fears about food safety but are short on science. So, what's the truth?

First of all, there's no question that heavy pesticide use poses a threat to the environment, independent of its effects on the food we eat. The EPA places concerns about the environmental effects of pesticides high on its list of environmental problems.[9] Based on that alone, it makes sense for the government to impose stricter controls on pesticide use. And more restrictive regulatory programs are underway. No one wants a "silent spring."

But when you hear or see a new media piece bashing a particular food or pesticide, what do you do? How do you decide?

It all boils down to an understanding of the difference between *toxicity* and *hazard*.

Toxicity is defined as the capability of a substance to harm living organisms. In its broadest sense, toxicity can apply to nearly everything. For example, a very high dose of vitamin C is *toxic*. But vitamin C is necessary for health, so a certain intake of vitamin C is needed. Should you stop eating food containing vitamin C because too much vitamin C is harmful?

Water is essential for life, but, under certain conditions, too much water produces water intoxication, a form of toxicity. Should you stop drinking water?

Similarly, a certain level of a pesticide prevents a fungus from destroying a plant. The pesticide is toxic to the fungus at a certain level, and it's probably toxic to humans at an extremely high level. But it's not toxic to humans at the level needed to control the fungus. Should you stop eating the vegetable or fruit from the plant because of the pesticide?

What do *you* think?

Dealing with Risk

Humans forever walk the line between safety and unsafety. Crossing the street, boarding an airplane, driving a car, riding a motorcycle, having sex—everything presents some level of risk. Yet, we find ways of rationalizing these risks. Somehow, the risk of pesticide residues seems to rouse emotions rather than rationalizations.

The fantasy of a risk-free world is just that—a fantasy. It's hard for those of us who think in absolutes to accept the reality of a risk-ridden world, a world in which, theoretically at least, one can never be completely "safe."

But just as we all accept risks when we travel in a car, board an airplane, engage in sex, or ride a motorcycle, we must come to terms with the risks inherent in our food. Many of these risks are infinitesimally small—such as the risk of cancer from consuming apple juice made with Alar-sprayed apples. But some risks are considerable, such as that of food poisoning from eating meat thawed at room temperature.

When you learn of nonfood risks, you make decisions: "I won't fly often," or "I'll use protection when I have sex," or "The emotional/psychological benefits of motorcycling outweigh the risks, so I'll keep riding (with a helmet)." When food-related risks are discovered, we're challenged to make other decisions: How often will I eat eggs (Salmonella and cholesterol risks)? Will I eat Caesar salad (raw eggs—risk of Salmonella)? Will I thaw meat on the counter (food poisoning)? Will I forgo fruits and vegetables (pesticide residues)?

Making decisions is your right. Seeking accurate information on which to base those decisions is your responsibility. Once you have information, you have choices: Is this a risk I'm willing to take? Do the benefits outweigh the foreseeable risks? Am I willing to change my behavior if the risks outweigh the benefits? How much am I willing to change?

Ultimately, you decide. If you choose to live dangerously, you have the right to ignore all risks. If you choose to be a "purist," you might aim to avoid *all* controllable risks, no matter how small. If you're like most people, you'll probably pick and choose your "causes," avoiding some risks, rationalizing others, and ignoring the rest. But all good decision-making starts with accurate information.

One helpful notion as we wade through the murky waters around this issue is the term *hazard*. Hazard is the ability of a chemical to produce injury under the conditions of its use.[10] For example, at the levels used, a fungicide (the type of pesticide used to fight fungus) is *hazardous* to a fungus that's attacking a plant, but it's not hazardous to humans. At a much higher level, or, perhaps, if combined with some other chemical at high enough levels, it *might* present a hazard to humans.

The term *hazard* is useful when we consider the arguments for continuing to drink water, despite the risk of water intoxication, or to eat vitamin C–containing foods, despite the threat of vitamin C toxicity. It is equally helpful when we consider arguments regarding pesticides.

The Risks

Pesticide risks fall into two categories: immediate and long term.

The primary immediate health risks linked with pesticide use are for people exposed to large quantities of these substances—farmers and agricultural workers.[11] Diseases such as non–Hodgkins lymphoma (a form of cancer); generalized poisoning involving the liver, kidneys, lungs, and/or intestinal tract; and seizure disorders have occurred with concentrated exposure to various pesticides.[11]

Aside from these human risks, the most concerning pesticide risks are environmental.

Long-term pesticide risks befall wildlife, particularly honeybees, wild bees, predatory birds (e.g., the eagle), and a wide variety of endangered plant and animal species.[11] Honeybees and wild bees are extremely valuable for their pollinating activities on billions of dollars worth of crops.[11] Estimates of economic losses due to honeybee elimination resulting from pesticides have climbed to at least $135 million.[11] Another compelling example of the effects of pesticides on wildlife is the bald eagle, whose historic decline in the 1960s and 1970s was reversed after the cancellation of a group of pesticides called chlorinated hydrocarbons.[11]

More critical long-term effects of pesticides involve more serious disruption of the ecosystem, that fragile balance of natural forces designed to ensure the earth's survival. Broad-spectrum insecticides wipe out beneficial insect populations along with the villainous ones, leading to population explosions of previously inoffensive species that may then work devastating damage.[11] Herbicides, when used generously, eliminate grass and weeds that had retained topsoil; their loss leads to soil erosion.[11]

One of the more frightening effects of pesticide use is the evolution of strains of pests that are resistant to even the most powerful pesticides.[11] By 1986, over 440 species of insects and mites and more than 70 species of fungus had been shown to be resistant to some of the pesticides designed to control them.[11] This problem is expected to worsen, leading to heavier doses and more frequent applications of pesticides, as well as the use of stronger, potentially more hazardous chemicals.[11]

Additionally, groundwater contamination by pesticides and other agricultural chemicals, including organic fertilizers such as manure, continues to be a public health concern.[11]

The Common Chemicals

Pesticides currently see wide use in treating crops for human and animal consumption. Pesticides are also used in treating pastureland for livestock, and they are applied to harvested fruits and vegetables to protect them from insects and fungi.[12] Weeds, insects, fungi, bacteria, and rodents are the targets of these chemicals. Additionally, chemicals used to regulate growth and to simplify harvesting are classified as pesticides. Here's a glossary of terms:

Pesticide: the broad term for chemicals used to control pests, to regulate plant growth, or to simplify harvest.

Herbicide: pesticide used to control weeds.

Insecticide: pesticide used to control insects.

Fungicide: pesticide used to control fungi, sometimes applied to waxes used to coat fruits and vegetables.

Nematicide: pesticide used to control nematodes (roundworms).

Rodenticide: pesticide used to control rodents.

Dessicant: substance used to simplify harvest.

Approximately 289 pesticides are currently used on food crops grown in the U.S.[12] Some of these have been used for several decades.

In 1985, the EPA identified 53 potentially oncogenic (tumor-causing) pesticides. This number represents 18 percent of all pesticides used on foods.[12] These 53 pesticides, and the crops on which they are used, are listed in Table 1. Some of these pesticides, most notably daminozide (Alar), have been removed from the market since the release of this list. Additional deletions and additions will continue to occur as the EPA receives and analyzes new research data.

It jars most consumers to contemplate this list. How could our food carry so many ominous-sounding substances? How can we possibly feel safe eating foods "tainted" with residues from so many chemicals?

Finding the "Hot Spots"

A group of pesticides that have generated particular consumer concern have been dubbed EBDCs. This group includes the chemicals amobam, mancozeb, maneb, metiram, nabam, and zineb. Commonly used on fruits and vegetables, these fungicides were spotlighted in 1989 and 1990 when their use on tomatoes became a media topic. Because tomatoes are concentrated into processed products, such as tomato paste and tomato sauce, concern arose regarding their accompanying concentration of EBDCs. Additionally, as with Alar, EBDCs exposed to heat, as in food processing, produce a cancer-causing metabolite called ETU.

TABLE 1. Pesticides with Potential Tumor-Causing Ability

Chemical name (common or trade name)	Crops on which used
Acephate (Orthene)	Citrus
Acifluorfen (Blazer)	Soybeans
Alachlor (Lasso)	Corn, soybeans
Amitraz (Baam)	Cattle
Arsenic acid	Cotton
Asulam	Sugar cane
Azinphos-methyl (Guthion)	Peaches, apples, pears, quince
Benomyl (Benlate)	Citrus, rice, soybeans, and peaches, cherries, plums, apricots (stone fruits)
Calcium arsenate	Stone fruits
Captafol (Difolatan)	Apples, cherries, tomatoes
Captan	Almonds, apples, peaches, seeds
Chlordimeform (Galecron)	Cotton
Chlorobenzilate	Citrus
Chlorithalonil (Bravo)	Fruits, peanuts, vegetables
Copper arsenate	Vegetables
Cypermethrin (Ammo, Cymbush)	Cotton
Cyromazine (Larvadex)	Poultry
Daminozide (Alar)	Apples, peanuts
Diallate	Sugar beets
Diclofop methyl (Hoelon)	Soybeans
Dicofol (Kelthane)	Citrus, cotton
Ethalfluralin (Sonalan)	Soybeans
Ethylene oxide	Spices, walnuts
Folpet	Cherries, fruits, vegetables
Fosetyl Al (Aliette)	Pineapples
Glyphosate (Roundup)	Hays, orchard crops
Lead arsenate	Apples, orchard crops
Lindane	Avocados, pecans
Linuron (Lorox)	Soybeans
Maleic hydrazide	Onions, potatoes

TABLE 1. (*Continued*)

Chemical name (common or trade name)	Crops on which used
Mancozeb (Dithane M-45)	Fruits, small grains,* vegetables
Maneb	Fruits, small grains
Methanearsonic acid	Cotton
Methomyl (Lannate)	Citrus, cotton, vegetables
Metiram	Fruits, small grains,* vegetables
Metolachlor (Dual)	Corn, soybeans
0-Phenylphenol	Citrus, orchard crops
Oryzalin (Surflan)	Soybeans, vineyards
Oadiazon (Ronstar)	Rice
Paraquat (Gramoxone)	Rice, soybeans
Parathion	Citrus, cotton
PCNB	Cotton, peanuts, vegetables
Permethrin (Ambush, Pounce)	Vegetables
Pronamide (Kerb)	Lettuce
Sodium arsenate	Pears
Sodium arsenite	Grapes
Terbutryn	Barley, wheat
Tetrachlorvinphos	Cattle, poultry
Thiodicarb (Larvin)	Cotton, soybeans
Thiophanate-methyl	Fruits, nuts, vegetables
Toxaphene	Cattle
Trifluralin (Treflan)	Soybeans
Zineb	Fruits, small grains,* vegetables

*Small grains: grains with small kernels (wheat, barley, oats, rice, rye).
SOURCE: Adapted from Ref. 11, pp. 52, 53.

ETU also causes thyroid disorders and birth defects, as well as tumors, in lab animals.[13]

In 1989, the EPA proposed a ban on certain uses of EBDCs, including their use on tomatoes, potatoes, bananas, and over 40 other crops. This ban was to remain in force until the EPA completed its testing of EBDCs to determine whether *all* uses of EBDCs should be banned.

The attention focused on EBDCs underscores an unfortunate fact of farm technology: fungicides are more toxic than insecticides and herbicides. In 1985, fungicides accounted for a mere 7 percent of all U.S. pesticide sales but a whopping 60 percent of all estimated tumor-causing risk from pesticides.[12] Further, fully 90 percent of all agricultural fungicides in use cause tumors in lab animals.[12] Because of these facts, and because of the contribution that fungicides make to agricultural production, fungicides represent a "special case" to regulators.

Fungicides seem to be indispensable for the growth of certain crops in humid regions, particularly the southeast and east.[12] Newer fungicides have been developed that are less toxic and more potent to fungi. They work by permeating the plant, not staying on the surface, which, unfortunately, means they can't be washed off. But because they are less toxic to lab animals than the older fungicides, they may present fewer risks to humans.

A comforting fact as we contemplate pesticide residues on tomatoes: California produces roughly two-thirds of all tomatoes consumed in the U.S. yet, because of its low humidity, uses less than 10 percent (by weight) of all oncogenic tomato fungicides used annually in the U.S.[12]

How Much Is Too Much?
Pesticide Residues

The National Research Council (NRC) of the National Academy of Sciences, a highly regarded private, nonprofit research body that advises policy makers, produced a well-researched and thought-provoking report in 1987 called *Regulating Pesticides in Food*.[12] The report raised concerns about regulatory inconsistency in pesticide control and addressed some frightening implications of the "one-by-one" approach to pesticide reform.[12]

One pivotal concept that this report underscored was the myriad interpretations, represented by conflicting regulations, of the Delaney Clause. This clause, cursed by many of those charged with enforcing it, prohibits the use of food additives that have been found to cause cancer in man or animal *in any amount*. We'll address this issue in more detail in Part I, Chap. 2, *Food Additives*, but it is a critical issue for agricultural producers as well.

The NRC report centers on the disparity between two critical sections of the Food, Drug, and Cosmetic Act that deal with pesticide residues. One section, Section 408, acknowledges the double-edged sword of pesticide use, using a risk–benefit balancing approach that allows tumor-causing pesticides to be used on fresh foods if the residues amount to what is considered *negligible risk*. Negligible risk is judged by conservatively-set maximum levels called *tolerances*, which are set by EPA.

Another section of the Food, Drug, and Cosmetic Act, Section 409, deals with processed foods. It invokes the Delaney Clause, disallowing *any* residues of tumor-causing (oncogenic) pesticides in processed foods, even at levels considered to pose negligible risk. Because of this, it sets no tolerances for any oncogenic pesticide in processed foods.[11] This leaves both farmers and regulators in a quandary.

Under these conflicting sections of the law, if a farmer properly uses an oncogenic pesticide allowed on fresh foods, e.g., tomatoes, those tomatoes cannot be sold to a tomato paste manufacturer because they would end up in a processed food. But the farmer can sell those tomatoes to a store, which will sell them as fresh tomatoes to consumers. Does this make sense? Is the risk really large enough to prohibit their use by manufacturers in tomato paste, or sauce, or ketchup?

A third section, Section 402, of the Food, Drug, and Cosmetic Act adds to the confusion. Called the "flow-through" provision, this section allows the Section 408 pesticide tolerances, representing negligible risk, in fresh foods to be used for the same residues in processed foods. This violates the Delaney Clause, but still protects consumers by ensuring negligible risk in processed foods.

Is this the best approach?

In essence, the zero-risk approach mandated by the Delaney Clause seemed quite realistic in the early days of toxicology, when traces of potentially harmful substances could only be detected in parts per thousand or parts per million. Today, the sensitivity of research methods has so improved that substances can be detected in parts per *trillion*— and that raises questions. What does the presence of Alar at two parts per trillion mean when you bite into an apple? The risk from the cyanide-containing apple seeds, if eaten, far outweighs any potential risk from such meager traces of a pesticide.

Today's society is not a risk-free environment. No society ever has been. But today we are more acutely aware of risks—at least certain ones. For some, this awareness has translated into fanaticism. For others, it has led to movement toward better consumer education.

Proposition 65

One example of the extreme of consumer awareness is Proposition 65, a law passed in California in 1986. This law, officially called the Safe

Drinking Water and Toxic Enforcement Act of 1986, requires the yearly revision and publication of a list of all chemicals known to cause cancer or reproductive toxicity. It also prohibits the release of any of these chemicals into water or onto land, where they can reasonably be expected to end up in drinking water.[14]

Under this law, consumers must be warned by mailing, labeling, or other notice *before* they are exposed to any chemicals known to cause cancer or reproductive toxicity.

The July 1990 list of these chemicals included nearly 500 substances, including such consumer surprises as vitamin A (listed as retinol and retinyl esters), alcoholic beverages, hydrazine (a component of mushrooms as well as some pesticides), and aspirin.[15]

The regulatory nightmare presented by this law is awesome. If scrupulously followed, warning signs must be posted wherever produce is sold, caution labels must appear on nearly every processed food, and even prescription drugs must bear warnings.

Does this improve consumer behavior?

One problem: *overload.* When people see warnings on nearly everything, they stop paying attention. Taken to its extreme, this law is probably not doing what its sponsors and promoters intended.

How Are We Doing?

A beacon of light in all this controversy has been the recent trend of declining amounts of pesticide residues from field to plate. In 1989, *no* pesticide residues were found in 65 percent of domestic foods sampled and in 67 percent of imported foods tested.[16] Roughly one percent of all domestic foods sampled contained "violative" levels of pesticide residues; that is, they exceeded the allowable tolerances. This amounted to 75 of the 7394 samples taken.[16]

Because of consumer concern about the safety of imported foods, the FDA has intensified its surveillance efforts on imported foods. In 1989, over 10,000 imported food samples were tested, and 3.5 percent contained violative levels of residues.[16]

Imported foods are suspected by some consumers of having been treated with pesticides that are banned in the U.S. but are still exported by U.S. companies to countries who later sell us their food. The perception is that Americans are ultimately exposed to these banned pesticides in the form of imported foods. Called *the circle of poison,* this concept has fueled U.S. consumer concerns about food safety.[17]

In reality, these fears appear to be unjustified. True, the stepped-up surveillance efforts have revealed a level of violation which exceeds that of U.S.-grown food. But the numbers still do not justify such concern. A 3.5 percent level of violation is still extremely low.

Despite the reassurance offered by intensified surveillance efforts, EPA has expanded its technical assistance to foreign countries to heighten their awareness of, and compliance with, U.S. pesticide regulations.[17] As for banning the sale of prohibited pesticides to other countries—the reality is that these pesticides are readily available from other countries, too, so stopping the U.S. supply would do little to stem the tide of their use.[17]

And what of our total exposure to pesticide residues from both U.S.- and foreign-grown food? The FDA's annual surveys include a Total Diet Study.[16] Four times a year, 234 foods that represent the diet of the U.S. population are purchased from local supermarkets in several geographic regions in the U.S. The foods are prepared as they would be in one's home (peeled, cooked, etc.), then analyzed for pesticide residues. From these tests, estimated dietary intakes of pesticide residues in eight age and gender groupings are calculated.

In the 1989 Total Diet Study, 53 pesticide residues were found, none at hazardous levels. The ones most frequently found appear in Table 2.

Every Total Diet Study to date has confirmed that, in all cases, estimated human dietary exposure in the U.S. is *far lower* (for most residues, over *1000 times lower*) than the Acceptable Daily Intakes (ADIs) set by the United Nations and the Reference Doses (RfDs) set by the EPA.[16] These standards (ADIs, RfDs) are revised whenever new scientific data demonstrates the need to do so. The RfDs used to assess the 1989 Total Diet Study were the April 1990 revision of these standards.

So, on the whole, we're doing quite well.

Minimizing Risk—
The New Agriculture

Whether or not we accept the need for pesticides in agriculture, we must accept the fact that their existence really does help ensure a bountiful supply of foods year-round. But consumer concern about pesticide safety has compelled many farmers to reduce their pesticide use.

A growing trend among farmers is a pest-control method called integrated pest management, or IPM. IPM is a strategy with both environmental and economic benefits. Rather than spraying pesticides based on a predetermined schedule, farmers using IPM monitor each crop's pest population to determine when spraying is actually *necessary* to pre-

TABLE 2. Most Frequently Occurring Pesticides
in the Total Diet Study in 1989

Pesticide	Percent of samples
Malathion	20
DDT	13
Chlorpyrifos-methyl	10
Diazinon	9
Chlorpyrifos	8
Dieldrin	7
Methamidophos	6
Endosulfan	5
Chlorpropham	5
Hexachlorobenzene	5
Dicloran	4
Lindane	4
BHC, alpha and beta	3
Carbaryl	3
Ethion	3
Quintozene	3
Acephate	3
Heptachlor	3
Dimethoate	3
Propargite	2
DCPA	2
Dicofol	2
Toxaphene	1
Omethoate	1
Parathion	1
Permethrin	1
Pirimiphos-methyl	1
Thiabendazole	1
Methomyl	1

SOURCE: Adapted from Ref. 15, p. 13.

vent significant crop losses.[11] Farmers save money by reducing their use of pesticides, consumers get food with fewer residues, and lower levels of pesticides enter the environment, reducing damage to the ecosystem.

IPM uses alternative pest-control techniques. For example, spraying grape fields with larvae of the green lacewing, which attacks crop-damaging insects, will control a wide variety of pests without pesticides.[4] To prevent a particular pest from establishing a steady population in a particular field, crops are rotated. Planting is timed to capitalize on low-pest periods. Alternatives to herbicides are used against weeds, such as cultivating by tractor.

When pesticides are used, careful thought goes into their application. For example, an apple grower will set pheromone traps to attract male codling moths, a devastating apple pest. When the first male moth is caught, the apple grower will plan the application of pesticide to coincide with the emergence of larvae from their eggs (when they are easiest to kill but haven't yet damaged the apples), and will use an extremely low level of an effective, environmentally acceptable pesticide.[18]

Another promising IPM method is the use of specially-designed vacuum cleaners to actually vacuum up bugs on lettuce crops. Aphids, worms, whiteflies, and several other scavengers are sucked into these high-powered vacuum cleaners and chopped into pieces. This method has proven superior to chemical pesticides in controlling certain pests, and it reportedly extends lettuce shelf-life.[19]

Some farmers feel that IPM is the best choice. Traditional farming may be too risky for the environment, and organic farming may be too risky for many farmers' pocketbooks. IPM offers the chance to produce excellent yields while minimizing risks to the environment. In fact, studies have shown higher crop yields from IPM farms versus traditional farms, and IPM growers often receive higher prices for their crops because of both high quality and low pesticide use.[11]

The Rise of Organic Foods

Beyond IPM is the organic growers' arena, where foods are grown with no pesticides at all. Consumers continue to express a preference for pesticide-free foods, particularly if they are priced similarly to traditional foods. A Harris poll conducted in 1989 for *Organic Gardening* magazine found that over 84 percent of those surveyed (1250 households) indicated that they would buy organically-grown fruits and vegetables if they cost the same as their traditional counterparts.[20]

A recent EPA-funded study of 681 households shows that some consumers will pay a premium for foods labeled *no pesticides*—as much as 37 cents more per pound.[21] This same study found that 30 percent of those surveyed were taking some action to reduce their intake of pesticide residues, with 10 percent buying organic, 10 percent attempting to remove residues from produce with soap and water* (ineffective for many pesticides), and 10 percent seeking out produce labeled *low spray*.[21]

The imperfect appearance of truly organically-grown foods has led

---

*The practice of using soap on produce is still debated and its effectiveness, beyond that of a plain-water scrub and rinse, in removing surface pesticide residues has not been firmly established. However, a recent FDA advisory encouraged consumers to reduce *Salmonella* risk by washing and scrubbing whole raw fruit and vegetable products with a dish detergent, then throughly rinsing.[22] Interestingly, the FDA revised this advice two weeks later, suggesting instead that consumers simply use plain water to clean raw produce.[23]

some would-be organic farmers, and the markets to whom they sell, to question the consumer acceptance factor. If perfect tomatoes appear alongside brown-creased, scarred "organic" tomatoes, and the perfect tomatoes are cheaper, which will the consumer buy?

Apparently, that depends. The above-mentioned EPA survey discovered that a high percentage of those surveyed would accept surface damage covering up to 12 percent of the surface of produce labeled *no pesticides*.[21] Others feel that the only real market for the stuff is among "those who are more knowledgeable about nutritional and environmental factors."[24]

Phone conversations with supermarkets and produce brokers reveal that the demand for organic produce in "mainstream" markets (i.e., not natural foods stores) rose dramatically during the Alar crisis, then dropped off sharply, leaving produce in special "organically-grown" store displays to rot.

Growers of pesticide-free produce endure a challenging livelihood. Genuine pesticide-free agriculture leaves crops vulnerable to many environmental changes that affect pest populations and crop growth. Weeding and other crop-maintenance tasks must be accomplished by people rather than chemicals, raising costs for the farmer. Year-to-year crop yields are more unpredictable than those for traditional and IPM farmers. All of these factors lead to higher costs for organically-grown foods.

Despite the challenges, when markets are ripe for organically-grown produce, the organic farmer can reap sizable economic benefits. Ripening those markets may depend on pesticide scares—or rising awareness among consumers of the environmental impact of pesticides. In any event, a continued, gradual increase in consumer demand has been observed in many markets, leading some growers to convert to pesticide-free methods.

Is It Really Organic?

The frenzy to jump on the organic bandwagon has led some food producers to enter the arena without complying with generally-accepted standards for what makes foods *organic*. From a purely biochemical perspective, *all* foods are organic, since the definition of organic is simply *containing carbon atoms*, which all living, or formerly living, things do. Consequently, consumers are left in a quandary: Is that bag of apples you're buying, labeled *organic*, really organic?

Happily, a growing number of states have laws or statutes which legally define *organic*. As of this writing, 20 states with such laws are known to the author. They are Alaska, California, Colorado, Connecticut, Iowa, Maine, Massachusetts, Minnesota, Montana, Nebraska, New Hampshire, North Dakota, Ohio, Oklahoma, Oregon, South Dakota, Texas, Washington, Wisconsin, and Vermont.

Confusingly, each state has a slightly different twist on what constitutes *organic*. The laws, currently, are not uniform. Nevertheless, a movement is afoot to pass legislation that would create a *national* definition of *organic*. This promises to improve the credibility of the organic marketplace.

In the meantime, independent certifying programs have emerged to verify the "organic" nature of foods so labeled. Despite the lack of a national standard, most of these groups require that the food be grown without the use of any synthetic chemicals and that soil fertility be maintained and replenished by the grower. Other requirements vary with the certifying organization, some mandating that soil be pesticide-free for a number of years before crops grown on it can be called "organic."

A trade association called the Organic Foods Production Association of North America (OFPANA) has evolved to lend some consistency to standards used by agencies that certify foods as "organic." OFPANA certifies the agencies that certify organic produce. But not all certifying agencies have OFPANA's seal of approval.

To make matters worse, organizations like NutriClean have emerged that inspect and certify produce on which no pesticide residues have been detected but which have not been truly organically grown. Such certification can mislead consumers who, for whatever reason, have opted for organically-grown fare and misinterpret the pesticide-free label.

The only way to be sure is to ask your grocer. If she or he doesn't know, find out who supplies the pesticide-free produce, and call that supplier. Find out how the produce was grown and who, if anyone, certified it. Then decide what's most important to you—price, no residues on foods, or the environment.

See Part V, *The Resource Corner*, at the back of this book, for a list of organic-food-certifying agencies in the U.S. as well as consumer-advocacy organizations that promote pesticide-free foods.

Unanswered Questions

Scientists still grapple with haunting issues such as: What happens when a bunch of chemicals from different sources gets together in our bodies? No one really knows—yet. Allowable pesticide levels are currently based on research on single pesticides—not combinations. Should you worry?

Well, yes and no. It all goes back to an understanding of risk. Since a high percentage of the foods tested each year by FDA have *no* detectable pesticide residues, the risk of major mixing of deadly combinations is probably low. But it's not yet clear whether pesticide mixing is truly benign to the human body.

What *is* clear is that a diet devoid of the nutrients found in produce *is* life-threatening. Most nutrition experts agree that the health risks from eliminating produce are far greater than the possible health effects of pesticide residues at the level to which American consumers are exposed.[25] Current recommendations emphasize produce intake, encouraging 5 to 9 servings per day.[26] And that recommendation makes the most sense for Americans.

Final Thoughts

The best approach for consumers regarding pesticides depends on your level of concern. For the consumer whose primary concern is the environment, low-pesticide (IPM) produce and organically-grown produce both fill the bill. The "purist" approach is to buy only organically-grown, but the environmental benefits of IPM methods are very similar.

If your primary concern is personal health, it probably doesn't really matter which type of produce you buy. Pesticide residues continue to be carefully monitored, and new research on health effects will continue to guide the EPA, FDA, and USDA policies that govern the use of pesticides and other chemicals in food production.

Finally, exposure to pesticides can be further reduced by certain food preparation techniques. We'll explore such issues in detail in a later chapter (Part III, Chap. 3, *Food Preparation*).

So, go ahead, eat that apple! The benefits far outweigh the risks. Just don't eat the cyanide-containing seeds...

Glossary

Pesticide-Free: usually means the produce itself has no detectable residues; is not equivalent to organically-grown; may be grown by traditional methods, IPM methods, or organic methods

Organically-Grown: depends on the state in which the produce was grown and on the agency, if any, that certified the food as organic; implies that the food was produced with no synthetic chemicals, including pesticides and fertilizers

Low Pesticide: no legal definition exists, but implies that the growing method employed limited pesticide use; often used to describe IPM produce

References

1. Parnell, Jack, Keynote Address presented at Journalists' Conference: Food Safety and Nutrition Update, sponsored by USDA and FDA, at National Press Club, Washington, D.C., June 25–26, 1990.

2. Food Marketing Institute, *Trends: Consumer Attitudes and the Supermarket 1990*, Food Marketing Institute, Washington, D.C., 1990.

3. "Poisoned Grapes on Sale," *New York Times*, September 25, 1891.

4. Gilbert, Susan, "America Tackles the Pesticide Crisis," *The Good Health Magazine/New York Times Magazine*, October 8, 1989.

5. Carson, Rachel L., *Silent Spring*, Fawcett Publications, Greenwich, Connecticut, 1962.

6. Natural Resources Defense Council, *Intolerable Risk: Pesticides in Our Children's Food*, Natural Resources Defense Council, New York, February 27, 1989.

7. Young, Frank E., FDA Commissioner, John Moore, EPA Acting Deputy Administrator, and John Bode, USDA Assistant Secretary for Food and Consumer Services, *Joint Statement*, March 16, 1989.

8. Lacadie, John A., Ph.D., Research and Development Director for Crop Protection Division, "Subject: Uniroyal Chemical Company Responds to a Food Safety Concern," *Statement to Nutritionists*, Uniroyal Chemical Company, Inc., March 1989.

9. Allen, Frederick, *Unfinished Business: A Comparative Assessment of Environmental Problems*, U.S. Environmental Protection Agency, Washington, D.C., 1987.

10. Hamilton, Eva May et al., *Nutrition Concepts and Controversies*, West Publishing Company, St. Paul, Minnesota, 1991.

11. National Research Council, *Alternative Agriculture*, National Academy Press, Washington, D.C., 1989.

12. National Research Council, *Regulating Pesticides in Food: The Delaney Paradox*, National Academy Press, Washington, D.C., 1987.

13. Environmental Protection Agency, *The EBDC Pesticides and EPA's Proposed Regulatory Decision: Facts for Consumers*, December 4, 1989.

14. California State Legislature, Division 20, *Miscellaneous Health and Safety Pro-*

visions, Chapter 6.6, "Safety Drinking Water and Toxic Enforcement Act of 1986," Proposition 65.

15. *Safe Drinking Water and Toxic Enforcement Act of 1986: Chemicals Known to the State to Cause Cancer or Reproductive Toxicity,* State of California Health and Welfare Agency, Sacramento, California, July 1, 1990.

16. Food and Drug Administration Pesticide Program, *Residues in Foods 1989,* Food and Drug Administration, Washington, D.C., 1990.

17. Fisher, Linda J., Assistant Administrator, U.S. EPA, *American Food Safety: A Global Issue,* presented at 1990 Journalists' Conference on Food Safety and Nutrition, June 26, 1990.

18. Wood, Stephen, "The Trials of a Fruit Grower," *EPA Journal,* 16(3):37–40, May/June 1990.

19. Bassi, Steve, "Vacuuming Up the Bugs," *EPA Journal* 16(3):41, May/June 1990.

20. Louis Harris and Associates, Inc., "The 2nd Annual Organic Index: An Exclusive Harris Poll," Organic Gardening Magazine, 1990.

21. van Ravenswaay, Eileen, and John P. Hoehn, *Consumer Willingness to Pay for Reducing Pesticide Residues in Food: Results of a Nationwide Survey,* Department of Agriculture Economics, Michigan State University, East Lansing, Michigan, 1991.

22. Food and Drug Administration, "FDA Issues Cantaloupe Advisory," FDA Talk Paper, Food and Drug Administration, Rockville, Maryland, July 3, 1991.

23. Retail Food Protection Branch, Food and Drug Administration, "Memorandum to Regional Program Specialists—Subject: Melons," Department of Health and Human Services, Rockville, Maryland, July 17, 1991.

24. Lane, Raymond, Food Editor, *Times-Journal Newspapers,* Springfield, Virginia, as quoted by Roy Popkin in "A Future for Pesticide-Free Foods?," *EPA Journal* 16(3):31–33, May/June 1990.

25. National Research Council, *Diet and Health: Implications for Reducing Chronic Disease Risk,* National Academy Press, Washington, D.C., 1989.

26. USDA and USDHHS, *Nutrition and Your Health: Dietary Guidelines for Americans,* 3d ed., U.S. Department of Agriculture and U.S. Department of Health and Human Services, Hyattsville, Maryland, 1990.

CHAPTER 2

FOOD ADDITIVES

*Are you skeptical about all the reports of rats and mice
getting cancer after eating enough of some polysyllabic
chemical to choke a horse?*
                                    Newsweek, *October 22, 1990.*[1]

Food labels have become a study in complexity. One look at an ingredient label, and you're bound to feel annoyed and confused. What is
calcium propionate, anyway? And what's it doing in your bread?

Confusion about the safety of food additives is not confined to consumers. Scientists, too, are locked in hot debate over both the safety of
food additives and the way safety testing is done.

Food additive testing relies on a branch of science called *toxicology*
and a brand of researcher called the *toxicologist*. For over 25 years, toxicology has tested substances by administering *megadoses* of the test substance to rats, mice, or rabbits, and observing the results. Tissues of the
test animals are then examined for evidence of abnormalities, particularly cancer.

But now scientists are raising the spectre that this megadosing system
is all wrong. Recent reports suggest that it's the megadose itself, *not* the
chemical being tested, that produces harmful results such as cancer.
The concept is a daunting one, particularly for regulators of the food
industry.

The Delaney Clause

Under current guidelines, *any* additive found to cause cancer in animals
or humans after administration of *any* amount, including "enough to
choke a horse," must be banned from use in the food supply. The legal
mandate for this guideline is the Delaney Clause, a section of the Federal Food, Drug, and Cosmetic Act.

Under the Delaney Clause, a substance must be banned "if it is found
to induce cancer when ingested by man or animal, or if it is found, after
tests which are appropriate for the evaluation of the safety of food additives, to induce cancer in man or animal."[2] There is a glaring lack of
specificity here regarding the methods to be used for determining the
cancer-causing ability, or *carcinogenicity*, of an additive. This lack of
specificity, borne of the fact that scientific methods and equipment were
much less sensitive when this clause was created than they are today,

has opened the door for the megadosing approach and has fueled both scientific and political debate.

The National Toxicology Program (NTP), which shoulders the responsibility for testing additives used in the U.S., recently published a study that highlighted the cancer-causing effects of megadosing itself, distinct from the effects of the chemical being tested. And the National Research Council was slated to release its own report on the megadosing issue in 1991. This gathering of scientific support has galvanized efforts to overhaul the outdated safety standards currently used to police food chemicals.

So while policy-makers ponder their next move, the search is on for better testing methods to determine the cancer-causing potential of additives. Future testing tools might include studies of molecular structure and other sophisticated techniques that promise more realistic predictive power.

Given this backdrop, food safety issues take on a new, less sinister look. Since some *natural* substances in foods may be more dangerous than the ones added to food (see Part I, Chap. 3), yet escape regulation because they are not additives, it seems ludicrous to waste vast amounts of anxiety on the likes of Polysorbate 80. Yet, given the emotionally charged nature of food safety concerns, and the continuing scientific debate on the issue, it's important that we explore food additives further.

What Is an Additive?

Before we proceed, it's critical to fully comprehend the all-inclusive nature of the term *food additive*. As defined in the Federal Food, Drug, and Cosmetic Act, an additive is:

> ...any substance the intended use of which results or may reasonably be expected to result, directly or indirectly, in its becoming a component or otherwise affecting the characteristics of any food (including any substance intended for use in producing, manufacturing, packing, processing, preparing, treating, packaging, transporting, or holding food; and including any source of radiation intended for any such use...[3]

Whew! Pretty amazing, huh? Based on this definition, *everything* in a food product might be said to be an additive. Thus, every ingredient on a food label might be considered fair game for safety testing. In reality, it's the *chemical* additives that are the target of the bulk of NTP's testing. But pesticide residues and packaging materials also fall under this definition.

Given this broad-based definition, scientists have divided additives into two functional categories: (1) direct or intentional additives, and (2) indirect or incidental additives.

Direct Additives

When a manufacturer intentionally places an additive in a food product, it's called a *direct* additive. Such additives include nutrients, sweeteners, artificial and natural flavoring agents, texturizing agents, stabilizers, thickeners, emulsifiers, colors, and preservatives, as well as a host of other foreign-sounding substances (like humectants and sequestrants). We're going to focus on the additives of most concern.

Sweeteners

It's impossible to discuss food additives without getting into the sweetener debate. Commercials by the sugar manufacturers would have us believe that a few spoonfuls of "pure, natural sugar" are preferable to the unknown hazards of chemical, artificial sweeteners. Well, are they?

The answer depends on who you are and what health problems you have.

First, let's identify the two categories of sweeteners: (1) nutritive and (2) nonnutritive. The term *nutritive sweeteners* applies to substances having greater than 2 percent of the caloric value of sucrose (table sugar) per equivalent unit of sweetening capacity (i.e., more than 0.32 calories per sweetening equivalent of one teaspoon of sugar).[4] This category includes traditional, "natural" sweeteners like sugar, brown sugar, "raw" sugar, turbinado sugar, corn syrup, honey, and molasses. It also includes other sugars appearing on ingredient labels, such as dextrose, lactose, fructose, high-fructose corn syrup, fructose syrup, invert sugar, refiner's syrup, and maltose. (For a complete listing, see Table 1.) The natural sugar in fruits and fruit juices is also comprised of nutritive sweeteners—a mixture of glucose, sucrose, and fructose.

Among the nutritive sweeteners, there are a few that are slowly absorbed. These sweeteners—xylitol, mannitol, sorbitol, and fructose—present minimal hazard to the individual who needs to restrict sugar intake due to its effect on blood sugar. However, all of these sweeteners contain calories, and therefore can, like sugar, contribute to body weight.

The term *nonnutritive sweeteners* refers to sweeteners having *less than* 2 percent of the caloric value of sucrose (table sugar) per equivalent unit of sweetening capacity (i.e., less than 0.32 calories per sweetening

TABLE 1. Nutritive Sweeteners[5]

Sugar (sucrose), beet or cane	Honey
Invert sugar	Maple sugar
Brown sugar	Dextrose anhydrous
Refiner's syrup	Dextrose monohydrate
Molasses	Glucose syrup
High-fructose corn syrup	Dried glucose syrup
Fructose	Lactose
Fructose syrup	Cane syrup
Maltose	Maple syrup
Maltose syrup	Sorghum syrup
Dried maltose syrup	Table syrup
Malt extract	Xylitol
Dried malt extract	Mannitol
Dried malt syrup	Sorbitol

equivalent of one teaspoon of sugar).[4] Nonnutritive sweeteners include *aspartame* (marketed under the brand names NutraSweet® and Equal®), *saccharin* (used in Sweet'n'Low® and Sugar Twin®), *acesulfame K* (marketed as Sunette®), and, before its removal from the list of additives approved by the Food and Drug Administration (FDA), *cyclamate*.

So, which should you use?

Choosing Sweeteners. For the person with diabetes, whether it's treated by diet or by a combination of diet and medication (pills or injections), artificial, or nonnutritive, sweeteners are a real ally. In fact, artificial sweeteners were first marketed with the sole intention of providing a safe sweetening alternative for diabetics. While research now suggests that judicious amounts of sugar-sweetened products *may* have their place in the diabetic diet (check with your doctor), artificial sweeteners are still seen by most health professionals as the least hazardous forms of sweetening for persons with diabetes. In addition, the nutritive sweeteners sorbitol, mannitol, and xylitol (called sugar alcohols), though they contain calories, can be safely used by the diabetic in moderate amounts. Excessive use of these three sweeteners can lead to diarrhea. For more information on diabetic diets, contact your local chapter of the American Diabetes Association, or consult a registered dietitian (R.D.). (See *The Resource Corner* in Part V for help in finding an R.D.)

Nutritive sweeteners may also prove villainous for the subsegment of the population that suffers from *reactive hypoglycemia,* a blood sugar disorder whose victims experience drastic plunges in blood sugar after consuming sugar-containing foods. Certainly, hypoglycemia was once the "chic" disease, being heavily overdiagnosed in the late 1960s and early 1970s. Books like *Sugar Blues* led many perfectly normal individuals to diagnose their own "hypoglycemia." Yet, the backlash from the medical community in the 1980s and 1990s has been to largely ignore this very real disorder. While the method of diagnosis remains somewhat elusive, a 5-hour glucose tolerance test is generally recommended to determine the presence of hypoglycemia. A blood sugar level of 40 milligrams per deciliter (mg/dl) or less during this test is generally considered sufficient to confirm the diagnosis. Yet many individuals experience the classic symptoms of hypoglycemia at blood sugar levels higher than 40 mg/dl, often in the 40 to 70 mg/dl range. As a result, some diagnosticians feel that the presence of symptoms is enough to diagnose the disorder, without confirmation by a blood test.

For all such individuals, whether hypoglycemia is confirmed by blood test or suspected by symptoms, most nutritive sweeteners, if consumed without a meal, can be devastating. A cup of sugar-sweetened hot cocoa in midafternoon can lead to severe fatigue, sweaty palms, heart palpitations, dizziness, or lightheadedness a few hours later. A doughnut or syrup-drenched pancakes for breakfast could cause the same symptoms by midmorning. Virtually all individuals may notice vague changes in energy level a few hours after consuming something sweet, particularly when taken on an empty stomach. But the true hypoglycemic will experience crippling fatigue and severe mental fuzziness, often to the point of falling asleep or actually fainting. In all cases, productivity is seriously reduced until the blood sugar climbs back to a normal level.

As a result, the hypoglycemic, or the person with hypoglycemic tendencies, can benefit from an alternative to nutritive sweeteners. For such individuals, if sweetened foods are desired, artificially sweetened foods and beverages, or foods sweetened with sugar alcohols, are reasonable choices for snacks, or for anytime a food is eaten on an empty stomach. (For more detailed information on managing hypoglycemia, consult a registered dietitian.)

Hyperactivity. For years, agonized parents have tried restricting the sugar intake of their children in an attempt to curb *hyperactivity.* Leading researchers over the last decade generally agreed that this was futile. But, in 1990, one small study revealed that sugar does trigger the release of adrenalin in children, possibly contributing to the "sugar crazies" many parents report. However, the significance of this research remains somewhat hazy, since the overwhelming majority of studies *disproves* any association between sugar and hyperactivity. In fact, the most compelling evidence against sugar is its cavity-causing ability. So, what do you use to replace the sugar? Are artificial sweeteners okay for kids?

And what about the rest of the planet? What if you just want to watch your weight? How safe is NutraSweet®? Saccharin?

Safety Issues. Until the nonnutritive sweetener cyclamate was banned in 1969, artificial sweeteners enjoyed nearly boundless consumer acceptance. Diet sodas had become increasingly popular, with virtually no consumer concern about long-term health effects. But with the advent of consumer advocacy groups like Ralph Nader's, the dangers of food additives became a serious national concern. The FDA's GRAS list, a list of food additives *generally recognized as safe*, had been developed in 1958 in an effort to subdue concerns about food additives that were considered benign. The removal of cyclamate from the GRAS list in 1969, due to animal studies revealing its cancer-causing abilities, made a huge impact on unsuspecting consumers.

Long believed to be totally benign, diet sodas and other artificially-sweetened products had up to that point been liberally consumed by weight-conscious Americans. Suddenly, a veil of safety had seemingly been lifted, and a crisis in public confidence arose. Could the government be trusted to protect us from unsafe food ingredients?

The answer is *yes*. Consumers generally have little understanding of the sophisticated testing now required of food additives before approval by the FDA. Starting in 1969, the Food and Drug Administration began reexamining this list of additives called GRAS, subjecting them to more rigorous testing procedures. It was this new policy that uncovered the cancer-causing ability of cyclamate.

But remember our earlier discussion about the *amounts* of these substances that are used to determine their cancer-causing properties. As with pesticide testing, lab animals are virtually *infused* with overwhelming amounts of the food additive being tested. In the case of saccharin, this testing method showed a tendency for male rats to develop bladder tumors. Despite this, and due to a combination of consumer and food industry outcry, Congress overrode the legal requirement to ban saccharin in 1977, so saccharin continues to be used in foods at levels considered safe. The Commissioner of the FDA wields the power to remove saccharin from the list of approved additives and is awaiting the results of long-term saccharin studies now taking place in Canada.[6]

Aspartame, marketed as NutraSweet®, has also been the target of safety concerns. Some research suggests that this sweetener impairs brain function in developing fetuses, children, and adults. For *children,* the level established as the maximum approved intake is five servings of NutraSweet®-sweetened products per day, or the equivalent of five cans of 100 percent NutraSweet®-sweetened soda per day. For adults, headache, mood changes, and irritability have reportedly resulted from aspartame use. Other potential side effects include allergic reactions and, after consistent use of aspartame for long periods, disordered responses to sugar and other caloric sweeteners when eaten. Studies are still under way to determine the extent to which these complaints are actually due to aspartame. In a 1984 report evaluating aspartame-related consumer complaints, the Centers for Disease Control concluded that aspartame consumption by humans is safe, and that the number of individuals who have allergic or other untoward symptoms is quite small.[7] Several other researchers have more recently attempted to either confirm or dispute reports of negative reactions triggered by aspartame, with conflicting results.[8-11] Maximum approved intakes for adults are the equivalent of 17 twelve-ounce cans of 100 percent NutraSweet®-sweetened soda per day.

For aspartame, the FDA's general maximum "safe" level, for both adults and children, is based on weight. The above figures are based on *reference* persons—a 50-pound child and a 154-pound adult. The actual safety level has been set at 23 milligrams per pound per day. A twelve-ounce 100 percent aspartame-sweetened diet soda contains approximately 200 milligrams of aspartame.

Additionally, phenylketonurics, those who suffer from an inability to metabolize phenylalanine (one component of aspartame), might be at special risk. However, the amount of phenylalanine in a serving of aspartame-sweetened products is extremely small.

Safe Sweetener Use. Regulations governing nonnutritive sweeteners continue to treat them as special additives whose primary role is to sweeten the lives of folks with special dietary needs. Unfortunately, the world treats them as calorie-saving commodities appropriate for general use. Conflicting research sheds both doubt and hope on their effectiveness as weight-loss tools, and most consumers are convinced that their lives are enhanced by them.

Walking the tightrope between safety and unsafety has become a habit for all of us. Nonnutritive sweeteners, at the levels consumed by most Americans, appear to be safe. But it appears wise to restrict the consumption of artificial sweeteners by children, particularly non-diabetic children, given the lengthening human lifespan and uncertainty about cumulative effects of 50 or more years of liberal artificial sweetener use.

Certainly, anyone who has undesirable reactions to a specific artificial sweetener should avoid the offending sweetener. And those who prefer to avoid artificial sweeteners altogether are entitled to their concerns. Phenylketonurics should avoid aspartame.[12] But, barring a 3-six-pack-a-day diet soda habit, adult consumers are probably safe with their artificial sweetener use. Children should be supervised to control their intake to less than five servings per day, or less if they weigh less than 50 pounds.

Fat Substitutes

Newer on the additives agenda are fat substitutes. One such additive, marketed as *Simplesse®*, won FDA approval in February 1990. The other current contender, to be marketed as *Olestra®*, is still undergoing rigorous testing to determine its fate.

Simplesse® is actually a substance called *microparticulated protein product*. Using egg white and/or milk protein, manufacturers employ a patented process combining controlled heat and high-speed blending, followed by rapid cooling, to produce a creamy substance remarkably like fat. Simplesse® has been approved for use in frozen desserts and as a thickener or "texturizer" in other foods.

One drawback of Simplesse® is that, once produced, it can't be heated, since further heating would coagulate the protein, resulting in a rubbery texture. So, its uses must be confined to chilled or frozen foods.

Enter Olestra®, the not-yet-approved "miracle fat" that can be subjected to high temperatures with no untoward effects. Olestra®, a liquid oil-like fat substitute, is a food manufacturer's dream come true. Imagine frying french fries, potato chips, or chicken in calorie-free oil.

Olestra® is an artificial fat called *sucrose polyester*. Although oil-like in appearance and texture, sucrose polyester is a molecule so complex that human digestive enzymes can't digest it. As a result, it passes out of the body without being absorbed.

It is this quality of Olestra® that raises eyebrows among consumer advocates and nutritionists alike. What will that undigested fat-like stuff take with it? Fat-soluble vitamins are one possibility, and supplementation of Olestra® with some fat-soluble vitamins has been proposed. What about diarrhea if enough of this substance is consumed at one time?

These and other concerns have led the FDA to take a long, hard look at Olestra® before rendering approval. Long-term lab animal studies, including testing of genetic effects over several generations, are going on now to determine its safety.

Projections initially place Olestra® in snack foods, where it may replace all the regular shortening used to fry potato chips and corn chips. Uses in fast-food chains, where it might be used to replace up to one-third of the oil in deep-fat fryers, will require a separate review process.

Should you take advantage of fat substitutes?

The egg-white- and/or milk-protein-based Simplesse® is real protein, just mechanically altered to change its texture. Nothing ominous here.

Sucrose polyester, however, seems a little scarier. It differs from other additives in that it raises the prospect of introducing something totally artificial into the body in large amounts, not the micro-amounts consumed of such things as aspartame. If it clears the FDA approval process, consumers will still be left with questions of "how much?" and "how often?" Unless new research shows otherwise, the best advice: not much, not often.

Nutrition educators agree that the idea of fat substitutes is a shortcut for consumers. Why learn to eat healthfully, why bother to exercise, if manufacturers provide virtually calorie-free alternatives? But healthy food choices, without magic fat, are available everywhere. Artificial fats are an outgrowth of the healthy focus on fat reduction, but let's be reasonable! Many nutrition experts, including this one, fear that these products go a little too far.

Preservatives

Among the first additives to grace the scene were preservatives, designed to prevent bacterial spoilage of food. Early preservation methods used the additives *sugar* and *salt* to inhibit bacterial growth. Drying, canning, and smoking were other early methods of food preservation that survive today.

Preservatives often come under attack these days because of consumer suspicion that they are simply a shelf-life extension ploy to fatten food industry wallets. While this may motivate a percentage of their use, preservatives help make reasonably-priced foods possible for consumers. Preservative-free bread doesn't last long, either at the store or at home, rapidly transforming into a moldy mass if not properly refrigerated. The extent of such losses in the store increases costs to manufacturers, which translates into higher prices for consumers.

Mold inhibitors used in bread include *calcium propionate* and *sodium propionate,* forms of a naturally-occurring component in dairy products called propionic acid. These additives inhibit the growth of mold in some cheeses as well as in bread and other baked goods. They appear to be unquestionably safe.[13]

Sulfites are more controversial. Long believed to be benign, sulfites were banned for use on fresh, raw fruits and vegetables in 1986 due to adverse reactions reported in a number of consumers. First hitting the news as the sinister ingredient in salad-bar vegetables (to prevent browning of fresh salad ingredients), sulfites earned a notorious reputation. Asthmatics are particularly sensitive to sulfites, an estimated 4 to 8 percent of whom react to sulfites with respiratory symptoms that make breathing difficult.[14]

Used as multipurpose preservatives in many foods, sulfites are added to a wide variety of products, from wines to frozen french fries. They minimize browning and other discoloration, prevent bacterial spoilage, and inhibit the growth of undesirable microbes during fermentation (as during winemaking).

Labeling regulations now require that products containing at least 10 parts per million of sulfites be labeled to warn consumers. However, foods purchased in restaurants need not be labeled. Some fresh foods, particularly raw, cut-up fruits and vegetables prepared in a variety of cafeterias and public eating establishments, are treated with a sulfite solution to keep them looking fresh. Potatoes, once the target of a partial ban on sulfite use, recently won a reversal of the ban and may once again be treated with sulfites.[15] (Unpeeled potatoes are not treated with sulfites, since the browning that sulfites prevents occurs only after peeling.)

Nitrites and nitrates, discussed in the next chapter (*Natural Toxins in Food*), are still used in smoking of certain meat and fish products, both commercially and in homes. The concerns related in the following chapter center around the ability of nitrites (and nitrates, which convert to nitrites) to combine with protein in food or in the stomach to form a carcinogen called nitrosamine.

Nitrites and nitrates are used to inhibit the growth of a particularly vicious microorganism called *Clostridium botulinum,* the "bug" responsible for botulism poisoning. It is this function that compels manufacturers to use it at the high levels at which it must be used to control the botulism organism.

The solution, of course, is to limit use of smoked products like bacon, smoked fish, and smoked meats.

Preservative Wrap-Up. The major benefit of preservatives for consumers is a degree of protection against food poisoning. This benefit is offset by potential dangers from some of the additives, if consumed in excessive amounts. But even such additives as nitrites and nitrates, still the target of some consumer concern, are naturally present in many foods. And the concentration of other natural toxins in foods is amazingly high. So avoiding preservative-containing foods is no insurance that potentially-hazardous substances won't enter your body.

Flavorings

Flavorings are a huge subcategory, accounting for perhaps 1700 different additives.[13] Usually divided into two subgroups—*natural flavors* and *artificial flavors*—they are used to create desirable flavors and to mask disagreeable ones in a product.[13]

Natural flavors include *essential oils,* which are the concentrated essence of various plants such as wintergreen or spearmint, *oleoresins,* which are extracted from spices, and *extracts,* which are usually derived from fruits or berries.[13]

Artificial flavors may be completely synthetic or may be a combination of synthetic and natural flavors.[13] An example of a popular synthetic flavor is *vanillin* or *ethyl vanillin,* a vanilla flavoring that is less expensive than vanilla extract.

Over the years, the FDA has identified a few flavorings whose safety has warranted their removal from use. One such flavoring is *safrole,* a natural flavoring derived from sassafras bark, which had been an ingredient in sassafras tea as well as a primary flavoring agent in root beer.[13] It was banned in the 1970s due to research exposing its carcinogenicity.[16]

Another flavor-associated ban occurred when *coumarin,* formerly an ingredient in artificial vanilla flavor, was found to cause hemorrhaging when taken in large amounts.[13] Coumarin is chemically related to a blood thinner used medically to reduce the tendency of blood to clot in patients with heart and blood vessel diseases.

Monosodium glutamate (MSG), still the focus of consumer concern, is a flavor enhancer. Used for many years in China and other Asian cultures, it is a form of the amino acid *glutamic acid.* MSG is derived commercially from glucose or from wheat, corn, soybean, or sugar beet proteins.[13] Experiments where infant mice were force-fed MSG produced brain abnormalities and damage to the central nervous system.[13] These results led to a withdrawal of MSG from baby foods.

MSG contains some sodium, but, compared to salt, the amount of sodium in MSG is tiny. The most famous side effect of MSG is *Chinese restaurant syndrome,* first identified by a set of symptoms shared by a number of individuals after eating at Chinese restaurants. These symptoms—burning sensations, a creeping back-of-head headache, neck ache, and facial and chest pressure—are experienced by a small number of people after consuming food laced with significant amounts of MSG. Asian food restaurants now frequently offer consumers the option of requesting food without MSG.

Other sources of MSG include seasoning powders, salty snacks, packaged gravy and sauce mixes, soups,...the list goes on. Glutamate, the major "ingredient" in MSG, is also naturally present in many foods. If you're truly sensitive to MSG, take a careful look at labels before buying nearly any nonsweet processed food—MSG is widely used. Research suggests that sensitivity to MSG is rare. In fact, the European Communities' Scientific Committee for Food recently released a report reaffirming MSG's safety as a food additive.

Flavor Wrap-Up. Currently, flavors are usually listed on food labels in one lump, such as "natural and artificial flavors," making identification of any individual additive impossible. However, new FDA labeling proposals, pending approval as of this writing, will require labels to list flavorings that have allergy-inducing potential.

Concern about the safety of flavor additives remains, both for natural and artificial flavors. Because natural toxins in natural flavors may exist, the words *natural flavors* on an ingredient label do not assure safety, any more than the words *artificial flavors* assure hazard. However, because flavorings comprise such a tiny percentage of any product, their ability to cause harm, except in allergy-prone individuals, appears minimal.

Texture Enhancers

Food products often contain thickeners. One of these is *carrageenan,* a seaweed-derived compound used as an emulsifier, thickener, stabilizer, and gelling agent.[17] This substance is considered to be safe.

Modified food starch often appears in foods as a thickener, and it has been the subject of continued safety debates. Produced by subjecting regular starch, derived from foods, to special chemical processes, modified starches help manufacturers control the thickness, flavor, stability, and clarity of the final product.[13] Safety testing has shown mild diarrhea, slightly reduced growth rate, incomplete digestion, and calcium deposits in the kidneys in lab animals fed very high levels of these starches.[13]

As with other additives, one must consider the quantity of this substance given to lab animals to produce these results. Normal human intake of modified starches is a tiny fraction of one's daily food intake. At the levels humans, including infants, consume, modified starches appear to present negligible risk.

Propylene glycol and *propylene glycol monostearate* are used in blending food ingredients and in enhancing spreadability.[13] They are classified as emulsifiers and stabilizers, and they're found in cake batters and icings, margarines, and whipped toppings.[17] These substances are metabolized as carbohydrates and appear to be completely safe.[13]

Polysorbate 60, 65, and *80* are three substances often found on ingredient labels. The chemical-sounding name raises eyebrows among many concerned consumers. These substances are called *sorbitan derivatives* because they are derived from sorbitol,[13] a sugar alcohol discussed in the *Sweeteners* section. Their purpose is to emulsify or disperse fat droplets in foods such as dairy products, whipped toppings, coffee whiteners, and frozen desserts.[13] No safety concerns have been uncovered through extensive research.[13]

Antioxidants

BHA, BHT, and *TBHQ* are called *antioxidants.* Their primary function is to protect fats in foods from becoming rancid.

BHA and BHT are used to extend shelf-life of products like potato chips, breakfast cereals, baked goods, chewing gum, crackers, and vegetable oils. Research shows that, at extremely high intakes, enlarged livers have been produced in lab animals.[13] Contrasting research shows a protective effect of both BHA and BHT on liver tumor incidence.[12,13] But some research shows the ability of both BHA and BHT to enhance tumor progression in lab animals where cancer has already been chemically induced.[12]

Some manufacturers have stopped adding BHA and BHT to foods, and are, instead, treating packaging materials with these compounds, where they can exert a protective effect without leaving a significant residue in foods.

TBHQ appears to be a safer antioxidant, showing no hazardous effects even at extremely high levels in lab animal diets.[13]

Vitamin E is also used as an antioxidant and is harmless under most conditions.

As you'll see in the next chapter, rancid fats present their own risks to humans, particularly in relation to cancer. Antioxidants, by preventing rancidity, help reduce consumer exposure to the risks associated with rancid fats.

Colors

Artificial colors continue to take a great deal of consumer heat. In 1990, yet another food color bit the dust—*Red Dye Number 3.*

A familiar agent used to color fruit cocktail cherries, pistachio nuts, chewing gums, beverages, and cosmetics, Red Dye No. 3 was found to cause thyroid tumors in lab rats. The quantity that caused the tumors? The human equivalent of eating all the cherries in 2000 one-pound cans of fruit cocktail every day for 70 years.[18] Were *you* at risk?

The banning of this and other dyes has occurred, once again, due to the technical interpretation of the Delaney Clause discussed earlier. Until proposed changes in the interpretation of this clause actually occur, regulators are forced to submit to the increasingly sensitive testing techniques that uncover tumors in lab animals force-fed ridiculous quantities of such additives as Red Dye No. 3.

In reality, some uses of Red Dye No. 3 are still legally permissible, depending on the formulation and method of application of the dye.[19] But all the uses of the dye are being re-evaluated as a result of the thyroid-tumor research.[19]

Some consumers continue to argue that dyes are purely a marketing ploy and are, therefore, a waste of potential risk. Others counter that people buy products which look appealing. Regardless of your position, you may want to know which colors are out there and how they're used, since food labels do not currently require listings of the names of most artificial colorings added to foods.

Such lists are available from:

Division of Colors and Cosmetics
FDA (HFF-442)
200 C Street, S.W.
Washington, DC 20204

Before we close our discussion of color additives, let's touch on one more dye that is still in the food supply but has seen regulatory action. A yellow coloring, called *FD&C Yellow No. 5,* also known as *tartrazine,* must be identified on food labels if it is present in a food.[16] This is because tartrazine is hazardous to some individuals, leading to allergic reactions in susceptible consumers. Usually, individuals who are allergic to tartrazine are also allergic to aspirin,[13] which may be the best way to determine whether you're at risk.

Indirect Additives and Contaminants

Irradiation

As a different approach to food preservation, irradiation has emerged. Foods exposed for a brief time to low doses of radiation, like x-rays, emerge free of the bacteria that cause food spoilage. Designed to reduce the use of additives and to extend shelf-life of a variety of products, irradiation has been approved (as of this writing) for use in killing microorganisms in herbs and spices, for control of the *Trichinosis* organism in fresh pork, to destroy insects in stored food, and to control enzymes that produce rotting in fresh produce. Labeling must appear on containers of irradiated food, accompanied by a special logo.[20]

A significant benefit of irradiation could be reduction in the use of other additives currently used to preserve foods.[21] Additionally, irradiation provides a great deal of protection against *Trichinosis,* a deadly form of food poisoning.

Understandably, consumer opposition to the use of radiation on foods has been strong. Consumers see it as dangerous, equivalent to direct exposure to x-rays, or, worse, to radioactive fallout or nuclear emissions. In reality, the radiation retained by the food is negligible. But many consumers remain staunchly opposed, charging that the effect on humans of even tiny amounts of residual radiation in food has not yet been adequately studied. To deal with this area of concern, research continues. As of this writing, irradiation is used only on herbs and spices in the United States.

The ultimate role of irradiation in food technology will depend on consumer response to its use. Industry and consumer groups alike will continue to pay close attention as government regulators determine the future of irradiated food.

Decaffeinated Coffee

Controversy over decaffeinated coffee has recently centered on more than the chemicals used to remove caffeine, but let's focus on those chemicals for now. At one time, *methylene chloride* was used to decaffeinate coffee. However, when the public learned that this chemical causes cancer, coffee companies sought alternatives, despite the FDA's contention that the residues remaining in decaffeinated coffee presented negligible risk.

Today, four major decaffeination processes are widely used. One involves *ethyl acetate*, a naturally-occurring chemical found in fruits. Another uses *liquid carbon dioxide*. A third method uses *coffee oils*, natural constituents of the coffee bean. A fourth method, called the *Swiss water process*, involves soaking coffee beans in water, allowing the caffeine to leach out. Then, the "coffee-water" is poured over activated charcoal, which removes the caffeine. Finally, for flavor and aroma, the coffee beans are rejoined with the now-decaffeinated coffee-water.[22]

All of these methods appear to be safe.

The most recent eyebrow-raising issue regarding decaffeinated coffee was the Stanford Lipid Research Clinic's discovery that men drinking three to six daily cups of decaffeinated coffee experienced a rise in low-density lipoproteins (LDLs), or "bad" cholesterol, whereas men drinking the same amount of regular coffee or no coffee experienced a drop in LDLs. These results have fueled media fanfare but have not been accepted by scientists as conclusive proof of decaffeinated coffee's supposedly "villainous" nature.

Some recommendations suggest that everyone limit their intake of all types of coffee to two cups per day[22]—and that's probably the best approach.

Packaging Materials

One of the areas of increasing research is the impact of packaging materials on foods. Fears that small amounts of toxic substances may migrate from packaging to the food within continue to rise.

One such substance, found in margarine containers and other plastic packages, is *acrylonitrile*. In the U.S., acrylonitrile has been detected in olive oil, margarine, and nuts.[12] Some research shows increased risk of cancer, particularly lung cancer, in humans and lab animals exposed to large amounts of acrylonitrile.[12] Still, we're talking large quantities here.

Special *microwave browning materials* in packages of certain microwavable foods (popcorn, pizza, pot pies, etc.) have been targeted for further FDA investigation. Research has shown that these substances, called *heat susceptors,* may migrate into foods during cooking, particularly if the temperature of the browning material rises to 400–500 degrees Fahrenheit (°F).[23] Initial FDA approval for heat susceptors was based on products heated to temperatures under 300°F. The danger of migration is greatest if foods are microwaved for longer than package recommendations, if the browners are reused, of if the browning material itself is browned or charred after cooking.[23] Avoiding all of these risky situations offers some protection until FDA investigations are complete and new regulations are in place.

Lead was once a popular material for "gluing" together the edges of cans used as food containers. However, since the mid-1980s, food canning plants have, for the most part, dropped lead-soldered cans in favor of lead-free cans. Statistics for 1989 show that, during the first half of that year, only 4 percent of all canned foods in the U.S. contained lead solder.[24] Americans are still exposed to can-associated lead from many imported foods, dry foods such as nuts and coffee, and odd-sized cans such as hams and bulk luncheon meats.[24] Food may also pick up lead from reused plastic bread bags, particularly if the bag is turned inside out, since lead paint is used on a high percentage of bread and bagel bags.[25] Other sources of lead for Americans include automobile exhaust (diminishing because of unleaded fuels), dust, paint, some drinking water, many ceramicware products, and whiskey.[12]

Polyvinyl chloride (PVC) has received some consumer attention. A chemical derivative of PVC may migrate from food-packaging materials into the food held in containers made of PVC. Oils, margarine, butter, and drinking water may contain PVC.[12] Health risks are associated with workers exposed to PVC vapors,[12] but there are no estimates of average daily dietary exposure to PVC and no estimates of the risk PVC presents to the average consumer.[12]

So, What's the Upshot?

Despite some pockets of concern, the average daily intake of additives in the U.S. appears to present minimal risk to consumers. Considering the protective effects of some additives, it's hard to blacklist the lot of them. Against a backdrop of natural toxins in food (discussed in Part I, Chap. 3), and the real risks of food poisoning (presented in Part I, Chap. 4), food additives appear as a faint blip on the health-concern radar screen. Ongoing research and sophisticated monitoring techniques ensure that risks from additives will continue to be minimized.

References

1. Begley, Sharon, "These Rats Die for Our Sins," *Newsweek,* October 22, 1990, p. 68.

2. Federal Food, Drug and Cosmetic Act, as amended October 1976.

3. Federal Food, Drug and Cosmetic Act, as amended October 1976, Section 201(s).

4. 21 CFR 170.3 (revised as of April 1, 1990).

5. 21 CFR 131.111, 21 CFR 168, 21 CFR 172.395, 21 CFR 184.1835, (revised as of April 1, 1990).

6. 21 CFR 180.37 (revised as of April 1, 1990).

7. Center for Health Promotion and Education, "Evaluation of Consumer Complaints Related to Aspartame Use," Centers for Disease Control, Atlanta, Georgia, November, 1984.

8. Garriga, M. M. et al., "A Combined Double-Blind Placebo-Controlled Study to Determine the Reproducibility of Hypersensitivity Reactions to Aspartame," *Journal of Allergy and Clinical Immunology* 87(4):821–827, 1991.

9. Lipton, R. B. et al., "Aspartame as a Dietary Trigger of Headache," *Headache* 29(2):90–92, 1989.

10. Janssen, P. J., and C. A. van der Heijden, "Aspartame: Review of Recent Experimental and Observational Data," *Toxicology* 50(1):1–26, 1988.

11. Schiffman, S. S. et al., "Aspartame and Susceptibility to Headache," *New England Journal of Medicine* 317(19):1181–1185, 1987.

12. National Research Council, *Diet and Health: Implications for Reducing Chronic Disease Risk,* National Academy Press, Washington, D.C., 1989.

13. Freydberg, Nicholas, Ph.D. and Willis A. Gortner, Ph.D., *The Food Additives Book,* Bantam Books, New York, 1982.

14. Giffon, E. et al., "Suspicion on Sulfites," *Revue des Maladies Respiratoires* 6(4):303–310, 1989.

15. Gershoff, Stanley N., Ph.D. (ed.), "Sulfite Ban Deemed Null and Void," *Tufts University Diet and Nutrition Letter,* October 1990, p. 1.

16. Cliver, Dean O., *Foodborne Diseases,* Academic Press, New York, 1990.

17. Lewis, Robert J., Sr., *Food Additives Handbook,* Van Nostrand Reinhold, New York, 1989.

18. Gershoff, Stanley N., Ph.D. (ed.), "Food Manufacturers are Seeing Red...Still," *Tufts University Diet and Nutrition Letter,* May 1990, pp. 1–2.

19. Blumenthal, Dale, "Red No. 3 and Other Colorful Controversies," *FDA Consumer,* May 1990, pp. 18–21.

20. 21 CFR 179.26 (revised April 1, 1990).

21. Lindroth, S. and S. S. I. Ryynanen (eds.), *Food Technology in the Year 2000,* Vol. 47 of *Bibliotheca Nutritio et Dieta,* J. C. Somogyi (ed.), Karger, New York, 1990.

22. Nierenberg, Cari, M.S., R.D., "Decaffeinated Coffee Causes a Stir," *Environmental Nutrition,* April 1990, p. 2.

23. Gershoff, Stanley N., Ph.D. (ed.), "Avoid Being 'Burned' by Microwave Browning," *Tufts University Diet and Nutrition Letter,* August 1990, p. 7.

24. Webb, Densie, R.D., Ph.D. (ed.), "Q and A," *Environmental Nutrition,* October 1989, p. 3.

25. Webb, Densie, R.D., Ph.D. (ed.), "Potentially Harmful Paint Found in Bread Packaging," *Environmental Nutrition,* January 1991, p. 3.

CHAPTER 3

NATURAL TOXINS
IN FOOD

> *It was all very well to say "Drink me," but the wise little*
> *Alice was not going to do that in a hurry. "No, I'll check*
> *first," she said, "and see whether it's marked 'poison' or*
> *not;" for... she had never forgotten that, if you drink*
> *much from a bottle marked "poison," it is almost certain*
> *to disagree with you, sooner or later.*
> LEWIS CARROLL,
Alice's Adventures in Wonderland, 1865.

In the collective American consciousness, there are really only two food safety concerns: food additives and pesticide residues. Harboring great resentment that chemicals are actually *put into* our food, many American consumers are incensed that this practice continues—*without* consumer consent and, in some cases, without consumer knowledge. But by focusing outrage on the *addition* of chemicals to food, consumers may overlook an important fact: There are many toxic substances that are *naturally present* in foods. Taken together, these substances are called *natural toxins,* and their study has evolved into a growing segment of toxicology.

Bruce Ames, a widely recognized biochemist at the University of California at Berkeley, asserts that we regularly consume at least 10,000 times more *natural* pesticides by weight than manufactured pesticide residues.[1,2] Such allegations are a revelation to most environmentally-aware Americans. The sheer volume of such exposure is enough to rouse concern.

Here, we'll cover many of the common potentially-harmful natural chemicals in foods and examine their prevalence in the American diet. We'll also address methods to reduce our exposure to them. But, a word of caution: Despite the care we may exercise in *selecting* foods, a variety of dangerous substances are *produced* when we cook foods in certain ways. Many of these food preparation concerns will be dealt with here. [Some will be saved for a later chapter (Part III, Chap. 3, *Food Preparation*).]

So, let's get educated.

Aflatoxin

For years, many consumers have heard the word *aflatoxin* and have, appropriately, connected it with peanuts. But even "aware" Americans have little perspective on this mold-produced toxin.

Aflatoxin is one of a whole class of toxins called *mycotoxins,* which are produced by mold. Mycotoxins have been described as "antibiotics in the microbiological struggle for survival,"[1] meaning that they are the mold's way of ensuring it will survive. Mycotoxins are produced in response to plant stress. Unfortunately, many mycotoxins are carcinogens (cancer causers).[1-5] Aflatoxin is one of them, and it is considered by some to be the most prevalent and dangerous mycotoxin in the human diet.[1]

There are actually several types of aflatoxin that food scientists and toxicologists have identified, all produced by various species of a genus of mold called *Aspergillus*. The various aflatoxins differ in their ability to harm living organisms, with a type called aflatoxin B_1 considered to be the most toxic.[2-4] This is also the one most commonly found in peanuts, corn, other high-carbohydrate grains, and, to a lesser extent, sweet potatoes.

The prevalance of aflatoxin depends on the weather conditions where corn, other feed grains, and peanuts are grown and stored. Aflatoxin production skyrockets when high temperatures or humid conditions prevail. These conditions are common in tropical and subtropical countries, where economies depend on exports of these products.[3] Drought conditions in the southern U.S. have also been known to produce aflatoxin-contaminated corn.[4]

Aflatoxin exposure has been implicated in several diseases, including jaundice, liver cancer, lung cancer, colon cancer, cirrhosis, kwashiorkor, Reyes syndrome, and impaired immune function.[3] Not only is aflatoxin particularly toxic to the liver, it is also a *teratogen* (capable of causing defects in developing embryos), *mutagen* (capable of inducing genetic mutation), *nephrotoxin* (harmful to the kidneys), and a carcinogen.[4] Unfortunately, toxicity studies have focused on animals, leaving wide disagreement about concomitant effects in humans.

Nevertheless, the National Research Council, in its groundbreaking 1989 report *Diet and Health: Implications for Reducing Chronic Disease Risk*, mentions the link between aflatoxin-tainted foods and human liver cancer in sub-Saharan Africa and southeast Asia, where primary liver cancer (cancer that *starts* in the liver, rather than spreading there from other tissues) is common.[6] However, a recent comprehensive study of diet, nutrition, and disease in China sheds doubt on the ability of aflatoxin to cause human liver cancer, asserting instead that lingering infection with hepatitis B virus is the cancer-causing culprit in such settings.[7]

Despite all this controversy, and because liver cancer is just one of the risks associated with aflatoxin consumption, interest in aflatoxin remains high among toxicologists, food regulators, and many consumers.

Many industrialized countries, including the U.S., import corn and peanuts from tropical and subtropical countries, largely for use as animal feed. In fact, research on the toxicity of aflatoxin began in the early 1960s in the U.K. as a result of disease outbreak in poultry that had been fed an aflatoxin-contaminated batch of peanut meal imported from Brazil.[3,8] Liver disease was also identified in the early 1960s in U.S. trout hatcheries where trout had been fed aflatoxin-contaminated imported feed.[3,9] In the same period, an aflatoxin-related compound was found in the milk of dairy cows fed an aflatoxin-contaminated diet.[3,10]

Fortunately, the mold that produces aflatoxin is visible and lends a moldy taste and odor to foods, thereby deterring people from knowingly consuming tainted foods. Even livestock tend to reject moldy feed (unless it's the only feed available), thus reducing the risk of animal transmission into the food supply.[4] Unfortunately, aflatoxin-contaminated foods cannot *always* be detected by appearance, taste, and odor, particularly when levels of contamination are low.[4,11]

Also unfortunate is the fact that aflatoxin is stable at both high and low temperatures, being resistant to destruction by cooking and baking (such as roasting peanuts) as well as by freezing.[4]

So, how does all of this affect you, the consumer?

Most experts agree that true risk from aflatoxin exposure is highest in tropical countries (i.e., not the U.S.) where the local diet is comprised largely of high-risk grains and lower-quality peanuts during certain parts of the year. And, despite widespread disagreement regarding the potential human effects, aflatoxin residues are carefully regulated in peanuts, peanut butter, and feed grains intended for use in the U.S.

Because peanuts and peanut butter are the most likely routes of U.S. consumer exposure to aflatoxin, the Food and Drug Administration (FDA) set an upper limit of 20 parts per billion (ppb) for peanuts and peanut products in 1969. Since 1972, the Consumers Union, publisher of *Consumer Reports,* has been checking for aflatoxin in peanut butter. They note that the levels of aflatoxin vary from year to year, partly due to changes in weather conditions. Their most recent sampling shows that the national brands they tested contained no more than 1 ppb, the lowest levels found, while more than half of the store brands and regional samples contained over 5 ppb. The "grind-your-own" peanut butters purchased by Consumers Union in one supermarket and two health food stores had the highest levels, averaging more than 10 ppb.[12]

What does this mean? Unless you eat peanut butter more than once or twice a week, your risk of cancer is probably not *significantly* increased regardless of the peanut butter you choose. But if you are a real peanut butter fanatic, consuming large quantities on a near-daily basis, it would be wise to stick to the widely advertised national brands of peanut butter, despite their added cost over store brands. Of those tested by Consumers Union, one widely advertised national brand of "old-fashioned" peanut butter (no sugar, salt, or hydrogenated fat) (Smuckers®) got high marks, with less than 1 ppb of aflatoxin in all samples tested.[12] So, if you crave the "just-ground" taste of natural peanut butter, but want to avoid the higher levels of aflatoxin in the grind-your-own variety, Smuckers® Old Fashioned Peanut Butter has received Consumers Union's seal of approval. And, in general, it's wise to moderate your peanut butter intake (a nearly impossible task for true peanut butter aficionados!).

Also, avoid peanuts with a moldy appearance or odor: These are not likely to appear on supermarket shelves, but may be part of the harvest produced by the green-thumbed of the southern U.S. for at-home consumption. And if you're a real sucker for the grind-your-own type of peanut butter, ensure the highest level of safety by purchasing roasted peanuts vacuum-packed in a can or jar and grinding them at home. If you choose this route, be sure to thoroughly clean your grinder after use: the ground-peanut residue left behind will rapidly become a rancid film that'll be picked up by your next batch of peanut butter.

As for other possible routes of aflatoxin ingestion, in the U.S. aflatoxins have been detected in corn, figs, grain sorghum, cottonseed, and certain nuts that grow on trees,[11] primarily in supplies destined for use as animal feed. As previously mentioned, people in tropical and subtropical countries who depend on consumption of corn and peanuts for survival have been known to consume suboptimal (i.e., moldy) corn and peanuts, with resulting illness and, in some cases, death.[11] As of this writing, none of these foods has been implicated in any human disease in the U.S., where consumption of such unappetizing items as moldy corn-on-the-cob is virtually nonexistent.

Certain foods contain substances that may help the body counteract the carcinogenicity of aflatoxin.[4,13-15] For example, large amounts of cauliflower reduced the toxic response to aflatoxin in one rodent study, thereby reducing liver cancer.[4] For a more complete discussion of cancer inhibitors, see Part II, Chap. 3, *Fiber and Cancer*.

Glycoalkaloids

The humble potato has been getting a lot of attention these days, now that most health-minded consumers have become aware of the virtues of *complex carbohydrates* (starches). But, in addition to avoiding the fatty toppings that originally adorned the familiar spud, consumers should become aware of the natural toxins produced by potatoes.

Glycoalkaloids are chemicals produced by potatoes as a defense against insects and fungi. The glycoalkaloid most common to consumers is solanine, a substance produced when potatoes are exposed to light, leaving a greenish tinge on the surface of the potato. Bruised and diseased potatoes produce another glycoalkaloid, chaconine. Both solanine and chaconine are potent inhibitors of cholinesterase, an enzyme critical for muscle relaxation in both animals and humans. These substances are also potential teratogens (capable of causing defects in developing embryos).[6,13]

Because these substances are produced by the potato as a plant-survival strategy, a higher concentration enhances the survival of the potato—but not of the consumer. In fact, a certain strain of potato which had been bred for its insect resistance had to be withdrawn from the market several years ago because its level of glycoalkaloids was too high for human consumption.[6]

Some evidence suggests that high levels of glycoalkaloids in cooked potatoes can be detected by a bitter taste and a burning sensation in the throat.[16–18] Research also indicates that, once consumed, absorption of these compounds from the intestinal tract is quite poor, and excretion via urine and feces is rapid.[18,19]

What to do? Avoid green-tinged potatoes, or at least cut off the green portions. Also, remove bruised sections of potatoes, or avoid bruised potatoes entirely. Potatoes with evidence of mold or past insect infestation should undergo "culinary surgery" to remove the diseased or formerly infested portions. If, while eating cooked potatoes, you detect a bitter taste or a burning sensation in the throat that is not due to the temperature of the potato, don't panic: discard the remaining portion of the potato, but don't become obsessed about your safety. Studies to date provide some assurance that whatever poisons you've consumed from that tainted potato will undoubtedly find their way out of your body.

Hydrazines

Most consumers, while justifiably wary of Grandma's hand-picked wild mushrooms, don't bat an eye when it comes to the common commercial mushroom. Found both fresh and canned in grocery stores, the common white mushroom, *Agaricus bisporus*, contains natural toxins called hydrazines. One such compound, agaritine, is a mutagen that can be converted by the mushroom into a potent carcinogen.[13] In laboratory studies, this carcinogen caused stomach tumors in 30 percent of the mice exposed.[20] Other hydrazines in mushrooms have been shown to cause bone, liver, and lung tumors in male and female mice.[21]

At an exposure level of one 15-gram (half-ounce) raw mushroom daily for life, the *possible* risk of human cancer based on animal studies is estimated to be 0.1 percent, or one in a thousand.[1] It remains uncertain how closely human risk parallels rodent (lab animal) risk, even after adjusting for body size differences. Of particular interest is the contention that, at low rates of exposure to carcinogens that affect rodents, human susceptibility to cancer may be fundamentally different from rodent susceptibility.[1] Fortunately or unfortunately, definitive studies to determine true human risk will never be done due to ethical issues.

The National Research Council estimates that, if only 1 percent of the mushrooms sold in the U.S. were eaten raw, cancer risk associated with mushrooms would be less than one per million per lifetime in the U.S.[6]

So, given the information we have, what's the best course to take?

Since raw mushrooms harbor more carcinogens than cooked or canned mushrooms, it seems prudent at this point to limit your consumption of raw mushrooms. However, since mushrooms, raw or cooked, most often comprise a small portion of a final product, undue concern about the effects of hydrazines appears to be unwarranted.

Polycyclic Aromatic Hydrocarbons

Perhaps you've caught wind of health concerns associated with charcoal-broiled foods. Since the early 1980s, charcoal-broiled and smoked foods have been on the National Academy of Science's list of foods to avoid to reduce cancer risk.[22] Most consumers don't know why. Well, here's the story.

Charcoal broiling and smoking of foods produce a significant level of carcinogenic compounds called polycyclic aromatic hydrocarbons, or PAHs for short. PAHs are also common contaminants found in fresh meats, roasted foods, leafy and root vegetables, vegetable oils, grains, plants, fruits, seafoods, and whiskies.[22] PAHs have been associated with cancer of the skin and lungs,[22] but these associations have been true only in studies of humans exposed occupationally to PAHs, for example, from soot in chimneys and from petroleum products.[22] PAHs have been shown to cause stomach cancer in lab animals,[6] with absorption of PAHs being enhanced if accompanied by a high salt intake.[6]

Home-smoked meat and fish products contain higher levels of PAHs than commercially smoked foods.[6,22] Studies have shown that population groups that consume large amounts of smoked meats and fish have higher rates of stomach cancer.[22] While some of this increased cancer risk might be attributed to PAHs, most studies into this issue have not separated out the effects of other carcinogenic compounds, such as ni-trite and N-nitroso compounds, which are particularly prevalent in smoked foods.[22] These compounds were discussed in Part I, Chap. 2, *Food Additives*, and will be discussed later in this chapter.

In the U.S. diet, grilled protein foods appear to be the biggest source of PAHs. Grilling produces large amounts of PAHs by three methods. First, when food is subjected to high temperatures, PAHs are formed on the surface of the food.[23] Second, certain fuels used as a source of heat in cooking, such as crumpled paper, logs, or pine or spruce cones, may be only partially burned, with the rising smoke depositing a layer of PAH-containing ash on the food.[23] Charcoal and gas grills produce only small amounts of PAHs,[23] but log fires are particularly abundant sources of PAHs until reduced to embers, which emit only moderate amounts of PAHs.[23] In addition, if foods are exposed to petroleum products, such as lighter fluids used to start charcoal fires, this in-creases the level of PAHs.[6]

Finally, and most importantly for U.S. consumers, PAHs are con-tained in the "spray" of burned fat particles, or fatty smoke, flying up from the heat source. If the food being grilled contains fat, fats dripping onto the heat source, located below the food (flames, charcoal, lava rocks, etc.), undergo a chemical change called *pyrolysis*. The smoke gen-erated by this pyrolyzed fat coats the food with PAHs.[6] If the food is protected from the smoke generated by the burning fat, exposure to PAHs can be reduced.[6] Unfortunately, the taste we appreciate in char-broiled foods is the taste of PAH-containing substances.

Even simple broiling of foods under an oven broiler produces other carcinogens, called heterocyclic amines, in the blackened material formed on the food.[2,6,22,24] These compounds will be discussed in the following section.

Despite some concern about the effects of PAHs on humans, no reli-able studies have been done to examine how consumption of low levels of PAHs might impact on the development of human cancer.[22] PAHs are not currently monitored by the FDA, and an acceptable limit for daily intake has not been established.[6]

So what's the best course?

Given current knowledge, it appears wise to limit consumption of grilled foods, particularly those grilled over open flames or with char-coal or gas grills. When grilling foods, the National Cancer Institute (NCI) advises us to remove fat and skin from meats and poultry before cooking and to avoid fat-containing basting sauces.[25] NCI also recom-mends that we wrap the food or the grill with foil before grilling, or put the food in a pan, to eliminate exposure to fat-generated smoke and petroleum-containing fumes.[25] Moving food away from the heat source, such as positioning grill racks at highest settings, is also recommended.[25] Finally, cooking foods at a lower temperature for a longer time also reduces PAHs.[23]

And what about smoked foods? Commercially smoked foods, while not recommended in large amounts or with great frequency, appear to be a better choice than home-smoked foods, since home-smoking methods typically produce a larger quantity of PAHs than commercially-used liquid smoke.[6,22]

Heterocyclic Amines

Besides PAHs, charbroiling produces another class of toxic compounds called heterocyclic amines.[6,24] Burnt and browned material on broiled foods, whether grilled or oven-broiled, contains these compounds.[2,6] Fried protein foods, such as fried beef and pork, also contain these compounds.[24] In fact, any protein-containing food, if heated at a sufficiently high temperature to produce browning, will produce heterocyclic amines.[6]

Heterocyclic amines have been shown to be mutagenic (capable of inducing genetic mutation) and carcinogenic (capable of inducing cancer) in lab animals.[24] Liver cancer and connective-tissue cancer have been caused by heterocyclic amines in rodent studies.[6,24]

Studies have also shown that the more browned or burnt matter there is on a cooked protein food, the more mutagenic activity there is in the food.[6]

A useful observation in scientific studies on these compounds has been the protective influence of certain food substances in inactivating the mutagenicity of heterocyclic amines. Vitamin A, plant fibers, and certain fatty acids (oleic and linoleic) have been found to inactivate, or detoxify, heterocyclic amines.[24] Some of these "protectors" will be discussed in greater detail in Part II, Chap. 3, *Fiber and Cancer*.

Information to date suggests that heterocyclic amines make up a small part of most U.S. consumers' diets,[6] leaving the issue of risk at the bottom of the list. However, with the growing popularity of blackened foods in U.S. eating establishments, the year-round use of gas grills in many U.S. homes, and the national fondness for broiled and fried meats and fish, our individual exposures could be considerable.

Given what we know, it makes sense to moderate our intake of meats and fish containing charred, burned, and browned material. When we cook meats and fish, we should use methods like microwaving, steaming, boiling, and poaching more often to reduce our exposure to these toxins. Finally, increasing our intake of plant foods, particularly those high in vitamin A and fiber, and choosing high-oleic-acid oils, such as olive, will help protect us from the heterocyclic amines we do ingest.

Nitrites, Nitrates, and *N*-Nitroso Compounds

Bacon, due to its considerable content of nitrites and nitrates, used to be the focus of a great deal of consumer attention. But the complete story on nitrites and nitrates is more far-reaching than just bacon.

Nitrites and nitrates, while added to foods as curing agents and preservatives, are *naturally* present in many foods.[2,26] Foods such as beets, celery, lettuce, spinach, radishes, and rhubarb all contain significant amounts of naturally-occurring nitrate.[2,26] The problem with nitrites and nitrates, as discussed in Part I, Chap. 2, *Food Additives*, is their ability, when combined with protein, to form compounds called *nitrosamines* and other N-*nitroso compounds* in the intestinal tract. These compounds are carcinogens, and may induce cancer anywhere in the body, but are particularly linked to stomach and esophageal cancer.[6]

Until recently, beer was the single largest dietary source of already-formed nitrosamines, but new methods in the malting process have greatly reduced beer's contribution to our nitrosamine intake.[6,22]

Nitrate, the compound found in vegetables, is not mutagenic by itself.[6] However, bacteria in our saliva convert roughly 5 percent of all ingested nitrate into nitrite.[22] Nitrite apparently can be mutagenic,[6] thereby enhancing the potential for cancer. Besides coming from foods and saliva, nitrites are present in the urine of people with bladder infections,[6] and are allegedly carcinogenic to the bladder.[22]

So, what does this all mean? Should you give up spinach, beets, and the other vegetables listed above? No. The key appears to be in preventing the formation of nitrosamines once nitrite- and nitrate-containing foods are eaten. Vitamin C (also known as ascorbic acid) or vitamin E, if present in the stomach at the same time that nitrite and/or nitrate are consumed, can prevent the conversion of nitrite and nitrate to nitrosamine, thereby reducing their cancer-causing potential.[22] However, vitamin C will not deactivate the nitrosamines already formed in such products as bacon and smoked meats. This leads, therefore, to the recommendation to reduce intake of smoked protein foods, as previously discussed.

Scombroid Fish Poisoning

Perhaps you've caught one of those news stories about people dying of *scombroid fish poisoning*. Perhaps not. Either way, here's the scoop.

Fish of the suborder Scombroidea, including albacore, mackerel, tuna, and skipjack, have high levels of a special substance called *histidine* in their flesh. Histidine, an amino acid, can be transformed by certain bacteria into histamine, a substance released by humans during allergic reactions. When fresh fish of this class are not refrigerated promptly after being caught, the flesh begins to decompose, paving the way for the transformation of histidine to histamine. The illness that results when this decomposed fish is eaten is called *scombroid intoxication* and includes symptoms such as burning of the throat, elevated blood pressure, rapid pulse, flushing, headache, numbness and tingling of the lips, nausea, and vomiting.[27] Though usually not fatal, this reaction can lead to sudden death for the individual with a weakened heart, high blood pressure, or propensity to stroke.

Scombroid intoxication is most common in coastal regions, though it has occurred inland as a result of consumption of canned tuna that had decomposed before canning.[27]

Partially as a result of some well-publicized sudden deaths associated with this type of poisoning, U.S. fish inspection regulations are being tightened. The FDA and U.S. Department of Agriculture (USDA) have assumed new responsibilities in these matters, and new regulations were being devised as of this writing. A movement is afoot to pass stricter laws that would mandate uniform fish inspection. With tighter control over fish inspection, scombroid fish poisoning should become a thing of the past in the U.S. Still, enforcement of tighter regulations will continue to present problems, largely due to underfunding of U.S. regulatory agencies.

Outside the U.S., fish inspection regulations may or may not exist. If they do exist, they may not be as strict as those in the U.S. Prudence would suggest avoiding the scombroid fish listed above when abroad if you suffer from high blood pressure or a heart condition. Imported foods present even greater obstacles to regulatory enforcement, more easily slipping through the cracks at crowded commercial ports,[28] so caution should be exercised when selecting such foods as imported canned tuna and imported canned mackerel.

Tyramine

Tyramine, like the histamine formed in scombroid fish, is a substance called a *pressor amine*. It can be produced in food from an amino acid called tyrosine. People who take medications called *MAO* (monoamine oxidase) *inhibitors,* including certain drugs to treat depression and tuberculosis, must avoid foods containing large amounts of tyramine. In combination with MAO inhibitors, tyramine can produce drastic elevations in blood pressure. These drastic elevations, called *hypertensive crises,* may be accompanied by such symptoms as excruciating headaches, rapid heartbeats, and, tragically, even bursting blood vessels in the head.[29,30]

Small amounts of tyramine are naturally present in fruits and vegetables, including pineapples and carrots.[27] However, foods that contain the most significant amounts of tyramine (as well as other pressor amines that should be avoided by those taking MAO inhibitors) include aged cheeses (especially brie, camembert, cheddar, ementhaler, gruyere, processed American, and stilton), aged meats, anchovies, bananas, beer, broad beans (fava beans and Italian green beans), chicken liver, pickled herring, raisins, sausages, sour cream, soy sauce, chianti wine, sherry wine, yeast extract, and yogurt.[29,31] Also, some experts recommend that chocolate and caffeine-containing substances be avoided, as should contaminated fish due to possible histamine content (see earlier section on *scombroid fish poisoning*).[29]

Drugs that fall into the class of MAO inhibitors include Marplan, Parnate, and Nardil.[31] People who take these drugs are generally cautioned by their health care provider regarding foods to avoid.

Rancid Fats

As most consumers know, over time, fats become rancid. You're probably familiar with the telltale odor of a rancid fat, a sort of acrid smell that tells you something is not quite right. Nuts, "old-fashioned" peanut butter, and nonpreserved vegetable oils are common victims of rancidity.

Rancidity occurs at an accelerated rate in fats which are heated, such as cooking oils (even those containing preservatives) and meat fat.[6] Unsaturated fats and cholesterol are particularly prone to rancidity.[13]

When one consumes rancid fats, one is consuming a large number of mutagens, carcinogens, and promoters of the cancer process.[6,13] As a result, the digestive tract and the colon (large intestine) are forced to be in close contact with cancer-causing substances.[13] While rodent studies have not produced conclusive evidence of cancer from rancid fats,[13] this exposure may produce some damage to digestive tract tissue.

Clearly, the prudent course would be to avoid rancid products. Foods as diverse as candy bars and bacon, if kept too long, will undergo rancidity reactions. Crackers, chips, cereals, nuts, nut butters, and oils are other likely targets for rancidity. Preservatives like BHA and BHT are used to prevent rancidity. Even the process used to produce hydrogenated fats came about as a means of preventing rancidity.

So, when your nose detects an off odor in a fat-containing product, don't take chances—toss it out. Don't reuse old fat for frying. Keep oils and fat-containing products, particularly those not containing preservatives, under refrigeration. And don't keep fat-containing snacks like chips and crackers in the cupboard too long. Rotate supplies and discard off-smelling leftovers of such items.

Cottonseed Oil

Cottonseed oil has been a bone of contention among consumer advocates and health-conscious folks for many years. Most people who register concern about cottonseed oil point only to cottonseed's status as a nonfood grain, since it is a by-product of cotton production, and disputedly is not held to the same agricultural and manufacturing standards as food grains like corn.

Despite this level of concern, cottonseed oil is manufactured according to "good manufacturing practices" (an FDA term) and is wholesome for human consumption from that standpoint. However, there are substances naturally present in cottonseed that might cause concern.

Crude cottonseed oil contains a substance called *gossypol* that causes sterility in males during use and was reportedly being tested in 1980 as an inexpensive male contraceptive in China.[13] However, only very crude cottonseed oil contains this substance, not the refined product used in the U.S.

Two toxic fatty acids, sterculic acid and malvalic acid, are also present in cottonseed oil.[13] These fatty acids are also found in fish, poultry, eggs, and milk from animals fed cottonseed.[13] Animal studies have shown that these fatty acids increase the carcinogenicity of aflatoxins consumed, cause hardening of the arteries in rabbits, and have a variety of other toxic effects.[13] It has been suggested that these effects are the result of the ease with which these fatty acids can be oxidized (become rancid) and their readiness to form *free radicals*, which can damage cells.[13]

Based on current research, it is unclear what impact, if any, these fatty acids might have on humans. Also, no reliable evidence exists regarding how widespread they are in the typical U.S. diet. The profile of other fatty acids in cottonseed oil is fairly favorable from a heart disease standpoint, containing a moderate amount of unsaturated fat and an acceptable level of saturated fat. As with all fats, moderation should be the watch word here.

Algal Poisoning

A particular type of fish poisoning occasionally occurs when large amounts of shellfish are consumed. The condition, known as *clam* or *mussel poisoning, paralytic fish poisoning,* and *mytilointoxication,* is caused by clams, oysters, and mussels heavily feeding on specific species of blue-green and golden-brown algae during times when these algae bloom.[27] These algae produce a compound known as *saxitoxin,* which concentrates in the organs and gills of the shellfish that consume it.[27]

Soon after large quantities of shellfish containing saxotoxin are consumed, the victim will feel a tingling and numbness of the lips and tongue, overall loss of muscular strength, and temporary paralysis of the arms, legs, and neck.[27] Rarely, the muscles between the ribs will also become paralyzed, leading to an inability to breathe—and death by asphyxiation.[27] Usually, the victim recovers without treatment within a few hours.[27]

When these algae bloom, they lend a characteristic color to the waters in coastal areas. Currently, harvesting of shellfish during blooms of these algae is prohibited,[27] which makes cases of this poisoning quite rare.

Another alga, this one with a green color and which grows in salt waters, produces a toxin called *ciguatoxin.* This toxin is consumed and stored by over 400 species of fish. If consumed by humans, ciguatoxin causes a cluster of symptoms that mimic metal poisoning, gastroenteritis, and the flu. Mental depression, temporary blindness, lack of limb coordination, and paralysis result.[27] As with saxitoxin poisoning, recovery usually occurs within a few hours.

Canavanine

A toxic substance called *canavanine* is a natural constituent of all alfalfa sprouts.[13] Canavanine is incorporated into the protein in alfalfa sprouts in place of a nontoxic amino acid, arginine.[13] In monkeys, eating alfalfa sprouts causes a severe lupuslike syndrome, and this effect is thought to be caused by canavanine.[13] There is no evidence that canavanine has a similar effect in humans.

Alcohol

Without even considering alcohol's potential for abuse and the widespread existence of alcoholism, there are several health risks associated with consuming *ethanol,* the type of alcohol in alcoholic beverages.

Alcohol consumption increases risk of several cancers, including cancers of the lip, tongue, mouth, pharynx, larynx, esophagus, rectum, liver, and breast.[6] People who smoke cigarettes and regularly consume alcohol are at greater risk for all types of cancers.[6] It has been theorized that alcohol acts both as a direct carcinogen and as a promoter of the cancer process in damaged tissue.[6,13]

Other disorders associated with alcohol consumption include fetal alcohol syndrome and other birth defects, liver disease, cirrhosis of the liver, chronic renal (kidney) disease, gout, elevated blood pressure, altered blood sugar levels (elevated or lowered), damage to the nerves of the extremities, alcoholic dementia, and malnutrition.[6] There is conflicting evidence regarding the impact of alcohol consumption on heart disease risk.[6] Alcohol consumption greatly increases our national death toll from motor vehicle accidents, drowning, falls, assault, and suicide.[6]

Given all these dangers, the National Research Council encourages "prudence in alcohol consumption and even abstention" (Ref. 6, p. 453).

Cabbage Family Toxins

Foods with a "cabbage-y" or sharp, biting taste contain their own set of natural toxins. Ironically, these are the very same foods that contain natural anticancer properties.

The plant family Brassicaceae, also called Brassica or Cruciferae, contain substances called *glucosinolates*.[32] These substances, when digested, become *isothiocyanates*, which have been shown to interfere with thyroid function.[32,33] The significance of this in rabbits, cattle, and rats has been shown,[33,34] resulting in goiter[33] and delayed behavioral development.[34] To date, human risk appears to be low, since huge amounts of cruciferous vegetables need to be eaten, along with a low iodine intake, to create significant problems with thyroid function, such as goiter.[33] However, scientists express concern about the impact of glucosinolates on people taking certain drugs, since glucosinolates change the way the body handles specific drugs.[32]

Also, some researchers have pointed to the levels of thiocyanates (by-products of glucosinolates) in the milk from cows who have grazed on cruciferous pastures as a contributor to hypothyroidism in certain geographic regions.[33] Still, a great deal of controversy remains.

Isothiocyanates appear to be a plant-protection strategy, with more of these chemicals being produced by cruciferous plants in response to fungal attack and to a growth abnormality called clubroot disease.[32]

The general recommendation, pending further research, is to ignore the goiter-causing properties of cruciferous vegetables and to consume them in considerable amounts, along with other plant foods, as an anticancer strategy.[25]

Vegetables in this family include cabbage (white and green, savoy, red), Chinese cabbage, bok choy, broccoli, brussels sprouts, cauliflower, turnips, certain greens (mustard, turnip, kale, collard), kohlrabi, and rutabaga.[25]

Other members of this family include the condiments horseradish and mustard.[6,13,32] The isothiocyanates in mustard seed and horseradish have been shown to be mutagenic in animal experiments.[6,13] In fact, isothiocyanates in high concentrations lend a strong, bitter taste and smell to the foods that contain them[32]—so, in general, the stronger the mustard or horseradish, the more isothiocyanates there are. Given this bit of information, avoiding large amounts or frequent intake of strong mustard and zingy horseradish appears advisable, but no human data have been collected to confirm this.

Tannins (Polyphenols)

Most consumers have heard of tannins in tea. But did you know that several other edible items contain tannins?

Beans, especially broad beans (fava), carob, and sorghum are food sources of tannin. In large amounts, tannins have been shown to retard growth in animals and to reduce the quality of protein consumed.[33]

Tea, coffee, and cocoa also contain small amounts of naturally present tannins.[6,33] While tannins have been implicated in certain forms of cancer when injected into animals, there are no reliable studies—human or animal—on the carcinogenic effects of tannins when consumed orally.[6]

Tannic acid may function as an *antivitamin,* reducing the body's ability to use thiamin (vitamin B_1).[33] Tannin may also bind up iron, preventing its absorption.[35] However, some studies show that it's actually tea, not just tannic acid, that blocks iron absorption,[36,37] sometimes leading to anemia.

These facts suggest that excessive intake of foods and beverages containing tannins be avoided.

Mutagenic Flavonoids and Flavonoid Glycosides

The edible portions of most food plants contain substances known as *flavonoids.* Many of these flavonoids are capable of altering cells genetically, so they're called *mutagenic* flavonoids. A special form of mutagenic flavonoid, called *flavonoid glycoside,* is considered by some to be carcinogenic. These flavonoid glycosides go by odd names such as quercetin, kaempferol, and galangin. Rutin, a substance present in many plant tissues, particularly citrus fruits, is also a flavonoid glycoside.[6,22]

In animal research, flavonoid glycosides have caused tumors of the intestine and the bladder.[22] Other research has shown no increase in tumors in animals fed large amounts of these substances throughout life.[22]

Flavonoid-containing foods include citrus fruits, berries, leafy vegetables, roots, tubers, spices, cereal grains, tea, and cocoa.[6] One researcher has estimated that about 25 percent of the U.S. flavonoid intake comes from tea, coffee, cocoa, fruit jams, red wine, beer, and vinegar.[22]

Because of the inconclusiveness of research into these matters, it is difficult to estimate the true impact of these substances on U.S. consumers. Since many of the major contributors to our intake of flavonoid glycosides are not considered particularly healthful products—e.g., coffee, tea, beer, red wine—these items should not be major parts of our diets anyway. If you're looking for a reason to reduce intake of one of these beverages, perhaps you've found it! More reasons follow...

Coffee and Tea

Besides the mutagens already mentioned, coffee and tea contain other questionable substances.

One such substance is chlorogenic acid. This compound, like tannin, is an antivitamin, interfering with the body's ability to use thiamin.[33] Chlorogenic acid may also be a catalyst for the creation of mutagens and carcinogens,[13] thus indirectly increasing risk of cancer. Both caffeinated and decaffeinated coffee contain chlorogenic acid.[33]

Another mutagen, methylglyoxal, is also present in both caffeinated and decaffeinated coffee.[6,13]

Caffeine, a stimulant present in coffee and, to a lesser extent, tea, remains a controversial food component. The greatest individual contributors to caffeine intake in U.S. adults are coffee and tea.[6] Soft drinks and chocolate provide a substantial, but comparatively smaller, chunk of adult caffeine intake.[6] In U.S. children, soft drinks and tea (including iced tea, the standard year-round beverage in the southern U.S.) are the biggest caffeine sources.[6] Caffeine is also found in nonprescription drugs, particularly cold relief and pain relief medications, and some over-the-counter appetite suppressants.

Some studies have shown that caffeine damages the body's ability to repair damaged genetic material, leaving the body more vulnerable to cancer.[6,13] Animal studies have shown increased numbers of tumors in caffeine-fed subjects.[13] And birth defects as a result of caffeine intake were reported in at least one study,[13] although more evidence is needed before one can add caffeine to the list of "don'ts" for pregnant women.

Theobromine, another stimulant found in tea as well as in cocoa, appears, like caffeine, to inhibit the body's ability to repair damaged DNA (genetic material).[13] In rat studies, theobromine caused testicular atrophy (shrinking of the testicles) and other reproductive abnormalities in male rats.[13]

Coffee has been linked, although inconclusively, to bladder cancer in humans.[6] Tea-drinking has shown no relationship to bladder cancer in several studies of human populations.[6]

Both coffee and tea have been linked to colon cancer, and tea has been linked to rectal cancer.[6] Risk of pancreatic cancer had been shown in coffee drinkers, but repeated studies have failed to show a significant relationship.[6] Tea-drinking, except in the British Isles, has not been connected with cancer of the pancreas.[6]

Research into coffee's impact on heart disease has been contradictory. This issue is discussed in more detail in Part II, Chap. 1, *Cholesterol and Heart Disease*.

On the flip side, surprising new evidence shows tea exerting *protective* effects against some diseases, including cancer,[38–45] stroke,[46,47] and elevated cholesterol levels.[48,49] Some evidence suggests that at least some of these beneficial effects may only occur when unprocessed green tea is used, not the variety available commercially,[48] but further research is needed to clear up the details before recommendations can be made.

Disease risk aside, many people are sensitive to the restlessness and jangling nerves that coffee and strong tea can cause. For people with blood sugar disorders, caffeine and theobromine can cause or aggravate symptoms.

Prudence would suggest a conservative approach to the consumption of stimulant-containing products. And, given the presence of mutagens in coffee and tea, both with and without caffeine, it makes sense to go easy on these beverages.

Avidin

As a result of the widely publicized increase in *Salmonella* bacteria in raw eggs, many consumers have resorted to eating their eggs well-done, forgoing runny yolks. Still, there remains a bastion of consumers who prefer their eggs raw, particularly in milkshakes. For those who still consume raw eggs, here's another risk to nudge you into reconsidering your position.

Raw egg *white* contains a substance called avidin. This substance is one of the most well-known antivitamins.[33] Avidin binds with a vitamin called *biotin*, making it unavailable to your body. Fortunately, biotin is widely distributed in our food supply, making it impossible to bind all of one's biotin supply with an occasional raw egg.[33] However, for those rare individuals who may consume several raw eggs daily as their primary source of food, it is possible to cause a biotin deficiency,[33] although this scenario is highly unlikely one. When heated, the avidin in egg white is inactivated.

While avidin may present a minor risk, *Salmonella* bacteria in raw eggs presents a major one. If you consume raw eggs, consider this carefully. A more thorough discussion of *Salmonella* appears in the next chapter, *Food Poisoning*.

Pyrrolizidine Alkaloids

Certain herbs that are used as folk remedies contain toxic substances called *pyrrolizidine alkaloids*. These toxins have been shown to produce liver tumors in rats and in certain pregnant African tribal women who are given herbal mixtures.[6] These substances also cause lung tumors.[13] Comfrey tea and comfrey tablets are among the more commonly-consumed members of this group of herbs containing pyrrolizidine alkaloids.[1]

The point here is to use caution when considering herbs as a remedy for any health condition. Certainly, herbs are valuable—in fact, so valuable that they form the basis for modern drug therapy. But don't be fooled into thinking that herbal remedies are inherently safe!

Even some herbal teas, such as those containing comfrey (mentioned above) and sassafras (discussed below), are considered hazardous.[50] Other potentially-hazardous herbs used in some herbal teas include, woodruff, foxglove, oleander, senna, buckthorn, dock, aloe, horsetail, shave grass, burdock, catnip, juniper, hydrangea, licorice, and jimson weed.[51]

Alkyl Benzene Compounds

Related to the previously-discussed toxins is another class of toxins called *alkyl benzene compounds*. Herbs and spices such as sweet basil, tarragon, sassafras, black pepper, and cloves contain these compounds. These substances cause cancer in rodents.[6,13] Several years ago, sassafras tea was taken off the market because of its high concentration of safrole, an alkyl benzene compound.

Does this mean that you shouldn't use herbs and spices? No. But *extremely heavy* use of herbs and spices, particularly black pepper,[13,52] may not be in your body's best interests, pending the results of further research. Moderation, even in herb and spice use, seems to be in order here as well.

Legumes

A particular type of bean that is popular in the Mediterranean is the fava or broad bean. This bean contains toxic substances called *vicine* and *convicine*, which can lead to a severe type of anemia in which red blood cells are destroyed.[6,13] Only certain people are genetically susceptible to these toxic effects, since a genetic deficiency of a particular enzyme (glucose-6-phosphate dehydrogenase) is required before this anemia can develop.[6,13] This enzyme deficiency is prevalent in geographic regions where malaria is common, since this deficiency seems to provide some protection against malaria.[13]

Another group of toxic substances, *phytohemagglutinins*, which are present in many types of beans, cause agglutination, or sticking together, of the red blood cells. These substances, found in castor beans, soybeans, black beans, peanuts, red kidney beans, and wax beans, are mostly destroyed by acids and enzymes in the human digestive tract, and only very small amounts are absorbed.[53,54]

Ethyl Carbamate

Ethyl carbamate, also known as urethane, is produced in fermented foods and beverages. Wines, beer, other alcoholic beverages, breads, and yogurt are among the common urethane-containing foods in the U.S. diet.[6]

Rodent studies have shown that oral consumption, inhalation, and injection of ethyl carbamate all cause tumors in a wide range of tissues (lung, lymph, skin, liver, mammary gland).[6]

The role of ethyl carbamate in human cancer is not known, but the levels we are exposed to are much lower than those used to produce tumors in lab animals.[6,22]

Bracken Fern

A particular type of fern called *bracken fern* contains several toxins that have mutagenic and carcinogenic activity.[6] This fern is eaten by humans in several parts of the globe, particularly Japan.

Cancers of the esophagus in humans have been linked to consumption of bracken fern, and damage to bone marrow and intestines have been found in cattle that graze on bracken fern.[6] Rodents fed milk from cows which had regularly grazed on bracken fern developed cancer of the intestine, bladder, and kidney.[6] Fiddleheads are a relative of bracken fern and are consumed as a delicacy in the U.S. A Canadian study of humans found no link between fiddleheads and bladder cancer.[6]

Based on these studies, U.S. consumers appear to be at extremely low risk for toxic effects of bracken fern because of our very low consumption rate of bracken fern and fiddleheads. However, consumers in Japan are at considerably higher risk.

Cycasins

A palmlike tree growing in tropical and subtropical regions is the cycad tree. Nuts produced by this tree are used to produce a flour that is used in foods eaten by humans in these regions, and livestock also consume nuts of the cycad.[6]

Cycad nuts contain a potent carcinogen called *cycasin,* one of the most potent cancer causers in plants.[6] When eaten, cycasin has been shown to cause liver, kidney, and colon cancer in many species.[6] Some researchers feel that cycasin is an important contributor to human liver cancer in certain parts of the globe.[6]

Consumers do not appear to be exposed to cycasins in the U.S.

Tryptophan

Tryptophan is an essential amino acid—that is, it is required in the human diet. Studies in dogs, rats, and mice have shown cancer-causing effects of tryptophan in all three species, with bladder cancer being the most common result.[6] Nevertheless, no research has clearly linked excess tryptophan with bladder cancer in humans.[6]

In 1989, tryptophan supplements were taken off the market due to a specific blood disorder that developed in people who took these supplements. The blood disorder, eosinophilic-myalgia syndrome, results in severe muscle and joint pain, swelling of the arms and legs, fevers, skin rashes, shortness of breath, and, occasionally, death. Until L-tryptophan supplements became available, this blood disorder was extremely rare.

Many other widely available supplements can cause toxic side effects, but that discussion is beyond the scope of this book. See Part V, *The Resource Corner*, for reliable sources of information on vitamin supplements.

Quinones

A group of toxins called *quinones* are present in many foods, notably rhubarb and coffee.[13] These substances can alter genetic material; produce free radicals, which damage cell membranes; and generate mutagens and carcinogens.[13] All of these toxins are promoters of the cancer process.[13]

Psoralens

When celery is exposed to light, a group of plant toxins with carcinogenic potential are activated. These carcinogens, taken together, are called *linear furocoumarins* or *psoralens*. Celery produces large amounts of these compounds when the plant is damaged by mold or pink-rot disease.[55] In fact, people exposed to mold-damaged celery on a regular basis—such as celery-pickers and produce-checkers—can develop a psoralens-related skin rash.[1,13,55]

Other plants producing psoralens include carrots, parsnips, parsley, and figs.[13,55] It is only when these compounds are exposed to sunlight that they become carcinogenic. To date, no scientific evidence exists that normal everyday exposure to psoralens from any source produces any increased risk of cancer or other disease for consumers. At this point, psoralens exposure appears to present increased risk of skin rashes only for agriculture and produce workers who are in continual contact with psoralens-containing plants. Nevertheless, this remains an area of continuing study.

Phytate

A naturally-occurring plant substance called *phytate* remains the center of a bit of controversy. Phytate is found in whole-grain products and in wheat bran. For years, phytate has been studied for its alleged inhibition of mineral absorption, particularly zinc absorption.[33] Early research suggested that calcium absorption was inhibited by phytate, but later studies seemed to show that yeast action in bread and enzymes from the human intestine eliminated phytate's threat.[33] Still, large amounts of phytate produce both calcium and zinc losses.[33]

Because high-phytate foods are also high-fiber foods, more recent studies have explored a possible link. These studies have determined that the mineral-absorption inhibiting effect is due to both phytate *and* fiber.[33]

Just how important phytate is remains unclear. However, research seems to point to the fact that you *can* get too much whole-grain food, and that the dual action of phytate and fiber may result in at least mild deficiencies of zinc and calcium.[33]

So, sprinkling wheat bran over everything and having bran bread at every meal appear to have some drawbacks. A good goal is to focus intensely-bran-containing foods, like bran cereal, at one meal such as breakfast, leaving other meals for the non-phytate-containing fiber of fruits and vegetables.

Oxalate

Like phytate, oxalate is a controversial substance. Present in beets and beet tops, rhubarb, Swiss chard, lamb's quarters, parsley, tea, spinach, and beans, oxalate allegedly combines with calcium, rendering it unabsorbable. Many consumers are familiar with oxalate from kidney stones, a large percentage of which are calcium oxalate stones.

Oxalate has been studied extensively, with more recent studies suggesting that a high oxalate intake must be combined with a low calcium diet and a deficiency of vitamin D for a prolonged period of time before true calcium deficiency would occur.[55] Estimates of the impact of oxalate on calcium absorption in the British diet suggest that only 30 to 70 milligrams of calcium would be bound by the typical British diet, which includes five cups of tea.[55]

Excessive amounts of oxalate can have toxic effects, leading to death.[55] Rhubarb leaves contain an extremely large amount of oxalate, and consuming them can lead to convulsions and, occasionally, death.[54] Large numbers of sheep fed a range crop called halogeton have died due to the oxalate content of halogeton.[54]

Some population studies have shown a striking increase in oxalate stones among children in regions where native foods contain large amounts of oxalates.[54] The popular houseplant *Dieffenbachia* contains high levels of oxalate and may be a hazard to small children.[54]

In general, moderate amounts of oxalate-containing foods, combined with a high-calcium diet and adequate vitamin D via sun exposure or fortified dairy products, will prevent problems with oxalates.

So...What's Left to Eat?

The purpose of this chapter is not to strike fear in the hearts of consumers, although it may have done so. Truly, the goal is to sensitize all of us to the reality that toxic substances are all around us and we consume them daily—with, generally, no ill effects. But the risks from these natural toxins may parallel or exceed the actual risks from toxins of more pressing concern to most consumers—pesticides and additives. The bottom line is that very likely *all* of these toxins—both natural and manufactured—present minimal risks for most consumers.

References

1. Ames, Bruce N., Renae Magaw, and Lois Swirsky Gold, "Ranking Possible Carcinogenic Hazards," *Science* 236(4799):271–280, April 17, 1987.
2. Ames, Bruce N., "Food Constituents as a Source of Mutagens, Carcinogens, and Anticarcinogens," in Ib Knudsen (ed.), *Genetic Toxicology of the Diet*, Alan R. Liss, New York, 1986, pp. 3–32.
3. Neal, G. E., "Influences of Metabolism: Aflatoxin Metabolism and Its Possible Relationships with Disease," in D. H. Watson (ed.), *Natural Toxicants in Food: Progress and Prospects*, Ellis Horwood Ltd., Chichester, England, 1987, pp. 125–168.
4. Wilson, Benjamin J., "Mycotoxins and Toxic Stress Metabolites of Fungus-Infected Sweet Potatoes," in John N. Hathcock (ed.), *Nutritional Toxicology, Vol. 1*, of *Nutrition: Basic and Applied Science—A Series of Monographs*, Academic Press, New York, 1982, pp. 239–302.
5. Williams, Gary M., M.D., "Food-Borne Carcinogens," in Ib Knudsen (ed.), *Genetic Toxicology of the Diet*, Alan R. Liss, New York, 1986, pp. 73–81.
6. National Research Council, *Diet and Health: Implications for Reducing Chronic Disease Risk*, National Academy Press, Washington, D.C., 1989.
7. Campbell, T. Colin, Ph.D., "A Study on Diet, Nutrition and Disease in the People's Republic of China, Part II," *Contemporary Nutrition* 14(6): 1989.
8. Asplin, F. D., and R. B. A. Carnaghan, "The Toxicity of Certain Ground

Nut Meals for Poultry with Special Reference to Their Effect on Ducklings and Chickens," *Veterinary Record* 73:1215–1219, 1961.

9. Wolf, H. and E. W. Jackson, "Hepatomas in Rainbow Trout: Descriptive and Experimental Epidemiology," *Science* 142:676–678, 1963.

10. de Iongh, H., R. O. Vies, and J. G. van Pelt, "Milk of Mammals Fed an Aflatoxin-Containing Diet," *Nature* 202:466–467, 1964.

11. Cordle, Frank and Albert C. Kolbye, "Environmental Contaminants in Food," in John N. Hathcock (ed.), *Nutritional Toxicology, Vol. 1, of Nutrition: Basic and Applied Science—A Series of Monographs,* Academic Press, New York, 1982, pp. 303–325.

12. Consumers Union, "Hold the Mold: Aflatoxin in Peanut Butter," *Consumer Reports,* September 1990, p. 591.

13. Ames, Bruce N., "Dietary Carcinogens and Anticarcinogens," *Science* 221: 1256–1264, September 1983.

14. Moss, M. O. and M. Frank, "Prevention: Effects of Biocides and Other Agents on Mycotoxin Production," in D. H. Watson (ed.), *Natural Toxicants in Food: Progress and Prospects,* Ellis Horwood Ltd., Chichester, England, 1987, pp. 231–251.

15. Ariens, E. J. and A. M. Simonis, "General Principles of Nutritional Toxicology," in John N. Hathcock (ed.), *Nutritional Toxicology, Vol. 1, of Nutrition: Basic and Applied Science—A Series of Monographs,* Academic Press, New York, 1982, pp. 17–80.

16. Morgan, M. R. A. and D. T. Coxon, "Tolerances: Glycoalkaloids in Potatoes," in D. H. Watson (ed.), *Natural Toxicants in Food: Progress and Prospects,* Ellis Horwood Ltd., Chichester, England, 1987, pp. 221–230.

17. Sinden, S. L. and K. L. Deahl, "Effect of Glycoalkaloids and Phenolics on Potato Flavour," *Journal of Food Science* 41:520–523, 1976.

18. Zitnak, A. and M. A. Filadefi, "Estimation of Taste Thresholds of Three Potato Glycoalkaloids," *Canadian Institute of Food Science and Technology Journal* 18:337–339, 1985.

19. Claringbold, W. D. B., J. D. Few, and J. H. Renwick, "Kinetics and Retention of Solanidine in Man," *Xenobiotica* 12:293–302, 1982.

20. Toth, B., "Mushroom Hydrazines: Occurrences, Metabolism, Carcinogenesis, and Environmental Implications," in E. C. Miller et al. (eds.), *Naturally Occurring Carcinogens-Mutagens and Modulators of Carcinogenesis,* University Park Press, Baltimore, Maryland, 1979, and Japan Scientific Societies Press, Tokyo, 1979, pp. 57–65.

21. Toth, B., and J. Erickson, *Cancer Research* 46:4007, 1986.

22. National Research Council, *Diet, Nutrition, and Cancer,* National Academy Press, Washington, D.C., 1982.

23. Larsson, Bonny K., "Formation of Polycyclic Aromatic Hydrocarbons Dur-

ing the Smoking and Grilling of Food," in Ib Knudsen (ed.), *Genetic Toxicology of the Diet,* Alan R. Liss, New York, 1986, pp. 169–180.

24. Sugimura, Takashi et al., "Mutagens and Carcinogens in Cooked Food," in Ib Knudsen (ed.), *Genetic Toxicology of the Diet,* Alan R. Liss, New York, 1986, pp. 85–107.

25. National Cancer Institute, *Diet, Nutrition & Cancer Prevention: The Good News,* National Institutes of Health, Bethesda, Maryland, 1986.

26. National Research Council, *The Health Effects of Nitrate, Nitrite, and N-Nitroso Compounds, Report of the Committee on Nitrite and Alternative Curing Agents in Food,* Assembly of Life Sciences, National Academy Press, Washington, D.C., 1981.

27. Mundt, J. Orvin, "Hazards of Foodborne Bacterial Infections and Intoxications," in John N. Hathcock (ed.), *Nutritional Toxicology, Vol. 1,* of *Nutrition: Basic and Applied Science—A Series of Monographs,* Academic Press, New York, 1982, pp. 209–237.

28. Broihier, Catherine, M.S., R.D., "How Safe Are Imported Foods? 'Circle of Poison' Sounds a Warning," *Environmental Nutrition* 14(2):1, February 1991.

29. American Dietetic Association, *Handbook of Clinical Dietetics,* Yale University Press, New Haven, 1981.

30. Kuhn, Donald N. and Walter Lovenberg, "Psychoactive and Vasoactive Substances in Food," in John N. Hathcock (ed.), *Nutritional Toxicology, Vol. 1,* of *Nutrition: Basic and Applied Science—A Series of Monographs,* Academic Press, New York, 1982, pp. 473–495.

31. Hart, Bonita E., R.D., *Clinical Diet Manual,* 7th ed., Food and Nutrition Management Services, Irvine, California, 1988.

32. Heaney, R. K. and G. R. Fenwick, "Identifying Toxins and Their Effects: Glucosinolates," in D. H. Watson (ed.), *Natural Toxicants in Food: Progress and Prospects,* Ellis Horwood Ltd., Chichester, England, 1987, pp. 76–109.

33. Bender, A. E., "Effects on Nutritional Balance: Antinutrients," in D. H. Watson, *Natural Toxicants in Food: Progress and Prospects,* Ellis Horwood Ltd., Chichester, England, 1987, pp. 110–124.

34. Norton, Stata, "Effects of Food Chemicals on Behavior of Experimental Animals," in John N. Hathcock (ed.), *Nutritional Toxicology, Vol. 1,* of *Nutrition: Basic and Applied Science—A Series of Monographs,* Academic Press, New York, 1982, pp. 451–471.

35. el-Shobaki, F. A. et al., "The Effect of Some Beverage Extracts on Intestinal Iron Absorption," *Z Ernahrungswiss* 29(4):264–269, 1990.

36. Garcia-Lopez, J. S. et al., "Iron Retention by Rats from Casein-Legume Test Meals: Effect of Tannin Level and Previous Diet," *Journal of Nutrition* 120(7): 760–766, 1990.

37. Fairweather-Tait, S. J. et al., "The Effect of Tea on Iron and Aluminum Metabolism in the Rat," *British Journal of Nutrition* 65(1):61–68, 1991.

38. Imanishi, H. et al., "Tea Tannin Components Modify the Induction of Sister-Chromatid Exchanges and Chromosome Aberrations in Mutagen-Treated Cultured Mammaliancells and Mice," *Mutation Research* 259(1): 79–87, 1991.

39. Liu, X. L., "Genotoxicity of Fried Fish Extract, MeIQ and Inhibition by Green Tea Antioxidant," *Chung-Hua Chung Liu Tsa Chih* 12(3):170–173, 1990.

40. Jain, A. K. et al., "Crude Tea Extracts Decrease the Mutagenic Activity of N-Methyl-N′-Nitro-N-Nitrosoguanidine in Vitro and in Intragastric Tract of Rats," *Mutation Research* 210(1):1–8, 1989.

41. Yan, Y. S., "Effect of Chinese Green Tea Extracts on the Human Gastric Carcinoma Cell in Vitro," *Chung-Hua Yu Fang I Hsueh Tsa Chih* 24(2):80–82, 1990.

42. Han, C., and Y. Xu, "The Effect of Chinese Tea on Occurrence of Esophageal Tumor Induced by N-Nitrosomethylbenzylamine in Rats," *Biomedical and Environmental Sciences* 3(1):35–42, 1990.

43. Fujiki, H. et al., "New Antitumor Promoters: (-)-Epigallocatechin Gallate and Sarcophytols A and B," *Basic Life Sciences* 52:205–212, 1990.

44. Wang, Z. Y. et al., "Antimutagenic Activity of Green Tea Polyphenols," *Mutation Research* 223(3):273–285, 1989.

45. Ito, Y. et al., "Chromosome Aberrations Induced by Aflatoxin B_1 in Rat Bone Marrow Cells in Vivo and Their Suppression by Green Tea," *Mutation Research* 222(3):253–261, 1989.

46. Sagesaka-Mitane, Y. et al., "Platelet Aggregation Inhibitors in Hot Water Extract of Green Tea," *Chemical and Pharmaceutical Bulletin* 38(3):790–793, 1990.

47. Sato, Y. et al., "Possible Contribution of Green Tea Drinking Habits on Prevention of Stroke," *Tohoku Journal of Experimental Medicine* 157(4):337–343, 1989.

48. Ali, M. et al., "A Potent Thromboxane Formation Inhibitor in Green Tea Leaves," *Prostaglandins Leukotrienes & Essential Fatty Acids* 40(4):281–283, 1990.

49. Sheriff, D. S., and M. el Fakhri, "Tea Consumption and Serum Lipids in a Libyan Population in Benghazy," *Annals of Clinical Biochemistry* 25(Part 6): 670–672, 1988.

50. Tyler, V. E., *The New Honest Herbal: A Sensible Guide to Herbs and Related Remedies,* Stickley, Philadelphia, Pennsylvania, 1987.

51. Powers, Dorothy E., and Ann O. Moore, *Food Medications Interactions,* Food-Medication Interactions, Phoenix, Arizona, 1986.

52. Abraham, S., and A. T. John, "Clastogenic Effects Produced by Black Pepper in Mitotic Cells of Vicia Faba," *Mutation Research* 224(2):281–285, 1989.

53. Roslyn Alfin-Slater, Ph.D. (ed.), *Nutrition and the M.D.* 16(6):4, 1990.

54. Goodhart, Robert S. and Maurice E. Shils, *Modern Nutrition in Health and Disease,* 6th ed., Lea & Febiger, Philadelphia, Pennsylvania, 1980.

55. Beier, R. C. et al., "HPLC Analysis of Linear Furocoumarins (Psoralens) in Healthy Celery (Apium Graveolens)," *Food Chemistry and Toxicology* 21:163, 1983.

CHAPTER 4

FOOD POISONING

*[Not even] one-third of . . . shoppers think that spoilage and
germs are the greatest threat to food safety. [But] the Food
Safety and Inspection Service and the rest of the public
health community think bacteria pose the greatest risk to
the public health.*
> CATHERINE ADAMS, PH.D., R.D., ASSISTANT ADMINISTRATOR,
> FOOD SAFETY AND INSPECTION SERVICE.[1]

Fewer common physical experiences are more unsettling than a bout with food poisoning—that weak, "quivering" feeling, the endless trips to the john, that deep-down feeling of utter exhaustion. Yet, most Americans are far more concerned about the long-term effects of pesticide and additive exposure than they are about the far more common, almost immediate, well-documented, potentially lethal effects of food poisoning.

Wake up, America! Food poisoning is not a foreign disease! Food poisoning affects millions of Americans annually!

It's been estimated that six million Americans suffer the cruel effects of food-related poisoning annually, and a small percentage die each year.[2] Annual financial losses to U.S. companies for missed work days due to nonfatal food poisoning number in the millions. These figures, of course, don't even begin to describe the human anguish involved in all of this "down time."

Most people have no idea of the extent of food poisoning nationwide. Often, we assume that such well-off nations as the U.S., with excellent refrigeration facilities and good sanitation, are somewhat immune to such a primitive malady. In fact, because the typical case of food poisoning is far more like a 24-hour flu than a poisoning, most nonlethal cases of food poisoning are self-diagnosed by sufferers as "the flu."

Because of this, the annual cases of food poisoning, or *food-borne illness,* are vastly underreported, making it difficult for public health officials to get a real handle on the scope of the problem.[3]

All of this suffering and anguish—not to mention lost work and play time—is preventable. Each of us has within our power the ability to control, for the most part, our risk of food-borne illness. How, you ask? Read on.

The Biggies

The most frequent causes of reported bacterial food poisoning in recent years have been *Salmonella, Shigella, Staphylococcus, Streptococcus,*

Campylobacter, and *Clostridium perfringens.*[3] *Salmonella, Clostridium botulinum, Shigella,* and *Listeria* have been the most common agents in *deaths* from bacterial food poisoning.[3] Poisonous mushrooms and toxins in fish, including scombrotoxin (from scombroid fish, discussed in the preceding chapter, Part I, Chap. 3) and ciguatoxin (from fish that have consumed poisonous algae), caused most of the chemical-related food poisonings and deaths in recent years.[3]

Food poisoning is extremely serious in very ill, very young (fetuses, infants, and toddlers), and very old sufferers. Death, tragically, is a frequent outcome in such fragile victims of some seemingly benign types of food poisoning. It is the healthy adult who is most likely to survive an attack of one of these common food poisonings. But let's not minimize the ravages of a severe case of nonfatal food poisoning, one which renders its victim relatively useless for a matter of days or weeks, yet, mercifully, does not bring death.

Salmonella

Salmonella is by far the most common cause of food-borne illness. The ghastly truth about the *Salmonella* bacterium is that it originates almost exclusively in fecal matter. Rat, mouse, and human feces are all likely to contain *Salmonella* bacteria. *Salmonella* is easily passed into eggs through small cracks in eggshells, into poultry through feces-contaminated chicken feed and packing facilities, into shellfish through a polluted-water habitat, and into both fresh and processed foods through rodent droppings in some food-processing plants and storage facilities. Scientists also suspect that hens can transmit *Salmonella* into eggs before the shells are formed. It is also extraordinarily easy for *Salmonella* to enter food via the contaminated hands of food handlers. Insects, birds, and domestic pets may also spread *Salmonella.* The most common food carriers of *Salmonella* include poultry, eggs and egg products, meat, pet meat, and sausage.

By now you're squirming in your chair, pondering all the ghastly possibilities and contemplating never buying food again. But it gets worse!

The symptoms of salmonellosis, the food-borne illness caused by *Salmonella,* are fever, headache, abdominal pain, diarrhea, and vomiting lasting from one to eight days.[4] Because the symptoms are flulike, many victims have no idea that this is the source of the trouble. Symptoms may begin as soon as six hours after eating contaminated food, or as long as 36 hours later.[4] The longer the delay before symptoms begin, the more likely the victim will dismiss food as the cause.

With *Salmonella,* the key is growth of the bacteria before the food is consumed. Bacteria divide every 20 minutes or so, so 100 bacteria become 200, then 400, then 800, then 1600—leading to over one million within three and a half hours.

Food left on a counter to thaw is a common cause of salmonellosis. Well-meaning cooks pull a chicken out of the freezer in the morning and set it out on the counter to thaw all day while they're off at work or other activities. Consider the consequences! An extremely graphic depiction of a thawing chicken, presented by one of my professors during graduate school, was that of a fowl becoming coated with an ever-thickening blanket of wriggling bacteria as it thawed, with that bacteria-laden blanket progressing relentlessly to the center of the bird. A ghastly picture, indeed.

A very recent discovery places cantaloupes on the list of *Salmonella* carriers. In August 1991, the Food and Drug Administration announced that over 400 cases of *Salmonella poona*, a type of *Salmonella* associated with cantaloupes, had been reported during June and July 1991.[5] Many of the victims had eaten at salad bars where cantaloupe was served. Contaminated cantaloupe rinds from a particular crop of cantaloupes harvested in Texas were implicated. Once these melons were cut, the bacteria spread to the edible portion of the fruit and was then consumed by those who later suffered food poisoning.[6]

While this may seem to have been an outbreak stemming from a localized problem, the FDA felt strongly enough to issue recommendations to consumers to wash and scrub whole cantaloupes, in fact all produce to be served raw, with dish detergent, then to rinse before cutting and serving them.[6] Two weeks later, due to concern about the use of detergent on fruits and vegetables, this advice was changed to simply thorough cleaning of raw produce with water.[7]

Beside the above, the best "kitchen control" strategies for *Salmonella* include:[4]

1. Immediate re-refrigeration of high-risk foods after purchase
2. Thawing of high-risk foods in the refrigerator or microwave
3. Using one cutting board or cutting surface exclusively for meats, poultry, and fish; another for other foods
4. Careful washing of cutting surfaces and utensils that have been in contact with raw meats, fish, and eggs
5. Careful personal hygiene of those handling food, particularly thorough hand washing before handling food and between food-handling tasks
6. Thorough cooking of high-risk foods
7. Re-refrigeration of leftover high-risk foods within two hours of removal from heat or refrigeration

Shigella

Shigella is a bacterium commonly spread via the *fecal–oral route*, generally where unsanitary conditions prevail, but it can also spread to food through improper hygiene of a food handler. In the U.S., about 20,000 cases of shigellosis are *reported* each year, largely in toddlers.[8] However, this probably represents a mere fraction of the *actual* number of cases.

Some strains of *Shigella* are quite potent, with as few as *ten Shigella* bacteria causing illness.[8] Other strains require ingestion of as few as 100 bacteria to as many as 10,000 bacteria before illness strikes.[8]

Symptoms of shigellosis include everything from no symptoms at all (scary, since the victim may easily spread the organism) to violent, bloody diarrhea. Severe cases include bloody stools (complete with mucus and pus), fever, chills, vomiting, and dehydration.[8] Not a pretty picture.

Usually, symptoms begin within four days of consumption of *Shigella*-contaminated food, but they sometimes are delayed up to seven days. The whole episode may last up to two weeks from the onset of symptoms. In very young victims, or in cases with severe diarrhea, antibiotics are sometimes used to treat the illness.[8]

Because *Shigella* bacteria are easily destroyed by heat, most reported cases of shigellosis have been been traced to contaminated cold foods, usually salads, particularly those made with potato, chicken, tuna, or shrimp.[8] Even lettuce and watermelon have been carriers of *Shigella*, as have raw oysters, apple cider, cream puffs, and spaghetti.[8]

Generally, shigellosis outbreaks have been linked to improper hygiene of food handlers in food service establishments.[8] But hygiene is no less important at home, where busy cooks, especially those caring for diapered little ones, may skimp on that critical hand-washing task before handling food.

Staphylococcus

"Staph," particularly *Staphylococcus aureus,* comes primarily from the skin of humans handling food. The organism can be found in the nose, on the hands, in the throat, and in boils, burns, scratches, and lesions.[4] Staphylococcus is also sometimes carried in raw milk from cows and goats, and in cream and cheese made from raw milk.

With *Staphylococcus,* it is the organism's production of toxin that is critical to causing food-borne illness. As Staphylococcus bacteria grow in food, they produce a poisonous substance, or toxin, which, when consumed, induces violent vomiting, abdominal pain, diarrhea, and, occasionally, collapse.[4] Within two to six hours of eating food contaminated with Staphylococcus toxin, symptoms ensue, and the whole ghastly event is over within 24 hours. Staphylococcus poisoning is almost never fatal. A distinguishing feature is that it does not produce a fever in its victims.[4]

Controlling Staphylococcus is largely a matter of attending to the hygiene of those who handle food. Critical measures are to avoid touching cooked food with bare hands, to wash hands frequently while preparing food and after handling drippy noses and trips to the john, to store food carefully to prevent bacterial growth, and to clean kitchen equipment thoroughly after use.

Streptococcus

Streptococcus, particularly *Streptococcus pyogenes,* causes many human diseases, including scarlet fever, "strep throat," rheumatic fever, tonsillitis, and other infections.[8] Individuals recovering from any of these disorders often carry the organism in their throats for a period of time, paving the way for transmission to foods.[8] A massive food-borne outbreak of Streptococcus poisoning in Chicago in 1912, leading to over 10,000 infected people and 200 deaths, was caused by transmission of Streptococcus to milk by a number of dairy workers who were suffering from Streptococcus-induced pharyngitis.[8] Normally, pasteurization kills Streptococcus, but, in this incident, the pasteurization equipment wasn't functioning.[8]

Raw milk and cheeses made from raw milk may also spread Streptococcus. Other foods that have been known to cause food-borne Streptococcus outbreaks include shrimp and lobster salads, tuna salad with eggs, egg salad, potato salad, custard, ice cream, pudding, cheese, and meat sandwiches.[8] Contrary to popular belief, it's not the mayonnaise in the salads that increases bacterial growth, but protein foods, particularly eggs. (Mayo is acidic, which inhibits bacterial growth.)

Food-borne Streptococcus infection, like any Streptococcus infection, can cause Streptococcus throat, scarlet fever, or any of the other infections listed earlier. Because Streptococcus can now be treated with antibiotics, it presents less of a threat than in previous decades. Still, deaths continue to occur due to food-borne Streptococcus infections, usually resulting from raw milk or raw-milk cheese consumption.[8]

Critical here is to avoid raw milk and raw-milk products, and to practice proper food-handling hygiene when one is infected with Streptococcus.

Clostridium perfringens

Clostridium perfringens is found not only in human and animal intestinal tracts, but also in soil, dust, and insects, including flies.[4] Contamination often occurs in raw meat and poultry.

This organism produces spores that are "seeds" for new bacterial growth. These spores *survive* normal cooking temperatures, so thorough cooking does not ensure freedom from *Clostridium perfringens*. After boiling or slow roasting, the spores remain active. Also unlike the previously-discussed bacteria, *C. perfringens* grows without oxygen. This makes it more insidious, since these bacteria will grow even in dark, hidden places, such as joints of roasts, even when such foods are carefully wrapped and chilled.

Symptoms, beginning 8 to 22 hours after eating contaminated food, include severe abdominal pain and diarrhea, but no vomiting. The ordeal generally lasts one to two days, and may be fatal in elderly and ill victims.

Safety measures include those already listed for the above-mentioned bacteria, with one addition: Cooked foods should be rapidly cooled after cooking and serving to prevent bacteria from multiplying. A good idea is to cut up large roasts, including poultry, into smaller pieces and wrap the pieces separately for refrigeration, to hasten cooling.

Because of the possibility of soil contamination with *C. perfringens,* it's wise to remove soil that accumulates in vegetable bins, and to make sure all soil is removed when washing vegetables.

Campylobacter

Less well known than some of the other food-poisoning "bugs," *Campylobacter* is now recognized as the leading cause of one of the most common forms of intestinal infection, or *gastroenteritis,* in the U.S.[8]

A wide range of animals carry the *Campylobacter* organism. The list includes poultry, cattle, swine, sheep, goats, turkeys, ducks, cats, and dogs.[8] Major outbreaks of food-borne *Campylobacter* illness have been caused by undercooked chicken, raw clams, raw hamburger, unpasteurized milk, and processed turkey.[8] As with other food-borne pathogens already covered, raw (unpasteurized) milk is the most frequent culprit in *Campylobacter* poisoning.[8]

Symptoms of *Campylobacter* enteritis range from brief, mild diarrhea to a severe syndrome with bloody stools, resembling ulcerative colitis.[8] Most frequent symptoms in those who seek medical care for the illness include abdominal pain, diarrhea, fever, nausea, vomiting, and an all-over "sick" feeling.[8] The illness may occur from one to ten days after consumption of the offending food, and usually occurs within three to five days. The condition lasts from one day to a few weeks, usually resolving in less than a week.[8]

Campylobacter is destroyed at normal cooking temperatures and at temperatures used to freeze and store frozen foods. It won't grow in a salty environment, but salt doesn't *kill* the bacteria that are already there.[8]

While human carriers may occasionally contaminate food with *Campylobacter,* most often, undercooked or raw animal-based foods are the culprits in *Campylobacter* enteritis in humans.[8]

Preventing *Campylobacter* enteritis primarily involves avoiding raw milk and raw-milk cheese, and cooking meat, poultry, and fish thoroughly.

Listeria

In the recent past, *Listeria* contamination caused a major frozen dessert manufacturer to issue a product recall, which, ultimately, led to the demise of the product. *Listeria monocytogenes,* the responsible organism, is a poorly understood pathogen that is widely distributed among animals, birds, fish, ticks, and flies.[8]

Listeria can survive freezing temperatures, grows under refrigeration, and is killed only after holding the contaminated product at pasteurization temperature for longer than it takes to pasteurize milk.[8]

Contaminated milk products have been the most common causes of *Listeria* outbreaks, and outbreaks are more likely to occur in the summer months.[8] However, the first major outbreak in North America, in 1981, was reportedly caused by coleslaw made from cabbage fertilized with manure from *Listeria*-infected sheep.[8]

Symptoms of listeriosis depend on the type of person infected. Pregnant women infected with *Listeria* develop chills, fever, back pain, and headache, and may develop diarrhea and other symptoms.[8] Sometimes, pregnant women are infected with *Listeria* but have no symptoms. Usually, a pregnant woman's infection will spread to the fetus, leading to a widespread, life-threatening infection in the fetus.[8] Infected adults and newborns experience chills, fever, laryngitis, and blood disorders. Infants and older persons, particularly men over 50, may experience meningitis or meningoencephalitis due to *Listeria* infection, both of which lead to death in 70 percent of all cases where treatment is absent or started too late.[8]

Curiously enough, most people who are exposed to *Listeria* develop no infection and no symptoms at all. Properly functioning immune systems tidily destroy *Listeria.* But those who do become infected need prompt medical attention for proper diagnosis and treatment.[8]

Those most susceptible to *Listeria* infection include pregnant women, newborns, and those with suppressed immune systems such as the elderly and those suffering from acquired immune deficiency syndrome (AIDS).

Preventing *Listeria* from entering the food supply requires careful sanitation procedures, particularly in dairies. Recommendations for such procedures have been detailed by experts.[8] In the meantime, the relatively rare occurrence of *Listeria* outbreaks should serve to reassure those who feel vulnerable to this disorder.

Clostridium botulinum

C. botulinum is a particularly vicious food-poisoning bacterium that causes the often-fatal form of food poisoning called *botulism*. Fortunately, botulism is quite rare.

As with *C. perfringens*, the spores of *C. botulinum* survive cooking, and the spores and bacteria grow without oxygen, allowing them to survive in cans and other airless environments. *C. botulinum* is found in meat, soil, vegetables and fruits, and some fish.

Botulism is caused when one consumes the toxin produced by *C. botulinum* bacteria. Fatigue, muscle weakness, headache, and dizziness begin twelve hours to four days after eating contaminated food. There is usually no fever. Initially, diarrhea may ensue, but constipation is more common.[8] Then, the nervous system comes under attack, disturbing vision and speech. Within eight days, death often occurs due to paralysis of the muscles that control breathing, unless the antidote, called *antitoxin,* is given soon after initial symptoms begin.[4] The survivor of severe botulism may need several months to recover.[8]

The *toxin* produced by *Clostridium botulinum* is critical to causing botulism. If spores of the bacteria are present, but no toxin, it is rare that botulism will occur in adults.[8] Conditions that enhance growth of the bacteria, so that they can produce toxin, increase the likelihood of botulism.[8]

Infants under six months of age are more susceptible to botulism than are others. If *C. botulinum* bacteria or spores enter an infant's intestinal tract, they will grow and produce toxin because infants under six months of age haven't yet developed mechanisms to inhibit the growth of this organism, as older infants and others have.[1] Honey has been clearly implicated as a cause of infant botulism and should not be given to infants less than one year old.[9]

In the U.S., fruits and vegetables have been the most common causes of botulism.[3,8] Potatoes wrapped in foil, baked, and held at room temperature for several days, still wrapped, before being used in potato salad caused one outbreak, while a purchased container of garlic in oil that had not been refrigerated, despite label directions to do so, caused another.[8] Home canned fruits and vegetables have also been responsible for several botulism outbreaks.[8]

In Europe, ham is the most frequent cause of botulism.[8] This fact is attributed to the popularity of home-canned hams in European homes.[8]

Preventing botulism requires careful observance of procedures for home canning of all foods, particularly holding foods at the required canning temperature for the entire specified time period. Avoiding honey in an infant's diet is also critical. And it pays to pay attention to news stories of product recalls, regardless of the organism implicated, since avoiding the offending product can truly mean the difference between life and death.

Summing Up

The key components of a food-poisoning situation are (1) contaminated food, (2) sufficient bacterial growth to present a hazard, and (3) a vulnerable victim.

Contamination sometimes occurs before food is prepared for consumption, but often it's the result of careless hygienic practices on the part of someone preparing and handling food. This underscores the importance of thorough washing of hands and all surfaces placed in contact with foods before and after handling raw food. Pets, diapers, and careless after-john cleanups all contribute to food contamination.

Situations that favor bacterial growth include undercooking of foods, especially meats, failure to submit milk to pasteurization, holding cooked or raw food at improper temperatures, thawing foods at room temperature, failure to rapidly re-refrigerate grocery-store purchases and leftovers, and using improper methods of home canning. Meats, eggs, poultry, milk, and fish are among the most common carriers of food-poisoning pathogens. They should be handled with the utmost care.

Anyone can be a food-poisoning victim, but some people are more at risk than others. Fetuses, infants, toddlers, elderly, ill, and AIDS victims are all at higher risk of death from food poisoning than are healthy adults and older children. Pregnant women are likely to pass along their food poisoning to their fetuses, possibly leading to fetal death or severe abnormalities.

Final Tips

The bottom line with food poisoning is this: You can't be too careful. Practice vigilance at the grocery store and in the kitchen.

At the Grocery Store:

1. Avoid leaky, dented, or bulging canned foods.

2. Make sure the refrigerated foods you pick up are cold to the touch.

3. Don't pick up refrigerated items that someone has abandoned in the canned-goods aisle—notify the store manager, and make sure the products are discarded, not put back in the case.

4. Don't buy foods past their freshness date.

At Home:

1. Re-refrigerate perishable goods *as soon as* you get in the door from shopping.

2. *Never* thaw frozen meats, fish, or foods containing perishable goods at room temperature.

3. Never leave cooked or raw perishables at room temperature longer than necessary (*maximum* time: 2 hours).

4. Discard or return to the store canned or other foods that, after opening, emit a strange odor or have an unusual appearance.

5. Throw out all foods that have begun to produce off odors—they're spoiled, and they're not worth the agony of food poisoning.

6. Thoroughly cook all meats, fish, eggs, and products that contain them.

7. Discard eggs with detectable cracks in their shells.

8. Avoid raw milk and raw-milk products such as cheese.

9. Avoid leaving your Sunday dinner on the counter while you serve dessert—bacteria will have a field day!

10. Cut up cooked leftover roasts and wrap the parts separately to hasten cooling in the refrigerator.

11. Divide leftover large casseroles into smaller containers to hasten cooling.

12. Carefully follow all instructions when canning foods at home.

13. Wash hands thoroughly before, during, and after handling of raw and cooked foods and after pet cleanup, diaper changes, nose cleanups, and bathroom trips.

14. Make sure your refrigerator and freezer are set to proper temperatures—no more than 38°F for the refrigerator and no more than 0°F for the freezer.

15. Wash vegetables thoroughly before cooking or serving to completely remove soil.

16. Avoid giving honey to infants.

17. Pay attention to food-product recalls, and take them seriously!

18. Consult Part III, Chap. 2, *Food Handling*, for tips on how long to keep foods, along with other food safety gems!

References

1. Adams, Catherine E., Ph.D., R.D., "Using Science to Ensure the Safety of Meat and Poultry," presented at the Journalists' Conference, June 25, 1990, National Press Club, Washington, D.C.

2. Hathcock, John N., *Nutritional Toxicology, Vol. 1*, Academic Press, New York, 1982.

3. Centers for Disease Control, "Food-borne Disease Outbreaks, 5-Year Summary, 1983–87," *Morbidity and Mortality Weekly Report* 39 (SS-1):15–57, March 1990.

4. Hobbs, Betty C. and Diane Roberts, *Food Poisoning and Food Hygiene*, 5th ed., Edward Arnold, Baltimore, Maryland, 1987.

5. Centers for Disease Control, Public Health Service, U. S. Department of Health and Human Services, "Multistate Outbreak of *Salmonella Poona* Infections—United States and Canada, 1991," *Morbidity and Mortality Weekly Report* 40(32):549–552, August 16, 1991.

6. Food and Drug Administration, "FDA Issues Cantaloupe Advisory," FDA Talk Paper, Food and Drug Administration, Rockville, Maryland, July 3, 1991.

7. Retail Food Protection Branch, Food and Drug Administration, "Memorandum to Regional Food Program Specialists—Subject: Melons," Department of Health and Human Services, Rockville, Maryland, July 17, 1991.

8. Cliver, Dean O., *Foodborne Diseases*, Academic Press, New York, 1990.

9. Arnon, S. S. et al., "Home and Other Environmental Risk Factors for Infant Botulism," *Journal of Pediatrics* 94(2):331–336, 1979.

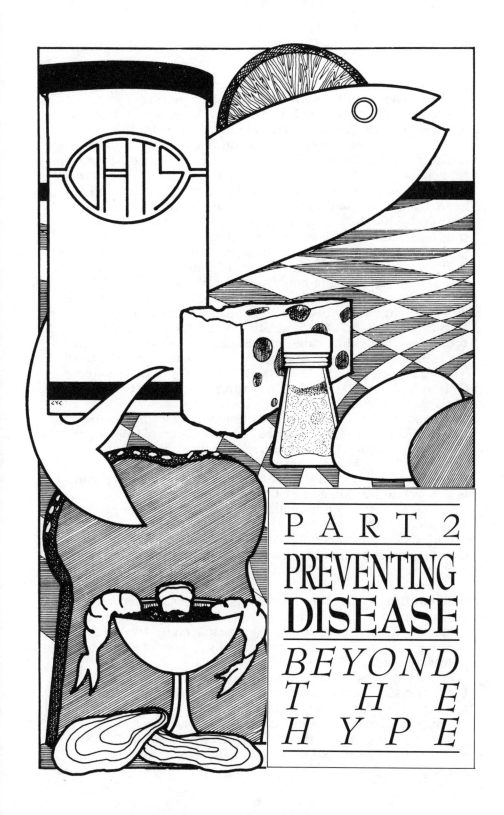

PART 2

PREVENTING
DISEASE

BEYOND

T   H   E

H   Y   P   E

Now that we've discussed the safety of our food supply, let's turn to some other profoundly important health issues.

Not so long ago, our leading causes of death were infectious diseases, like tuberculosis (TB), pneumonia, and influenza. Deaths during childbirth were also quite common. In large measure, problems like TB have come under such good control that cases are quite rare (except among the homeless, where an unusual frequency exists). And advances in obstetrics and neonatology have so drastically reduced the number of deaths during childbirth that such events are seen, thankfully, as rare tragedies rather than common occurrences.

That brings us to an entirely new set of leading causes of death.

Topping the list of current causes of death are heart and blood-vessel diseases, or cardiovascular diseases (CVD). This term encompasses heart attacks, strokes, high blood pressure, and rheumatic heart disease. Separated out, heart disease accounted for 513,700 U.S. deaths in 1987 alone,[1] making it the leading individual cause of U.S. deaths. Strokes accounted for 149,200 deaths in that same year,[1] making them the third leading cause of death. The total number of U.S. deaths from CVD in 1987 was 976,700, accounting for almost 46 percent of all deaths in the U.S. that year.

Occupying the number two position among leading causes of death is cancer. Estimates place cancer deaths in 1990 at 510,000 nationally.[2] Among causes of cancer deaths, lung cancer ranks highest for both men and women, with the rate of lung cancer among women continuing to rise. Colorectal cancer is the second leading cause of cancer deaths in the U.S., claiming an estimated 60,900 lives in 1990,[2] with an estimated 155,000 new cases occurring in the U.S. in 1990.[2]

Both CVD and cancer appear to have undeniable genetic connections, making them likely to occur more frequently within certain families. But *inheriting a predisposition* to one of these diseases and actually *having* the disease are two different things. Genetics only opens the door for the disease to occur—our behavior, including our diets, determines whether or not the disease develops. In fact, people often develop these health conditions *without* a prior family history of them, which points to our lifestyles as the main culprit.

Part II explores the nutrition links to heart disease, high blood pressure, and cancer. We'll also cover overweight, a risk factor for these and many other diseases.

Our goal here is to emphasize the extent to which we determine our own health, and to learn what we can do nutritionally to avoid or postpone life-threatening health problems.

References

1. American Heart Association, *1990 Heart and Stroke Facts,* American Heart Association, Dallas, Texas, 1989.

2. American Cancer Society, *Cancer Facts and Figures—1990,* American Cancer Society, Atlanta, Georgia, 1990.

CHAPTER 1

CHOLESTEROL &
HEART DISEASE

Read any good labels lately?

Cholesterol-free! No Cholesterol! A Cholesterol-Free Food!

The chorus of announcements from food labels is deafening. Can you remember (or imagine) life without *cholesterol-free* labels? Americans have come to depend on these bits of promotional excess.

Have you ever stopped to consider what these labels actually *mean*?

What most Americans believe about a food that screams "No Cholesterol!" is that it is low in fat, low in calories, and generally good for you. Right?

Wrong!

Unfortunately, it's not as simple as that. The phrase *cholesterol-free* does *not* mean *fat-free*. If you're surprised, you're not alone. All those cholesterol-free potato chips, crackers, and other goodies have *many* Americans fooled. So, what *does* "cholesterol-free" mean?

To answer that, we need to spend a few moments answering another question: What is *cholesterol*?

Cholesterol: A Thumbnail Sketch

Cholesterol, that dread substance reportedly avoided by two-thirds of American adults in a recent survey,[1] is a necessary, life-sustaining compound that our bodies actually manufacture. Believe it or not, unlike fat, it's calorie-free! Because it's calorie-free, removing it from a food does *not* reduce the calories in the product unless something else, such as fat, has also been removed from the product.

A waxy, fat-like substance, cholesterol regulates many body processes, such as growth and reproduction, in its vital role as a component of our hormones. It also speeds up the transmission of nerve impulses, as part of the special coating, called myelin, that surrounds our nerve fibers. Cholesterol performs vital functions in our brains, kidneys, adrenal glands (the tiny glands atop our kidneys that produce adrenalin), and other organs and tissues. In fact, without cholesterol, we wouldn't be here!

So what's the bad news? Obviously, our fear of cholesterol must have *some* basis in fact, right?

Well, sort of. Here's where the confusion starts.

Cholesterol is found in our blood. It's part of the little fat packages called *lipoproteins,* which our bodies use to transport fat around in the bloodstream. The cholesterol in the *blood* is what causes health problems.

Atherosclerosis

Blood cholesterol has been blamed for its unmistakable role in the process leading to heart disease. By plastering itself along the inside walls of our blood vessels, blood cholesterol creates *fatty streaks*. These fatty streaks initiate a process called *atherosclerosis,* or hardening of the arteries, through which fatty streaks develop into hardened areas called *plaques.*

In advanced stages, atherosclerosis clogs and narrows blood vessels, drastically reducing the flow of blood to various body parts. This leads to problems such as leg and chest pain, shortness of breath, and signs of senility. The biggest concern, however, is that small clots and other debris floating along in the bloodstream will become lodged in narrowed blood vessels, completely cutting off blood flow. When this happens, the tragic result is usually a life-threatening event, such as a heart attack or stroke.

History

Researchers started talking about the material that we now call cholesterol way back in 1769 when it was first discovered by a French chemist. In 1824, another French chemist named the substance *cholesterine.* (Later, its name was changed to *cholesterol,* the name we use today.) Still later, in the early 1900s, the first links between cholesterol and heart disease were tentatively drawn. What was known then, and now, is that cholesterol makes up the fatty streaks in blood vessels that are blamed for the disease process leading to heart attacks. But how cholesterol actually gets there—how it finds its way into our blood, and, eventually, into those fatty streaks—was still a mystery.[2]

Since the early 1900s, when cholesterol was first discovered in those fatty streaks, it has taken reams of additional research to shed light on the process of atherosclerosis, and some mysteries still remain. But scientists now feel somewhat comfortable with their knowledge of the process. One of the more interesting tidbits is that heart-disease risk is most clearly connected with the level of a certain type of fat package, or lipoprotein, in our blood called LDL, or *low-density lipoprotein.* This little detail will make more sense later, when we'll focus on diet–heart recommendations.

More recently, public interest in cholesterol has peaked whenever news of ground-breaking research has hit the media. And the frequent availability of public cholesterol screenings has kept interest and awareness alive. But it was in 1987 that the whole idea of preventing heart disease *really* caught fire.*

The National Cholesterol Education Program

In 1987, the National Heart, Lung, and Blood Institute of the National Institutes of Health (NIH) released the product of years of effort: the report that launched the National Cholesterol Education Program (NCEP).[4] This report was a landmark publication in several ways.

First, it redefined the levels of blood cholesterol thought to indicate increased risk of heart disease. By *redefined*, we're talking *lowered*. Until 1987, most adults with cholesterol levels of 240 had been told their heart-disease risk was no higher than that of a person with a cholesterol level of 180. The old standards even allowed for the tendency of blood cholesterol to increase with age, setting higher acceptable levels for people over 45 and higher still for those over 60. But, based on research showing progressively increasing risk of heart disease with higher blood cholesterol levels regardless of age, the NCEP abolished all age distinctions. Not everyone in the health field agrees with these new guidelines.[5]

Second, this new report encouraged health-care practitioners to check the blood cholesterol levels of *all* adults. The goal here was, and is, to catch problems early in the game, to prevent at least some of those freak "heart attacks out of nowhere." By identifying people with elevated cholesterol levels, practitioners could offer preventive measures *before* symptoms of heart and blood-vessel disease developed.

Finally, this report created the first set of clear guidelines for the health professional on what to do when an adult with high blood cholesterol is identified. The protocol includes a pattern for additional test-

---

*—or *heat*, depending on your perspective. The National Cholesterol Education Program (NCEP) was both a beacon to consumers and, to some others, a black hole of disappearing health resources. For further reading on some areas of disagreement, see *Heart Failure* by Thomas Moore,[3] a rather excessively critical analysis of the NCEP and other heart-disease prevention efforts. Yet, despite broad areas of disagreement, even the book, *Heart Failure*, and Mr. Moore's headline-grabbing *Atlantic Monthly* article ("The Cholesterol Myth," *The Atlantic Monthly*, September 1989, pp. 37–70), acknowledge the connection between elevated blood cholesterol and heart disease.

ing, a timetable for retesting after intervention, and guidelines for the use of diet and the use of drugs to help lower blood cholesterol.

The Magic Number

The new "magic number" set by the NCEP, and the cholesterol level still being used as a cutoff point for adults by most U.S. health-care practitioners today, is 200. According to the NCEP, if your cholesterol number, your measured total blood cholesterol, is *under 200*, your probability of developing heart disease because of blood cholesterol is considered to be low. As a result, your health-care practitioner will send you on your way without advice about changing your diet and without prescriptions for any drugs to lower your cholesterol.

If your cholesterol level is *200 or over*, your health-care provider may order additional tests and will recommend changes in your diet. After discussing other risk factors you might have, like high blood pressure or cigarette smoking, your doctor may send you to a nutrition professional for in-depth dietary instruction. If, after a time, no change in cholesterol is seen, you may be given a drug to help lower your cholesterol.

Some Don't Agree

Critics of the NCEP report suggest that the report and these guidelines have put too much emphasis on the role of blood cholesterol in heart disease. They suggest that important factors such as smoking and high blood pressure, both known to be more potent contributors to heart disease than high blood cholesterol alone, are camouflaged by this newer approach. Critics also suggest that this new standard of 200 is unrealistically, and unnecessarily, low,[5] or perhaps simply too arbitrary.

They may be right, in part. The cholesterol phobia that has gripped most health-conscious Americans has diluted the focus on smoking as a major risk factor for heart disease. In fact, most people believe that the only real risk from smoking is lung cancer—certainly a disturbing prospect, but not the whole picture. And high blood pressure may be fading in the public eye as a cause of heart and blood-vessel problems. Yet, high blood pressure remains the leading cause of both stroke and congestive heart failure. (We'll talk more about high blood pressure in the next chapter.)

As for the level of 200 being too low—research shows increasing incidence of heart attacks at levels of cholesterol over *140*. Now *there's* a low number. Perhaps the term *arbitrary* better fits the chosen standard of 200 than the term *low!*

Despite the criticism that the NCEP report has generated, many professionals in the health and nutrition fields feel indebted to the expert panel who developed these new guidelines. Through them, the NCEP has created an entirely new set of consumers who are concerned about their health—enough so to actually change what they're eating! Until cholesterol phobia hit the streets, health professionals had a hard time convincing many people of the importance of diet in health. Now, virtually everyone is somewhat interested in what they're eating, and an increasing number of people are seriously concerned about their diets.

The Diet–Heart Connection

The results of years of research on diet and heart disease have led scientists to make diet–heart recommendations, despite the controversy still buzzing around this issue. As more research accumulates, these recommendations will probably continue to be fine-tuned—in other words, *changed*. Changes in diet and health recommendations are understandably jarring to the public. Any change appears to confirm the commonly-held suspicion that scientists didn't have it quite right all along. Well, guess what—we still don't know everything. The true impact of dietary changes on the risk of heart disease is still a bit fuzzy. But that's no excuse to ignore the trends in research—and to miss out on our best shot at taking control of our health!

Misplaced Focus

Sadly, some early mistakes have survived into the present. The earliest diet–heart recommendations misleadingly amounted to simply this: Avoid foods containing cholesterol. Cholesterol phobia was born.

Why is avoiding cholesterol not enough? Why is this whole focus wrong?

A key distinction must be made here: What we've been talking about up to now is cholesterol found in the body, particularly the component of body cholesterol that contributes to heart disease, called *blood cholesterol* or *serum cholesterol*. From here on, whenever we refer to cholesterol in our *bodies*, we'll be calling it *blood cholesterol*.

The cholesterol in food is called *dietary cholesterol*. Dietary cholesterol, from a purely chemical standpoint, is the same compound as the cholesterol found in our blood. But its effect on our blood cholesterol, the key concern here, is not what most Americans think. Let's explore this.

Most people who've thought about cholesterol in food today have some idea of where it comes from. Most consumers seem to know that egg yolks and organ meats, such as liver, are high in cholesterol. But does peanut butter contain cholesterol? How about shellfish? Skim milk? Whole milk? Salad dressing? Coconut oil? Nuts? Palm oil? Margarine? Corn oil? And what does cholesterol-free really mean?

Let's take a quiz.[6]

1. If a food is labeled cholesterol-free, is it also:
   a. Low in saturated fat
   b. High in saturated fat
   c. Could be either high or low
   d. Not sure

2. Which kind of fat is more likely to raise blood cholesterol:
   a. Saturated fats
   b. Polyunsaturated fats
   c. Both of them
   d. Neither of them
   e. Not sure

3. Is cholesterol the same thing as:
   a. Saturated fat
   b. Polyunsaturated fat
   c. Neither of them

4. Where is cholesterol found?
   a. Vegetables and vegetable oils
   b. Animal products like meat and dairy
   c. All foods containing fat or oil
   d. Not sure

5. Are saturated fats usually found in:
   a. Vegetables and vegetable oils
   b. Animal products like meat and dairy
   c. Not sure

6. Are polyunsaturated fats usually found in:
   a. Vegetables and vegetable oils
   b. Animal products like meat and dairy
   c. Not sure

7. If a product is labeled as containing only vegetable oil, would it be:
   a. Low in saturated fat
   b. High in saturated fat

c. Could be either high or low

d. Not sure

8. Which kind of fat is more likely to be a liquid rather than a solid?
   a. Saturated fats
   b. Polyunsaturated fats
   c. Both the same
   d. Not sure

9. If a fat or oil is hydrogenated, has it become:
   a. More saturated
   b. Less saturated
   c. Not sure

10. Which kind of fat is higher in calories?
    a. Saturated fats
    b. Polyunsaturated fats
    c. Both the same
    d. Not sure

See page 104 for answers.

Confusion

Let's examine some common areas of confusion.

Dietary cholesterol is found *only* in animal products—milk, cheese, other dairy products, eggs, meat, fish, poultry, and animal-derived fats, such as butter, lard, and beef tallow. *There is no cholesterol in fatty foods that do not contain animal products,* such as peanut butter and margarine.

A food that is *high* in cholesterol may also be *low* in fat. For example, there's shrimp—a 3½-ounce serving (about 18 shrimp, cooked without fat) contains 195 milligrams (mg) of cholesterol, but only 1.1 grams (g) of fat.[7] Given the cost of shrimp, it's not common that one will eat 18 shrimp as one serving, so the actual cholesterol content of a *typical*, i.e., smaller, serving of shrimp would be lower. But the maximum cholesterol intake recommended by the American Heart Association and the NCEP is 300 mg per day, while the maximum *fat* intake is roughly 50 to 90 g, depending on calorie needs. So, shrimp contributes a hefty chunk of cholesterol, but almost no fat. It could be labeled as a *lowfat food,* but not a *low-cholesterol food.* But does that make it a good food?

Before we answer that, let's review the diet–heart recommendations from the National Cholesterol Education Program.[8]

To lower your high blood cholesterol:

1. Eat less high-fat food (especially food high in saturated fat).
2. Replace part of the saturated fat in your diet with unsaturated fat.
3. Eat less high-cholesterol food.
4. Choose foods high in complex carbohydrates (starch and fiber).
5. Reduce your weight, if you are overweight.

These guidelines were written in order of importance. Notice that reducing dietary cholesterol is *not* first on the list. Let's explore why.

A common misconception is that the cholesterol we eat automatically appears in our blood, much the way the gasoline you pump into your car ends up in the gas tank. It's not quite that simple. Only a fraction of the cholesterol we eat actually gets absorbed. And after it's absorbed, the body may get rid of it by dismantling it in the liver. So a pretty good percentage of the cholesterol we eat doesn't end up in our blood.

But the real kicker is that most of the cholesterol in our blood wasn't in our food at all. Most of it is produced in our bodies, by our livers. And what do our livers use as the raw material to create cholesterol? The primary fuel for our cholesterol-making machinery is fat, especially saturated fat. Here we're talking about the saturated fat in our diets, that villain found in all fats that are solid at room temperature, even some that you don't actually see. Coconut oil, butterfat, palm oil, palm kernel oil, meat fat—they all contain saturated fat.

Many people still believe that eliminating dietary cholesterol will *automatically* reduce blood cholesterol. This is not true! When a health-care practitioner says, "You need to change your diet to lower your cholesterol," these words don't mean "Eat a low-cholesterol diet." What they *really* mean is "Eat a cholesterol-lowering diet," which, in turn means "Eat less fat, saturated fat, and cholesterol." It may also mean "Lose weight" and "Exercise." All of these words may or may not come out of the doctor's mouth, but that's what needs to be done to lower blood cholesterol successfully.

Now, back to an earlier question: Is shrimp a good food? If you're not allergic to shrimp and your blood cholesterol is under 200 (under 175 for children and young adults up to age 19), then shrimp is a good food. It's a very low-fat source of protein, vitamins, and minerals. If your cholesterol is 200 or over, then shrimp should be eaten with more caution, no more than once per week. This same rule covers any other high-cholesterol food that is low in fat, such as organ meats and sardines. Egg yolks, a high-cholesterol, relatively low-fat food, should be limited to 4 to 7 per week for those with good blood cholesterol levels, and 2 to 3 per week for those with elevated blood cholesterol levels.

Focus on Fat

Heart-conscious consumers should focus on *fat*. In fact, consumers should be far more concerned about *fat* intake than they are about the amount of *cholesterol* in foods. Not only is fat the undisputed chief villain in the whole heart-disease scenario—fat is also a promoter of cancer. In addition, high-fat diets promote obesity, and obesity, in turn, increases risk of a host of other health problems, from diabetes to high blood pressure.

As you will note above, the *first* recommendation from the NCEP is to eat less high-fat food.

Total fat, animal fat, and saturated fat have been the focus of many incriminating studies, and all are associated with increased risk of heart disease.

MUFA and PUFA

Two types of fat, polyunsaturated fat (called PUFA) and monounsaturated fat (called MUFA), seem to *reduce* blood cholesterol. These fats come mainly from plants, like corn, soybeans, and olives. PUFA is the primary fat in most liquid vegetable oils. MUFA is the main fat in olive and canola oils. Together, MUFA and PUFA are called unsaturated fat.

Both polyunsaturated and monounsaturated fat contain the *same* calories as saturated fat, 9 calories per gram or 100 to 125 calories per tablespoon, so they are not *diet* food. But they are better choices than animal fats and should make up the bulk of our fat intake.

MUFA has the effect not only of lowering total blood cholesterol and LDL ("bad") cholesterol, but also of *maintaining* blood levels of "good" cholesterol called HDL, or *high-density* lipoproteins. PUFA, on the other hand, slashes *both* good (HDL) *and* bad (LDL) cholesterol, making it somewhat less desirable. By the way, HDL, or high density lipoproteins, act as scavengers in our blood vessels, scooping up cholesterol and whisking it away before it can get dumped into artery walls—hence the nickname "good" cholesterol.

Hydrogenated Fat

A type of fat called *hydrogenated fat* has received more attention recently. Ingredient labels often bear such words as *hydrogenated soybean oil* or *partially hydrogenated cottonseed oil*. The process resulting in hydrogenated fat is called *hydrogenation,* and it is used by the food industry to achieve a desirable texture in many food products. The down side is that hydrogenation creates a chemical change in the fat, producing what are called *trans* fatty acids. Some research shows that these changed fats produce effects in the body that are similar to those produced by saturated fat, but not all studies confirm this.[9] The prudent approach is to be cautious, going easy on foods containing hydrogenated fats.

Unfortunately, most hydrogenated fats aren't tallied up separately on the *nutrition* labels of products such as margarine and oil, where total fat, polyunsaturated fat, and saturated fat all appear as separate numbers depicting grams per serving. This is because, technically, most hydrogenated fats are, chemically, MUFA, which is neither saturated fat nor polyunsaturated fat and, therefore, needn't be listed. Even if MUFAs *were* listed separately, the issue would be further clouded by the fact that hydrogenated fats are an unnatural, or *trans*, form of MUFA, and do not behave in the positive ways that MUFAs do. So under current labeling regulations it's impossible to know how much of these changed, or *trans*, fats are in foods. The best approach is to notice if the words *hydrogenated, partially hydrogenated,* or *hardened* are used to describe oils on the *ingredient* label. If they are, then notice the total amount of fat in the product. If the amount of fat falls below the maximum levels we've illustrated at the end of this chapter, then don't worry about it, but eat it in moderation. If it exceeds these numbers, then, chances are, it's better left on the shelf, regardless of the type of fat it contains.

Fish Oil

Another flicker on the heart-disease scene is the use of fish oils to reduce heart-disease risk. Fish oils contain special types of PUFA called omega-3 fatty acids. These fats lower both blood cholesterol and another type of unhealthy substance in the blood called triglycerides which, if elevated, may be unhealthy. They also reduce the tendency for blood cells to get together and form clots, which can lodge in narrowed blood vessels and cause heart attacks and strokes.

However, one of the negative effects of large quantities of fish oils is a rise in the bad blood cholesterol called LDL.[9] Also, when taken in pill form, omega-3 fatty acids cause dangerous side effects like excessive bleeding. To take advantage of the positive effects of omega-3 fatty acids, the safest approach is to eat fatty fish often, twice a week if possible.* Fatty fish—including salmon and mackerel—are particularly

---

*Concern about contamination of fresh fish with hazardous chemicals in certain regions, such as dioxin in Lake Ontario salmon, may limit appropriate levels of consumption. For more information, check with your local office of the Cooperative Extension Service (see Part V, *The Resource Corner*).

good sources of omega-3 fatty acids. In addition, other foods, such as soybeans, soybean oil, canola oil,[9] pecans, walnuts, macadamia nuts, wheat germ, and wheat germ oil[10] all contain omega-3 fatty acids.

How Much Fat?

Current recommendations encourage us to keep our total fat intake under 30 percent of our total calories, which translates into a maximum intake range of 50 to 90 g of fat per day (based on calorie needs of 1500 to 2700 per day). On average, most adults should strive to keep total fat intake below 67 g per day. Of those grams of fat, fewer than ⅓, or 22 g, should be saturated fat, with the rest coming from PUFA and MUFA. A *minimum* of, on average, 22 g of *total* fat per day (10 percent of calories) is needed to promote hormone and cell-membrane production; so, in your zeal to reduce fat intake, remember this as a danger zone. Stay above 22 g of fat daily!

Fat-Free Product Bonanza

Many food manufacturers have jumped on the fat-free bandwagon, offering choices like fat-free frozen desserts, nonfat yogurt, fat-free salad dressings, no-fat baked goodies—the list keeps growing. This is a desirable trend in the food industry, and consumers can readily benefit. However, fat-free products are not calorie-free, and many of them contain a fair amount of sugar and other sweeteners, making them a dangerous choice for diabetics if consumed freely. Some fat-free products also contain more sodium than their traditional counterparts—a red flag for those with high blood pressure.

Oat Bran

There's no question—oat bran reduces blood cholesterol. But it's not the only food with this special power. The commercial attention given to oat bran has been nothing short of amazing, and consumers have been caught up in it since the first medical report touting oat bran's virtues.

The key to understanding oat bran lies in understanding some facts about fiber.

Fiber comes in many varieties. One of these types is called *gums,* a type of soluble fiber.* Gums appear to reduce the absorption of dietary fat and cholesterol from the digestive tract, leading to a reduction in blood cholesterol.

Oat bran, which comes from whole oats, is one of the products that contains this gummy fiber. *Rolled* oats also contain gums, as do all products made from whole oats. But pure oat *bran* has a particularly high concentration of gums, and much research has been done on the cholesterol-reducing effects of eating pure oat bran muffins.

Grocery stores, bakeries, and donut shops that sell oat bran muffins usually sell a product made largely from wheat flour with a mere sprinkling of oat bran in the batter and/or a sprinkling of rolled oats on top. These types of muffins have *not* been shown to reduce cholesterol. Only pure oat bran muffins, made using oat bran as the only type of flour ingredient, have been shown to be effective at reducing blood cholesterol. Recipes for pure oat bran muffins can be found on the boxes in which oat bran is purchased.

Research on oat bran shows that three to four pure oat bran muffins per day produce significant reductions in blood cholesterol, without the side effects of cholesterol-lowering drugs.[11]

Dissenting research shows that replacing fatty foods with *other* starchy foods *without* gummy fiber, such as farina, causes an effect on blood cholesterol similar to that of oat bran, implying that the true cholesterol-lowering effect is not from oat bran's special powers, but from the displacement of fat calories by fat-free calories. The particular study that demonstrated this has been criticized for its use of nutrition professionals, who already had excellent blood cholesterol levels, as subjects. Nevertheless, it makes a point—oat bran is not magic. It's merely another tool in the fight against heart disease.

Other Cholesterol-Reducing Fiber Foods

Oats are not the only sources of cholesterol-reducing fiber. Another source of fibers is *guar gum,* a substance used as a thickener in many foods. Guar gum, derived from a legume called guar, is now seeing limited use as a supplement to reduce cholesterol.

Legumes—kidney beans, chick-peas, dried beans, and dried peas—

---

*The term *soluble fiber* is used for types of fiber that dissolve in water, such as the type in oat bran.

all contain a type of fiber that produces similar results. Psyllium seeds—available in a few breakfast cereals, in some bulk-producing laxatives, and in health food stores—reduce blood cholesterol, too.

Pectin, a type of fiber found in apples, carrots, and citrus fruits, has been found to lower cholesterol. And rice bran, derived from brown rice, produces increases in good cholesterol, or HDL. Rice bran can be purchased in bulk in some specialty stores, but is more widely available in brown rice and brown rice-containing breakfast cereals. As with oat bran, the quantity of rice bran determines the effect. One study shows that a daily intake of 60 g (about 2 oz) of rice bran produces a desirable effect.[11]

One thing to keep in mind—the most effective way to lower blood cholesterol is to reduce fat intake. By eating more fruits, vegetables, and whole grains, even if they're not "pure" oat bran or "pure" rice bran, you will tend to eat fewer high-fat foods. The feeling of fullness produced by starch- and fiber-containing foods makes it easier to avoid or reduce fatty foods. This leads, in most cases, to favorable results for your blood cholesterol.

Overweight

The NCEP's last recommendation is to reduce weight if you are overweight. Not only the total weight but also the way the weight is distributed is important.

As we will discuss in more detail in Part II, Chap. 4, research has shown a marked increase in risk of certain diseases, including heart disease, when excess fat is distributed in the abdominal region. A simple calculation called the *waist-to-hip ratio* can be used to predict your level of risk. To calculate yours and to find your risk level, see Part II, Chapter 4, *Calories and Your Weight*.

What's Left to Eat?

The confusion produced by misleading food labels should come to a halt soon. New labeling regulations, projected to go into effect in 1993, will limit the use of such terms as *light, lite,* and *cholesterol-free*. They'll also require new pieces of nutrition and ingredient information that will help clarify what's inside the package.

Until then, your best ally is a pair of reading glasses. Check out those labels. If there's a nutrition label, look at the portion size. How realistic is it for you? Will your serving be larger or smaller? Look at the amount of fat, and compare it to the chart below for *your* serving size. Remember—the key issue for reducing blood cholesterol is fat, so keep the label's listings of fat grams in your sights, with a milder interest in the label's cholesterol numbers.

Meal Component	Fat, g (maximum)	Cholesterol, mg (maximum)
Entrees	10	100
Salad dressings	5	10
Margarine and spreads	6	10
Desserts	5	50
Crackers and cookies	3	5
Breads	1	5
Snacks	5	5
Cheeses	5	20
Milk	3	10

Remember, the daily goal for most adults is *less than* 67 g of fat and *less than* 300 mg of cholesterol.

In the final analysis, you'll find the easiest way to achieve a low fat intake is to eat more fruits, vegetables, grains, and pasta, use nonfat or low-fat dairy products, eat three-ounce portions of meat (if eaten), choose fish and skinless poultry (if eaten), and avoid fried, batter-dipped, and grease-laden foods.

Finally, ignore the "Cholesterol-Free!" labels emblazoned on foods. It's the amount of fat and saturated fat that really counts. Trust the *nutrition* label, not the promotional fanfare.

Caution with Niacin

To top off this discussion, here's a word about the use of niacin to control blood cholesterol.

A form of niacin called nicotinic acid, available in pill form, has been shown to reduce blood cholesterol levels in people with elevated levels of blood cholesterol. A best-selling book divulged this information to consumers, along with detailed information on how to do it yourself. As a result, hundreds of consumers have overdosed on niacin supplements, appearing in medical clinics all over the country with liver disorders. The book's author and publisher were slapped with a megabucks lawsuit. The point is this: Nicotinic acid, in the huge doses required to reduce blood cholesterol, is a drug. All vitamins, in high doses, have what is called a *pharmacological effect,* an effect beyond their functions as vitamins. When nicotinic acid is taken in doses of 500 mg or more per day, especially in sustained-release form, the possibility of liver damage is surprisingly high.

If you want to take nicotinic acid for your blood cholesterol, consult your doctor. The only safe way to do it is under a doctor's care, where periodic tests can monitor its effects on your liver.

Cholesterol Quiz Answers

Below are answers to the quiz on page 95. These questions were part of a 1988 Food and Drug Administration survey of 3200 U.S. adults. The numbers in parentheses indicate the percentage of 1988 survey respondents answering each question correctly.[12]

1. c (35% surveyed answered correctly)
2. a (56% answered correctly)
3. c (41% correct)
4. b (33% correct)
5. b (62% correct)
6. a (55% correct)
7. c (29% correct)
8. b (34% correct)
9. a (17% correct)
10. c (21% correct)

If you answered:

Eight or more correctly, you're a diet–heart whiz!

Four to seven correctly, you're a serious student!

Three correctly, you achieved the average score of those surveyed.[13]

Less than three correctly, you *really* need to read this chapter!

References

1. The Gallup Organization, Inc., *Gallup Survey of Public Opinion Regarding Diet and Health,* The Gallup Organization, Princeton, New Jersey, 1990.

2. Cooper, Kenneth H., M.D. *Controlling Cholesterol,* Bantam Books, New York, 1988.

3. Moore, Thomas, *Heart Failure,* Random House, New York, 1989.

4. The Expert Panel of the National Cholesterol Education Program, "Report of the National Cholesterol Education Program Expert Panel on Detection, Evaluation, and Treatment of High Blood Cholesterol in Adults," *Archives of Internal Medicine* 148:36–69, 1988.

5. Olson, Robert E., M.D., Ph.D., "A Critique of the Report of the National Institutes of Health Expert Panel on Detection, Evaluation, and Treatment of High Blood Cholesterol," *Archives of Internal Medicine* 149:1501–1503, July 1989.

6. Food and Drug Administration, *1988 FDA Health and Diet Survey,* Food and Drug Administration, Washington, D.C., 1988.

7. National Institutes of Health, *Facts about... Blood Cholesterol,* National Institutes of Health, NIH Publication No. 88-2696, U.S. Department of Health and Human Services, Bethesda, Maryland, revised November 1987.

8. National Cholesterol Education Program, "So You Have High Blood Cholesterol...," National Institutes of Health, NIH Publication No. 87-2922, U.S. Department of Health and Human Services, Bethesda, Maryland, September 1987.

9. National Research Council, *Diet and Health: Implications for Reducing Chronic Disease,* National Academy Press, Washington, D.C., 1989.

10. American Dietetic Association, *Handbook of Clinical Dietetics,* Yale University Press, New Haven, Connecticut, 1981.

11. Kestin, M., R. Moss, P. M. Clifton, and P. J. Nestel, "Comparative Effects of Three Cereal Brans on Plasma Lipids, Blood Pressure, and Glucose Metabolism in Mildly Hypercholesterolemic Men," *American Journal of Clinical Nutrition* 52(4):661–666, October 1990.

12. Blumenthal, Dale, "The Health–Diet Link: Charting a Rising Awareness," *FDA Consumer,* October 1989.

13. Levy, Alan S., Ph.D., "What Americans Know About Diet and Health: Trends from the 1979–1988 FDA Health and Diet Surveys," presented at the 1990 Journalists' Conference, June 25, 1990, National Press Club, Washington, D.C.

CHAPTER 2

SALT & HYPERTENSION

High blood pressure—"The Silent Killer." An estimated 60,990,000 Americans, some as young as six years old, suffer from high blood pressure.[1]

Also called *hypertension,* high blood pressure is one of the major ingredients in the deadly "recipe" that leads to heart and blood vessel diseases. Dubbed "The Silent Killer" because *it has no symptoms,* high blood pressure contributes more than any other single factor to deaths from congestive heart failure and stroke.

The American Heart Association estimates that over 46 percent of all Americans who have high blood pressure don't know they have it.[1] How tragic, since detection and treatment of this disorder are relatively simple and easily accessible by most Americans. But, because high blood pressure has no symptoms, it often goes undetected.

Statistics show that, in 1987, nearly 31,000 Americans died of high blood pressure. Another 149,000 died of stroke, and nearly 514,000 died of heart attacks.[1] Because of high blood pressure's effects on the heart and blood vessels, it contributes substantially to atherosclerosis (hardening of the arteries), heart attacks, and strokes.

High Blood Pressure: A Definition

Even people who know they have high blood pressure are hard-pressed to define it.

Blood pressure is the force exerted by the heart as it pumps blood through the miles of blood vessels in the body. When blood returns to the heart after its journey through your body, it gets pushed by a squeeze of the heart to your lungs to pick up a fresh load of oxygen and to get rid of carbon dioxide. Blood then returns to the heart to be pushed once again out into the body.

Each time your heart beats, the pumping action creates new pressure inside your blood vessels. This pressure, when measured, is the first, or top, number of your blood-pressure reading, called the *systolic* blood pressure. When your heart relaxes between beats, the pressure inside your blood vessels drops. This lower level of pressure is the second, or bottom, number of your blood pressure reading, called the *diastolic* blood pressure. Blood pressure is always stated as two numbers, such as 120 over 80. The second number is always smaller than the first. In a doctor's record, your blood pressure is listed as a fraction, like 120/80.

The generally-accepted level defined as high blood pressure is anything greater than 140 over 90 (or 140/90).[2] Depending on one's age, general health, gender, and other factors, medical professionals often do not prescribe medication until the blood pressure reaches higher levels. Borderline hypertension goes from 141 to 159 for the top number, and from 91 to 94 for the bottom number,[2] while true hypertension is 160 or above for the top number or 95 or above for the bottom number.[2]

Whether or not you take pills for high blood pressure, having high blood pressure is serious business.

When blood pressure rises, problems also arise. First, high blood pressure acts as a form of resistance to the heart's pumping action, forcing the heart to work harder. Such overwork can lead to a "wearing out" of the heart, often resulting in congestive heart failure—which can lead to death. Another problem results from the extra wear and tear on the blood-vessel walls as they endure the higher pressure exerted on them. This can lead to weakening and scarring of the blood-vessel walls, opening the door for a stroke or an aneurysm, both of which are life-threatening.

High blood pressure also hurries along the process of atherosclerosis (hardening of the arteries) by speeding up the process of plastering cholesterol onto the inner walls of arteries. This can hasten the onset of life-threatening events like a stroke or heart attack, or promote the development of an aneurysm.

Genesis of Hypertension

What actually causes 90 percent of the cases of high blood pressure is still something of a mystery. In most cases, tiny blood vessels called *arterioles* are thought to be in a perpetual state of constriction, which prevents easy blood flow through them. This causes a backing up of pressure inside the blood vessels, which in turn makes the heart push harder to pump blood.

Genetics appear to play a role in high blood pressure, with a tendency for the disorder to run in families and in certain races. Even if one has the genetic tendency to develop hypertension, however, it's possible that it will not develop unless certain other factors are present, such as excess weight, cigarette smoking, excessive alcohol intake, and/or a stressful or sedentary lifestyle.

Risk Factors and Prevention

Because high blood pressure may be a result of choices we make in our lives, it's important to explore "risky" choices.

Excess Weight

Excess weight seems to encourage elevated blood pressure. While not everyone who is overweight has high blood pressure, it is risky to become, and remain, overweight. A healthy choice is to achieve and maintain an appropriate weight for one's height. We'll address this further in a later chapter (Part II, Chap. 4, *Calories and Your Weight*).

Smoking

Smoking of tobacco products, especially cigarettes, increases blood pressure through the action of nicotine. Nicotine causes blood vessels to squeeze down on blood flowing through them, increasing pressure inside the veins and arteries. Although this effect is only observable while nicotine is still in the body, most habitual smokers always have a level of nicotine in the bloodstream, which means that, theoretically at least, there's always some effect on blood pressure.

In practice, research has shown that smokers typically have *lower* blood pressure than nonsmokers, possibly because they also, on average, weigh less.[3] However, when smoking is coupled with caffeine or alcohol, the elevating effect on blood pressure is dramatic.[3] Additionally, smoking reduces the effectiveness of some blood-pressure medications.[3] Another side effect of smoking is elevated blood cholesterol, which, in turn, speeds up the process of plastering cholesterol onto the insides of the blood-vessel walls. Ultimately, this too can increase blood pressure.

Alcohol

Excessive alcohol intake, defined as more than 2 drinks daily, also has the effect of raising blood pressure. The *critical dose* for most adults appears to be an ounce of *pure* alcohol per day, or approximately 2 average drinks.[3] For smokers, the dose that raises blood pressure is lower, equivalent to about 1½ drinks per day.[3] A level of 5 or more servings of alcoholic beverages per day, or roughly a fifth to a quart of 80-proof spirits per week,[2] is considered dangerously high for several reasons, not the least of which is its effect on blood pressure. Chronic heavy consumption of alcohol is linked not only to elevated blood pressure but also to increased risk of strokes.[2]

Alcohol intake not exceeding 2 drinks per day for men and 1 drink per day for women is considered "safe" from a blood-pressure standpoint.[4] Still, the truly, all-around safe alcohol dose for humans has yet to be defined, and may be none at all.[2]

Caffeine

Some scientific evidence shows that blood pressure increases with caffeine intake,[3] while other research suggests that, over time, tolerance to caffeine develops, and the blood-pressure effect is wiped out.[3,5] But one convincing piece of evidence comes from a study where blood pressure was taken after a nine-hour abstinence from caffeine and, again, within three hours of taking caffeine. There was no question—blood-pressure levels were significantly higher *after* the caffeine than before.[3]

Other studies have shown that no permanent tolerance to caffeine ever develops, and that, after 12 to 17 hours without caffeine, the blood pressure effect after taking caffeine is just as dramatic for the seasoned coffee drinker as it is for the first-time coffee drinker.[3]

Caffeine worsens the effect of tobacco smoking (nicotine) on blood pressure.[3] Caffeine also exaggerates the elevating effect of stress on blood pressure.[3]

Stress

The role of stress as a cause of high blood pressure is still somewhat fuzzy. However, it appears that individuals who have inherited the genetic tendency for high blood pressure may actually develop high blood pressure only when an array of factors are present at the same time. One of these factors may be psychological stress.[2] If this is true, then managing stress becomes a critical disease-prevention strategy.

Managing our lives to reduce stress, modifying our attitudes to limit negative emotions, and practicing relaxation techniques can be life-enhancing measures.[3] Behavioral techniques such as biofeedback, meditation, yoga, assertiveness training, progressive relaxation, and group psychotherapy, coupled with keeping track of one's blood pressure with a home blood-pressure monitor, have achieved significant drops in blood pressure, particularly when two or more techniques are combined and used regularly.[3]

Lack of Exercise

The "couch potatoes" of America are sprouting everywhere. The rising popularity of "cocooning" (getting home from work and cozying in for the evening) has punched the fitness boom right in the nose. With this growing trend has come an increase in the number of out-of-shape Americans, both children and adults, despite the billions of dollars being spent on home exercise equipment.

Being out of shape has far more than cosmetic consequences. For those at risk for high blood pressure, inactivity coupled with psychological stress spells *danger*. Rising blood pressure from a tough day at work or school doesn't abate while watching TV or playing video games. After a good walk or jog outside, or a romp on the treadmill, trampoline, ski track, bike, or rowing machine, blood pressure slides down as tension is released.

Physical activity is a potent ally in the fight against high blood pressure and is effective both in prevention and control of this disorder. However, power-oriented activities like weightlifting are dangerous for those with high blood pressure. Rather than reducing blood pressure, power activities actually *raise* blood pressure, sometimes resulting in strokes. If you have high blood pressure, consult a fitness professional before embarking on a bodybuilding program.

What about Salt?

Too many Americans point to salt as the key villain in high blood pressure. While it may be important, salt or sodium chloride is only one piece in the high-blood-pressure puzzle.

As we've already discussed, many factors seem to come together to increase risk of high blood pressure. High salt intake may be one of the factors that pushes blood pressure over the edge for some individuals.

For years, researchers have been telling us that certain individuals are *sodium-sensitive*. These folks are more likely than non-sodium-sensitive folks to experience significant rises in blood pressure as a result of increased salt intake. So, for these folks, consuming a low-salt diet for most of their lives appears to be a way to prevent high blood pressure. But the technology to *predict* who is actually sodium-sensitive is still being perfected, so it's not yet clear *who* should be cutting down on their salt intake as a means of preventing high blood pressure.

This dilemma has led to general, population-wide recommendations to control salt and sodium intake. Yet, the efficacy of this for the general public has never been proven.

Studies have shown that, in countries where salt intake is high, high blood pressure is more common than in countries where diets are low in salt. These findings have been used to fuel the argument that *everyone* should follow a low-salt diet.

There's no question that the average American takes in far more salt than is physiologically necessary. And there's no question that, if everyone really did eat a low-salt diet, those who are sodium-sensitive would benefit by experiencing lower blood pressures. Science also suggests that reducing salt intake is harmless for practically everyone, although one surprising new study suggests that some individuals may respond to *severe* sodium restriction (less than 500 milligrams per day) with *increases* in blood pressure.[6]

The larger issue is that Americans have become accustomed to eating salty foods. Is it fair to admonish *all* consumers to tow the line and forgo salty fare because, on average, *some* of them will benefit? And, further, if consumers *do* follow a low-salt diet, will they be misled into believing that this is all they need to do to prevent high blood pressure?

The committee who devised the latest *Dietary Guidelines for Americans* decided to perpetuate the general recommendation that all consumers eat a low-salt diet.[4] Basically, this meets with the approval of most health professionals. But the message to Americans needs to be clearer.

In fact, in this new edition of the *Dietary Guidelines for Americans*, some attention *is* given to the other risk factors for high blood pressure—excess weight, lack of exercise, and excessive alcohol intake.[4] But the spotlight remains on salt and sodium.

So, Now What?

One solution to the salt riddle is for each of us to consider our own individual risk factors. The best place to start is to have our blood pressure measured, and then to research the health condition of our blood relatives, both living and deceased.

If we come from a long line of hypertension sufferers, then the odds are good that we'll befall the same fate—if we allow enough risk factors to accumulate in our lives. A family legacy of high blood pressure may increase the chances that we are among the sodium-sensitive, and we should, therefore, be wary of salt and high-sodium foods.

But our efforts shouldn't end there. With a strong family history of hypertension, it becomes even more important to maintain a healthy weight, keep up a regular exercise program, and avoid excessive alcohol. Stress management and avoidance of tobacco products should also take center stage.

If we don't have high blood pressure now, and none of our blood relatives have ever had it, that still doesn't let us off the hook. Very-high-salt diets are a relatively new phenomenon. Our great-grandparents were never exposed to the levels of salt that we endure today. Theoretically, *anyone* could be sodium-sensitive. So, going easy on the salt is still a good idea.

For folks who have high blood pressure, reducing salt generally seems to reduce blood pressure. In fact, medications to control high blood pressure usually work better if people are also avoiding salt. Many high-blood-pressure sufferers think they don't have to worry about their diets, as long as they take their pills. While it's essential to take blood-pressure pills as prescribed, it's also critical, in many cases, to restrict salt.

Of course, all the things that help *prevent* high blood pressure also work in *treating* it. Here, we're talking regular exercise, proper weight, avoidance of alcohol, stress management, and smoking cessation. If conscientiously implemented, these nondrug methods of controlling blood pressure can eliminate the need for drug therapy, and, for people in the borderline category, they may prevent progression to true hypertension.[7]

How Much Is Too Much?

The question of "How low should you go?" when considering salt intake remains a tricky one.

Most recommendations agree that a level of around 2000 milligrams (mg) of sodium per day is an adequate level of restriction for adults. The 1989 edition of the *Recommended Dietary Allowances* lists 2000 mg as an estimated minimum requirement for healthy adults, yet explains in the text that levels as low as 500 mg per day are really enough.[8]

A landmark 1989 report from the National Research Council recommends that Americans limit salt intake to 2400 mg sodium per day, but adds that more health benefits would accrue with an intake of 1800 mg per day.[2] The American Heart Association recommends an intake of 1000 mg of sodium per 1000 calories per day, not to exceed 3000 mg per day.

The amount of sodium in one level teaspoon of salt is roughly 2200 mg.

Of course, salt is not the only source of sodium, and the above recommendations do not imply that we should all be sprinkling a teaspoon of salt on our food everyday. But comparing sodium to a quantity of salt may help you visualize what we're talking about here.

Everything we eat contains *some* sodium—even fresh, unaltered fruits and vegetables. But only certain foods are *concentrated* sources of salt, and all of them are processed foods. Much research points to the likelihood that salt, as in *sodium chloride,* is the *real* culprit in blood pressure concerns, rather than sodium in other forms.

Products that are particularly high in sodium chloride (table salt) include canned and dried soups (unless low-salt or salt-free), many frozen foods, soy sauce, salty snacks (chips, pretzels), canned vegetables (unless salt-free), cheese spreads, many cheeses, sauerkraut, pickles, tomato juice, vegetable juice, bouillon cubes and packets (unless salt-free), canned entrees (stews, pasta), dehydrated instant dinners, canned fish, beef jerky, cold cuts (unless low-salt), and frankfurters (including chicken and turkey).

Food-labeling regulations define such terms as *sodium free* and *low sodium.* See Table 1 for definitions. Also, *all* products on which nutrition labeling appears *and* products that make claims about their salt or sodium content *must* list the amount of sodium per serving on the label.[9] Additionally, new labeling regulations projected to go into effect in 1993 will require *all* processed foods to list their sodium content.

Research shows that, after two months of a mild salt restriction, our taste for salt changes. Studies show that people who had selected a relatively high level of saltiness as "most pleasant" in a taste test *before* two months of salt restriction *preferred* significantly lower levels of saltiness *after* the two months of restriction.[3] This is evidence that our preference for salt is *learned* rather than inborn, and it's a big ray of hope for those who must restrict their salt intake.

TABLE 1. Definitions — Sodium on Food Labels[9]

Sodium-free	Less than 5 mg of sodium per serving.
Very low sodium	35 mg or less of sodium per serving.
Low sodium	140 mg or less of sodium per serving.
Reduced sodium	Sodium reduced by at least 75% (label must compare sodium content of this product to that of the full-sodium product).
Unsalted, without added salt, no salt added	Processed without the salt usually used in similar products.
Low salt	This is not a regulated term as of this writing. Implies that the product contains less salt than the regular product. Does not mean *low sodium.*

"Lite" Salt?

Because of the growing health-conscious food market, new products keep springing up. A product (Salt Sense) that claims to have 33⅓ percent less sodium than regular salt has been on the market for a few years. Sounds good, right?

The problem with this product is that it's still salt. The only difference is that the crystals have been reshaped in such a way that fewer can fit on a spoon. Teaspoon for teaspoon, this product has less sodium than regular salt. But if you season foods to taste, rather than by measuring, you'll end up with the same amount of salt in your food as with regular salt.

Another lower-salt product (Morton's Lite Salt) contains half the normal amount of salt. The other half of the product is a salt substitute called *potassium chloride*. For some people, this is a better choice than the previous product, but it's not salt-free. Also, it's important to check with your doctor before using such a product to make sure that you don't have any health conditions, such as kidney disease, that might be worsened by increasing your potassium intake. In addition, if you are taking a particular type of medication for high blood pressure that *conserves* potassium in your body, using potassium chloride may be dangerous. Check with your doctor.

A third type of product is the potassium chloride salt substitute. This type contains no salt at all, and includes such products as the commercially-marketed No Salt and Nu-Salt. As with the half-salt product above, your doctor is the one to give you clearance to use this type of product to make sure it's safe for you. If it is, and you choose to try one, you might notice that the flavor of this type of product has improved over the years.

Finally, the safest of them all are the herb blends. These products are simply crushed herbs and spices creatively blended to provide a salt-free seasoning. When choosing one, make sure the label says *salt-free*. Also, check to see if the one you choose contains potassium chloride—if so, because of the medical concerns mentioned above, be sure to get clearance from your doctor. Most of these blends *don't* contain potassium chloride, and there are several to choose from. When you find one you like, use it in place of salt, or use it as a way of adding less salt to your cooking and at the table.

In addition, creative use of herbs and spices in cooking is a terrific alternative to salty seasonings. Check with your local chapter of the American Heart Association for informative pamphlets on salt-free cooking.

What Else Works?

Researchers continue to seek a clearer understanding of the nutritional links to hypertension. Some interesting findings have emerged.

Fish Oils

Studies of fish oil continue to enjoy wide popularity, and some scientists have demonstrated significant reductions in blood pressure with fish oil supplements.[10,11] However, not all research supports these findings.[2] The major drawback of the studies which show drops in blood pressure with fish oil is that they use very high doses of fish oil, doses that can cause significant side effects. One side effect is excessive bleeding,[10] which can present serious risks to an individual who enters surgery after taking high doses of fish oil supplements. Another possible risk is the production of rancid fats and free radicals when excessive fish oil is taken,[10] thereby increasing cancer risk. Other risks may be present, as well, but research to date is not extensive enough to clarify all of the possible drawbacks.[2,10] One additional snag—fish oil supplements at the doses used in experiments are expensive.

Eating fish is always an option (for those not allergic to fish), but the amount of fish oil in the quantities of fish we're likely to consume is far smaller than the amount shown to reduce blood pressure in experiments. Still, fish is low in fat, and a low-fat diet has been shown to reduce blood pressure, at least somewhat.[2]

Monounsaturated Fat (MUFA)

Evidence is beginning to accumulate on the possible blood-pressure-lowering effects of monounsaturated fats, or MUFAs.[2] Olive and canola oils are the richest sources of MUFA available to most Americans.

Until further evidence surfaces, it is unwise to use *any* oils with a generous hand. Stick, instead, to moderate amounts of *all* types of fat, and, if you haven't already done so, use moderate amounts of olive oil or canola oil in place of other fats.

Garlic

The "miraculous" properties of garlic have perhaps been overstated in recent years. But some research shows that garlic helps reduce the formation of blood clots, a key element in some strokes.[12,13] Some reports also suggest that garlic reduces blood pressure, but this remains an area of some controversy.

Garlic oil capsules do *not* seem to contain the health-enhancing ingredients that fresh garlic contains. So, to harness the potential therapeutic benefits of garlic, use fresh cloves of garlic rather than pills. Daily intakes ranging from three cloves to an entire bulb of garlic per day have been recommended, but the jury's still out on the best "dose." Also, abdominal pains, stomach distension, and flatulence may result in certain individuals after large garlic intakes, so caution is in order.

Potassium

Potassium, used in the salt substitutes described above, has a well-established track record of conferring protection against high blood pressure.[2,3] Besides directly lowering blood pressure, potassium exerts other protective effects on the blood vessels that reduce the risk of blood-vessel damage and stroke.[2]

Studies reveal that an intake of at least 3500 mg of potassium per day, found in five to seven servings of the high-potassium foods listed below, significantly reduces blood pressure and risk of stroke.[2] Furthermore, the beneficial effect is enhanced if *sodium* intake is kept low.[2] Excellent food sources of potassium are potatoes, dried fruits, prune juice, bananas, orange juice, and oranges, as well as leafy green vegetables. These foods are all naturally low in sodium, too.

Calcium

A controversial topic is the relationship between high blood pressure and calcium intake. Some researchers have suggested that people who ingest little calcium are more likely to have elevated blood-pressure levels, while high calcium intakes lead to lower blood-pressure levels. Animal studies seem to verify that blood-pressure levels go down in hypertensive lab animals when calcium supplements are given, but human data are less convincing.[2,3] Still, it's another area of exploration that may yield some useful results in the near future.

Magnesium

Magnesium, another mineral with physiological functions similar to those of calcium, shows similar tendencies to reduce blood pressure in experiments.[2] Again, the human data don't yet support this claim.[2,3]

Vegetarianism

Vegetarians have lower blood pressures than nonvegetarians.[2,3] Some studies have focused on *lacto-ovo-vegetarians,* vegetarians who eat milk products and eggs but no meat or fish. In all cases, their blood pressures are lower than those of *omnivores,* or those who eat meat as well as plant foods.[2,3] This finding holds even when vegetarians drink coffee, smoke, or are overweight.[3] No one has yet identified with any degree of certainty what it is about the vegetarian diet that reduces blood pressure. One possible answer is the vegetarian's higher intakes of purported blood-pressure-lowering minerals such as potassium, magnesium, and calcium.[3] Another is a possible blood-pressure-raising effect of animal protein.[2]

Fiber

No one's been able to confirm any drops in blood pressure just from increased intake of dietary fiber. Clearly, there are many other health benefits from increasing fiber, but, to date, reducing blood pressure hasn't been proven to be one of them. No animal experiments have been done to test this connection, but observational human studies always show lower blood pressures in those consuming high-fiber diets.[2] But because high-fiber diets are also different from low fiber diets in other ways—calories, fat, animal protein, minerals—there's no clear way to give fiber the credit.[2] Still, eating a high-fiber diet, if the fiber is consumed as foods rather than supplements, appears to confer some blood-pressure benefits because of the other things in—or not in—high-fiber foods.

Milk

Some research shows blood-pressure reductions with milk protein.[2] Diets with substantial amounts of milk protein appear to thwart the development of severe hypertension.[2] More research is needed to clarify this, but the consumption of skim milk, if you can tolerate milk, is an excellent choice if you want to try it for yourself.

Final Thoughts

High blood pressure is both preventable and controllable. A lifestyle that reduces risk of hypertension includes regular exercise, efforts to maintain proper weight, low alcohol intake, no smoking, moderate salt and sodium intake, high potassium intake (if not prohibited by certain health problems), and techniques to manage stress.

Research in which subjects with high-normal blood pressures worked to prevent an increase in blood pressure by reducing alcohol intake, losing weight, reducing salt and fat intake, and increasing exercise successfully prevented a rise in blood pressure and, in many cases, lowered their blood pressures further.[7] Drops in blood pressure in this group were most closely linked to the degree of weight loss.[7]

If hypertension is diagnosed, these preventive behaviors, along with whatever medicines a health-care professional may prescribe, are the keys to controlling it.

Newer areas of research promise to further clarify other possible roles of nutrition in prevention and control of high blood pressure.

References

1. American Heart Association, *1990 Heart and Stroke Facts*, American Heart Association, Dallas, Texas, 1990.

2. National Research Council, *Diet and Health: Implications for Reducing Chronic Disease*, National Academy Press, Washington, D.C., 1989.

3. Silverberg, Donald S., "Non-pharmacological Treatment of Hypertension," *Journal of Hypertension* 8(Suppl. 4):521–526, 1990.

4. USDA and USDHHS, *Nutrition and Your Health: Dietary Guidelines for Americans*, 3d ed., U.S. Department of Agriculture and U.S. Department of Health and Human Services, Hyattsville, Maryland, 1990.

5. Myers, Martin G., "Effects of Caffeine on Blood Pressure," *Archives of Internal Medicine* 148:1189–1193, 1988.

6. Egan, B. M. et al., "Neurohumoral and Metabolic Effects of Short-Term Dietary NaCl Restriction in Men," *American Journal of Hypertension,* 4(5, Part 1):416–421, 1991.

7. Stamler, R., J. Stamler, et al., "Primary Prevention of Hypertension by Nutritional-Hygienic Means," *Journal of the American Medical Association* 262(13):1801–1807, 1989.

8. National Research Council, *Recommended Dietary Allowances, Tenth Edition,* National Academy Press, Washington, D.C., 1989.

9. Office of the Federal Register, *Code of Federal Regulations (CFR) 21,* Parts 100–169, National Archives and Records Administration, Washington, D.C., April 1, 1990.

10. Knapp, Howard R., et al., "The Antihypertensive Effects of Fish Oil," *New England Journal of Medicine* 320(16):1037–1043, 1989.

11. Bonaa, Kaare H., et al., "Effect of Eicosapentaenoic and Docosahexaenoic Acids on Blood Pressure in Hypertension," *New England Journal of Medicine* 322(12):795–801, 1990.

12. Ali, M., et al., "Antithrombotic Activity of Garlic: Its Inhibition of the Synthesis of Thromboxane-B2 during Infusion of Arachidonic Acid and Collagen in Rabbits," *Prostaglandins Leukotrienes and Essential Fatty Acids* 41(2):95–99, 1990.

13. Bordia, A., "Effect of Garlic on Human Platelet Aggregation in Vitro," *Atherosclerosis* 30:355–360, 1978.

C H A P T E R 3

FIBER & CANCER

Cancer. Probably the scariest disease known to man. While it is the second leading cause of death in the U.S., it is the most feared.

Most people think of cancer as a sort of time bomb that a few unfortunate folks are just born with. The feeling is: Either you're going to get cancer, or you're not. Your lifestyle has nothing to do with it. Some supernatural power—or fate—just decides.

Well, it's not that simple. The reality is that *all* of us have the potential to get cancer. But some of us do things that *encourage* the development of cancer, and some of us don't. And some of us do things that *prevent* cancer, while some of us don't.

Of course, people who have an interest in taking control of their health want to know the "secrets" of preventing cancer. But even many health-minded people can't get over that eerie feeling that cancer is really just a matter of destiny.

A Change of Attitude

For example, you know that smoking causes cancer. But if you choose to smoke, perhaps there's this little voice inside you that says "It's not going to happen to me. If I haven't gotten cancer by now, after __ years of smoking, it's just not going to happen."

Yet, there's no question that smoking causes cancer. And the more years of smoking that accumulate, the greater your risk. Sure, not everyone who smokes gets cancer. But smoking causes 83 percent of all lung cancer in this country (1990 figures).[1] Smoking also contributes substantially to our nation's death toll from oral cancer, pancreatic cancer, stomach cancer, cancer of the nasal passages, throat cancer, liver cancer, skin cancer, and brain tumors as well as heart disease and—well, you get the picture. The rates of all of these health problems are also higher among *nonsmokers* in households where someone smokes than in smoke-free households.

It's undeniable: lifestyle *does* make a difference in cancer risk. You can't hide from the facts.

Making a Choice

With all health behaviors, we make a choice. When it comes to smoking, most people know the cancer risk. Consequently, many people choose not to smoke, or to quit, because they care about their health. Others choose to continue to smoke, ignoring or denying the health risks, or simply hoping that it doesn't happen to them. Unfortunately, hope is not a form of prevention.

When it comes to *nutrition* and cancer, most people really *don't* know the facts. How can you choose to change if you don't know what to change *to?* So, let's explore the connections.

Cancer: A Definition

Before we plunge into our exploration of nutrition and cancer, we need to understand what cancer is.

The simplest definition of cancer is this: Living cells growing out of control. Under normal conditions, worn-out body cells are destroyed, and the body is programmed to grow new cells in their places. After replacing these old cells, our bodies halt the growth process until the next time new cells are needed. In cancer, cell growth continues out of control. Instead of simply replacing old cells, the body keeps producing new cells until a mass, or tumor, is formed.

The theory is that cancerous cells are cells that have been taken over by some cancer-causing demon called a *carcinogen.* Carcinogens occur everywhere—in the air, in soil, in chemicals, in food, and even in our own bodies as by-products of digestion and bacterial action. When carcinogens enter cells, they tamper with the cells' reproductive machinery or DNA, damaging it and triggering uncontrolled growth. The genetic tampering is called *initiation,* while the process of uncontrolled growth is called *proliferation.*

When cells have been *initiated,* the body may simply destroy them. But if the right conditions exist to enhance their growth, then they begin to *proliferate.* Such enhancement of continued growth is called *promotion.*

Of course, not all tumors are cancerous. Sometimes the body produces a mass of extra, noncancerous cells that form a *benign* tumor. In such cases, the tumor is separated from the rest of the body by a thin layer of tissue called a *capsule.* This capsule keeps the tumor from spreading or *metastasizing.* In most cases, benign tumors can be surgically removed, and they do not spread to other parts of the body.

Cancerous tumors, on the other hand, are called *malignant* tumors. They have the ability to spread, or metastasize, to other parts of the body. Malignant cells also divert nutrients and blood away from healthy cells, interrupting body processes and interfering with normal body functions.

Treatment of cancer usually involves surgery, along with some attempt (chemotherapy, radiation) to prevent the continued abnormal growth of cells. Sometimes, surgery cannot be done because it is too risky or because the cancer has spread too far. In these cases, chemotherapy and radiation are considered.

Preventing cancer is the most effective defense against it. The key to prevention is minimizing the exposure of body cells to cancer-causing substances, or carcinogens, and maximizing our body's defense system.

Inhibitors and Promoters

Scientists have divided factors that affect cancer risk into two categories. Factors that reduce risk are called *inhibitors*. Factors that increase risk are called *promoters*.

Foods can be both inhibitors *and* promoters. Researchers estimate that at least 35 percent of all cancers are related to what we eat.

Let's begin our overview of nutrition and cancer with cancer inhibitors.

Cancer Inhibitors

Fiber. As early as 1973, a researcher named Burkitt published a now-famous report linking our low-fiber diet with cancer.[2] Since then, research into how diet affects cancer risk has mushroomed, with a number of new links being established.

Yet, despite burgeoning research into other cancer–nutrition links, the most widely publicized link is fiber's ability to reduce cancer risk, particularly risk of colon (large intestine) cancer. Since the mid-1980s, this connection has been heavily exploited in advertisements for breakfast cereals, leading to a rethinking of the Food and Drug Administration (FDA) policy that previously prevented food labels from espousing their disease-preventing properties. Proposed changes in such FDA regulations were still being pondered at this writing.

In spite of the well-established nature of the "fiber prevents cancer" notion, there remains some controversy about its accuracy. By examining cancer rates among people who live in different countries, and by conducting experiments on animals, a few researchers have discovered that a high-fiber diet is sometimes linked to *higher* risk of colon cancer.[3] The possible reasons for this are widely disputed, and the whole idea is the subject of continued controversy. And the bulk of current research *supports* the fiber recommendation.[4] Nevertheless, the possibility that fiber may be harmful remains, perhaps reminding us that one *can* get too much of a good thing.

Despite the controversy, both the American Cancer Society (ACS) and the National Cancer Institute (NCI) recommend that we increase our intake of dietary fiber. Recent national surveys have revealed that, on average, adult Americans consume only about 12 grams (g) of fiber per day. The ACS and NCI recommendations are 20 to 30 g of fiber per day.

How It Works. As most health-minded folks have heard, dietary fiber comes in several varieties. The more widely studied types include: (1) cellulose, (2) hemicelluloses, (3) pectin, (4) lignin, and (5) gums and mucilages. As we discussed earlier (Part II, Chap. 1, *Cholesterol and Heart Disease*), some of these fibers are helpful in reducing heart-disease risk. When addressing *cancer* risk, *all* types of fiber appear to be useful.

Cellulose, the structural material of plant cell walls, is the most abundant type of fiber in nature. Under a microscope, cellulose looks like flat, ribbonlike strands packed together into bundles that are woven together to form fibers. Because it is part of all plant cells, cellulose is found in plant foods, with carrots, legumes, apples, pears, and leafy vegetables having a high percentage of their fiber in the form of cellulose.[5] Wheat bran also contains an impressive amount of cellulose.

By attracting water and providing bulk, cellulose stimulates the bowel to eliminate waste products more rapidly. When we eat high-cellulose foods, we experience more frequent and larger stools. The advantage? Waste products in the intestinal tract frequently contain cancer-causing substances, like breakdown products of bile and certain types of fatty acids. By moving things through the large intestine more quickly, we reduce the time that the intestinal tract is exposed to these carcinogens. Also, by increasing the size of stools, we are effectively diluting the concentration of carcinogens in the stool, thereby reducing the exposure of each square inch of the large intestine to these carcinogens. Both speedier removal and dilution of these substances reduce the chances that these carcinogens will trigger cancer.

Lignin and *hemicelluloses,* found in many plant foods including whole-wheat and whole-rye products, strawberries, peaches, pears, plums, oranges, bananas, tomatoes, and cabbage, have an effect similar to that of cellulose, leading to more rapid elimination of wastes.

Pectin, with highest levels found in citrus fruits and apples, and *gums,* found in oat bran and in vegetables such as okra, seem to stimulate the bowel to get rid of by-products of digestion called *bile acids.* Bile acids are known to be cancer-causing to the bowel. By whisking them away, pectin helps defuse their carcinogenic effects.

By eating foods high in all kinds of dietary fiber, we substantially reduce our risk of cancer of the colon (large intestine). Some studies suggest that fiber reduces risk of stomach cancer and breast cancer, and it may contribute to decreased risk of ovarian cancer and endometrial cancer.[4]

In addition, unprocessed high-fiber foods are virtually fat-free. By eating fruits, vegetables, and whole grains, we are more likely to feel satisfied with fewer calories and less fat. As we'll see, both excess weight and dietary fat are linked to higher rates of many cancers.

Beta-Carotene.   Another star in the cancer-prevention line-up is a nutrient called *beta-carotene.* Beta-carotene, one of the substances responsible for the orange, yellow, and green colors in fruits, vegetables, and leafy greens, has been linked to lower rates of lung, esophageal, skin, breast, cervical, and bladder cancers.[4] Some research suggests that beta-carotene may also prevent cancers of the pancreas, prostate, and colon.[4]

Chemically, beta-carotene is a precursor of vitamin A, which means that the body can change beta-carotene into an active form of vitamin A, called retinol. Yet, despite beta-carotene's ability to become vitamin A, there appears to be something else about beta-carotene that reduces cancer risk. Some studies show reduced rates of cancer *only* with higher intakes of beta-carotene, but *not* with higher intakes of preformed vitamin A (retinol).[4] This finding may have something to do with fat. Many foods that contain preformed vitamin A (retinol) also contain fat—butter, sour cream, and eggs, for example[4]—while unprocessed beta-carotene-containing foods are virtually fat-free. (As we'll see, fat is considered a cancer promoter.)

The search for a reason that beta-carotene works has led to three possibilities: (1) beta-carotene may affect the way cells grow, protecting them from mutation; (2) beta-carotene, functioning as an antioxidant, may protect cells from being damaged by free-wheeling oxygen particles called *free radicals,* which can initiate cancer in cells; and (3) beta-carotene may enhance the body's immune system so that it is less vulnerable to carcinogens.[4]

Whatever the mechanism, beta-carotene's apparent effects have led both the ACS and the NCI to encourage consumers to increase intake of beta-carotene-rich foods. These foods include dark green leafy vegetables like spinach, broccoli, swiss chard, collard greens, turnip greens, mustard greens, beet greens, and kale; and yellow, orange, and red vegetables and fruits like pumpkin, winter squash (acorn, butternut, hubbard, buttercup), sweet potatoes, yams, carrots, cantaloupe, peaches, apricots, and tomatoes. Fortunately, these foods all contain other essential nutrients as well, making them good choices for health—even when cancer prevention isn't at the top of your list of concerns.

Vitamin C. In the minds of many consumers, vitamin C has long been linked with preventing colds. While the effectiveness of vitamin C in cold prevention remains controversial, its role in cancer prevention appears promising.

Vitamin C, also known as ascorbic acid, appears to reduce the risk of many types of cancer, including cancers of the esophagus, stomach, lung, bladder, and cervix, although the evidence for all except stomach cancer is somewhat inconsistent.[4,6]

One of vitamin C's tactics is to prevent the formation of certain cancer-causing substances in the stomach. In Part I, Chap. 3, (*Natural Toxins in Food*), we talked about nitrites and nitrates and their cancer-causing ability. Nitrites and nitrates become carcinogens *only* when they combine with protein elements and become *nitrosamines* in the stomach. This transformation is largely *prevented* when vitamin C is present in the stomach along with the nitrites/nitrates or proteins.[4,6]

Another mechanism that may account for vitamin C's effectiveness is its ability to prevent the transformation of certain chemicals into active carcinogens in the bladder,[6] although vitamin C's role in preventing bladder cancer remains speculative.[4]

Vitamin C supplements are not without risk. Intestinal disturbances, kidney stones, and altered drug metabolism are among the side effects of high-dose vitamin C supplements,[6] particularly in amounts above 2000 milligrams (mg) per day.

Because vitamin-C-and-cancer studies have focused on *foods* as sources of vitamin C, and because of the risks associated with high-dose supplements, both the ACS and the NCI have recommended increased consumption of fruits and vegetables, rather than supplements, as a defense against cancer. Particularly good sources of vitamin C include citrus fruits and juices, cantaloupe, red and green peppers, broccoli, and strawberries.

Vitamin E. Many people take vitamin E supplements for a variety of reasons. But not many vitamin E pill-poppers are aware of the cancer-preventive potential of vitamin E.

When carcinogens are working to subvert cells, vitamin E is one nutrient that comes to the rescue. Vitamin E appears to fortify the defenses of body cells, helping them to resist the effects of carcinogens.[6] Vitamin E also acts as a "scavenger" of oxygen particles called free radicals, which damage cells and weaken their defenses against carcinogens. As a result, cells are protected from being transformed into cancer cells.[6]

Another of vitamin E's skills, like that of vitamin C, is to prevent the formation of nitrosamines in the stomach.[6] Because vitamin E, unlike vitamin C, is fat-soluble, it can prevent nitrosamine formation when the nitrites/nitrates or proteins enter the stomach in fatty foods.[6]

In addition, vitamin E boosts general immunity in the body, further bolstering defenses against carcinogens.[4] Vitamin E may also regulate enzymes that determine how tissues differentiate, thereby exerting control over cell growth.[4]

Despite knowledge of vitamin E's potential protective mechanisms, research into cancer rates among people with low and adequate levels of vitamin E have failed to show any consistent protective effects when focusing on vitamin E alone.[4] However, when taking into account both vitamin E and selenium levels, a connection appears.[4] This finding seems to illustrate an essential collaboration between vitamin E and selenium in protecting body cells from cancer, particularly from cancers of the breast and lung.[4]

Naturally-good sources of vitamin E include wheat germ, wheat-germ oil, whole grains, green plants, egg yolk, vegetable oils, nuts, and seeds. Vitamin E is sensitive to heat and is destroyed by prolonged high-temperature heating.

Cruciferous Vegetables. A group of vegetables called *cruciferous* vegetables has been the focus of much cancer-prevention research. Studies in which subjects consumed large amounts of cruciferous vegetables showed higher levels of special enzymes called *glutathione* enzymes, which protect cells against free radicals and carcinogens.

The substances that appear to be largely responsible for the special cancer-inhibiting ability of cruciferous vegetables are called *indoles*. These compounds increase the activity of enzymes in our bodies that detoxify carcinogens.[7]

Cruciferous vegetables get their name from the crosslike shape of the flowers their plants produce. Members of the cabbage family, cruciferous vegetables have a distinctive cabbage-like taste, making them easy to identify.

The list of cruciferous vegetables is a long one, with some items being unfamiliar in the U.S. Commonly eaten cruciferous vegetables in the U.S. include Brussels sprouts, cabbage, broccoli, bok choy, cauliflower, collard greens, kale, mustard greens, turnip, turnip greens, and rutabaga. A less-familiar cruciferous vegetable, kohlrabi, is also available in many U.S. supermarkets.

Selenium. Selenium is comparatively new on the nutrition scene. Among its capabilities, selenium appears to protect against cancers of the lung, colon, rectum, bladder, esophagus, pancreas, breast, ovary, and cervix.[4] In fact, some studies show that it protects against *all* types of cancer.[4,7]

Selenium's tactics may center on its role as a component of specific enzymes. Glutathione-containing enzymes, which appear to protect our bodies against carcinogens and free radicals, are produced by the body under certain circumstances. When the selenium intake is adequate and cruciferous vegetable intake is high,[4] cancer-inhibiting enzymes are produced in greater amounts.

The selenium content of food is largely dependent on the content of volcanic ash in the soil on which the food was grown, with higher volcanic ash content yielding higher selenium levels. Soil that is irrigated by seawater, such as much of California's cropland, also contains higher levels of selenium. In general, soil in the western U.S. is high in selenium, while soil in the eastern U.S. is low in selenium. Check with your local Cooperative Extension Agricultural agent to find out about the selenium content of soil in your area. High-selenium soil may present some environmental problems due to its adverse effect on waterfowl reproduction.[8]

Selenium-rich foods include brewer's yeast; vegetables, fruits, and grains grown in selenium-rich soil (e.g., on the U.S. west coast); and meats from livestock that have been fed selenium-containing feed. It is not recommended that anyone take selenium supplements, since selenium is toxic in seemingly modest amounts (200 *micro*grams),[7] amounts that are easily obtained through supplements.

Folacin. Among the B-complex vitamins, a nutrient that goes by many names is *folacin*. Also known as folate and folic acid, folacin is a key nutrient in blood production and in cell division.

Cancer research has shown repeatedly that folate not only helps prevent liver tumors, it also helps *reverse* the cancer process in both breast and cervical cancers.[4] It is known for its ability to inhibit the growth of tumors in lab animals.[4]

Folacin may also block the initiation of cancer, preventing cells from being subverted by carcinogens into cancer cells.[4]

While folacin is available as a supplement, it is more advantageous to get it from foods. Most foods that are good sources of folacin also contain other cancer-preventive nutrients, as well as a host of other health-promoting compounds.

Great foods for folacin include leafy greens (broccoli, collard greens, kale, turnip greens, and mustard greens), legumes (mature beans, peas, and lentils), seeds (such as pumpkin, sunflower, and sesame), and liver.

Vitamin B$_6$.   One of the B-complex vitamins, vitamin B$_6$ has been studied for its effect on cancer prevention and regression. One study shows that vitamin B$_6$–deficient women with past breast cancer are more likely to have a recurrence of breast cancer.[4] Another report indicates that women with a certain type of uterine cancer live longer if given vitamin B$_6$ supplements.[4]

Research suggests that vitamin B$_6$ works to keep our immune systems strong, helping to resist carcinogens.[4] It also prevents cell mutations that could result in haywire cell growth, leading to tumors.[4]

A dilemma with vitamin B$_6$ is that supplements easily lead to side effects, the most distressing of which is irreversible nerve damage. Other side effects include irritability, headaches, numbness in fingers and toes, depression, and difficulty walking. Because many women take vitamin B$_6$ as a means of relieving premenstrual syndrome (PMS), more toxicity symptoms are being seen now than ever before. Incidentally, the link between B$_6$ supplements and relief of PMS remains tenuous.[9]

Rather than rely on supplements as sources of any nutrient, logic dictates that we choose healthier foods.

Good vitamin B$_6$ sources include green, leafy vegetables (sound familiar?), legumes, fruits, whole grains, fish, shellfish, poultry, and lean meats.

Calcium.   While calcium's role in cancer prevention remains uncertain, there is some evidence that adequate intakes of calcium may reduce the risk of colon cancer.[4]

One study, which focused on people who were considered to be at high risk for colon cancer, found that daily supplements of 1200 mg of calcium reduced the number of precancerous colon cells.[4]

To consume the 1200 mg of calcium used in the above study, one would need to consume three cups of yogurt, or one quart of any kind of milk, or an equivalent combination of these or other high-calcium foods.

Because our goal is to reduce fat intake, it's wise to choose lowfat foods as sources of calcium. Good choices include skim or 1% milk (including reduced-lactose versions), low-fat or nonfat yogurt, skim and low-fat cheeses. Other good calcium sources include sardines (with bones), canned salmon (with bones), and tofu containing calcium sulfate as a coagulator. In addition, many foods are now being fortified with calcium (orange juice, ice milk), which makes them good sources of calcium, too.

Cancer Promoters

As we discussed earlier, some food components have a cancer-promoting effect. Here, we're not addressing natural toxins or food additives or pesticides—these were covered in detail in earlier chapters. The harsh reality is that normal nutritive components of foods can encourage cancer.

Dietary Fat. There's no question about fat's role in promoting cancer. In fact, of all the possible links between diet and cancer, this link is the strongest.[4,7] The higher the total fat intake, the greater the risk of cancer.

Breast cancer and colon cancer are the two forms most clearly connected with fat intake.[4] Cancers of the pancreas, prostate, rectum, ovaries, and uterus are also linked to fat intake.[6] Many of these links have been repeatedly demonstrated in world-population studies, animal studies, and human studies.

What has been more elusive is the search for a "villain" within the types of fats. For a time, polyunsaturated fats were considered *more* effective at promoting cancer than other types of fat, a depressing prospect since these fats are also effective at reducing blood cholesterol. Yet, current research seems not to confirm this effect in humans eating a mixed diet.[4]

Recent research has confirmed that saturated fat does, indeed, promote cancer.[10] In fact, with one exception, *all* types of fat have been linked to cancer. The one exception is fish oil, rich in omega-3 fatty acids, which appears to inhibit the cancer process.[4] There also appears to be some reduction in cancer risk with monounsaturated fats, like those in olive oil. Still, scientists are continuing to tease out the differing effects of various fats on risk of cancer, searching for a clearer picture of how it all works.

The key here is reducing fat intake, which means moderating our intake of all types of oils, margarines, fat-containing salad dressings, fatty meat, poultry skin, nuts, seeds, nut butters, chocolate candy, chocolate chips, fat-containing baked goods, snack chips, fatty crackers, sour cream, full-fat cheeses, full-fat dairy products, and cream. Reducing fat has been addressed in earlier chapters and will be addressed further in later chapters.

Excess Weight. Being overweight carries risks far greater than anxiety at bathing-suit time. More and more research is linking excess weight with increased risk of several diseases. Cancer is no exception.

Excess weight, particularly in the abdominal region, is linked to increased cancer risk at many sites, including breast, colon, rectum, prostate, uterus, cervix, gallbladder, kidney, and thyroid.[6] Conversely, restricting calories appears to inhibit tumor growth, at least in laboratory animals.[3,6]

The mechanics of how all this happens are still a bit fuzzy, but scientists have come up with several possible explanations. One theory is that excess calories provide additional nourishment for cancer cells, enhancing tumor growth.[3,6] Another theory is that chemical carcinogens may hide in body fat, insidiously sneaking around to find organs and tissues to attack.[6]

A third explanation is the increased production of certain hormones in obese individuals. These hormones may stimulate cell growth in certain organs, possibly triggering uncontrolled cell replication.[6]

Now that excess weight has been linked to cancer, as well as to other diseases, new techniques have emerged to make it easier for people to estimate their level of risk. One such technique is to measure the *waist-to-hip ratio*, an easily calculated figure with impressive predictive value. Simply take your waist measurement, defined as the smallest circumference below the rib cage and above the navel. Then, measure your hips, defined as the circumference at the maximum protrusion of the buttocks.[4]

To find your waist-to-hip ratio, divide your waist measurement by your hip measurement. You'll get a number like 0.7 or 0.9 or 1.1. Compare this number to Table 2 on page 145 in the next chapter. In general, anything over 0.8 or 0.85 for women implies above-average risk of chronic disease, including cancer. For men, the high-risk figures begin at 0.95 or 1.0, depending on age.[4]

What we're measuring here is the *distribution* of fat on the body. A greater distribution of fat in the abdominal area indicates greater risk, while a greater fat distribution in the hip and buttocks area indicates lower risk. The farther below 1 the ratio is, the lower the risk.

People with large abdomens are called "apples," while those with large hip regions are called "pears." From a health standpoint, it's better to be a pear than an apple.

Animal Protein. The general scientific opinion is that too much animal protein increases risk of cancer. However, studies to confirm this have had trouble separating the effects of protein from those of fat, since many animal-protein foods are also high in fat.[4,6]

Bladder[7] and breast cancers[4,7] appear to be most closely linked with high-animal-protein diets, with prostate cancer also showing some connection.[4]

Even though research on this is inconclusive, it serves to confirm the negative effects of a high-protein, high-fat, low-fiber diet—a pattern far too familiar in the U.S.

The best approach? Limit animal protein foods, particularly those high in fat, such as fatty cuts of meat, poultry with skin, and full-fat dairy products.

Charbroiled Proteins. The effects of charbroiled protein foods on the cancer process were discussed briefly in an earlier chapter (Part I, Chap. 3, *Natural Toxins in Food*). Charbroiling on gas or charcoal grills or over an open flame all cause the production of cancer-causing substances in protein foods such as meat, fish, and poultry.

One group of these cancer-causing substances, as we discussed earlier, is referred to as polycyclic aromatic hydrocarbons, or PAHs. These are formed primarily by dripping fat, which burns when it hits the heat source and sends a smoky spray back onto the food, coating it with PAHs.

Pyrolyzed proteins are another type of cancer causer produced by charbroiling. High heat and long cooking periods produce mutations called pyrolyzed proteins. These damaged proteins are capable of triggering mutations in the body tissues of those who consume them, opening the door for the cancer process.

Techniques that reduce charbroiling time, such as partial cooking of foods before grilling, help minimize the formation of these unhealthy substances. Also, practices like covering the grill with foil, grilling only lean and skinless meats, avoiding fats and oils as basting materials, and devising a way to catch dripping fat before it creates smoke are all aids in reducing the formation of carcinogens.

Nitrates, Nitrites, Nitrosamines, and Smoked Foods. In a previous chapter, we addressed the cancer-causing potential of nitrates, nitrites, nitrosamines, and smoked foods. The bottom line: vitamin C helps reduce the formation of nitrosamines in the stomach, but does not defuse the cancer-causing abilities of nitrosamines already formed in foods. Refer to Part I, Chaps. 2 and 3, for a more thorough discussion of this issue.

Alcohol. There's no question that ethanol, the alcohol we drink, is harmful to health. Among the negative effects of ethanol is cancer, particularly cancers of the lip, tongue, mouth, larynx, esophagus, rectum, liver, and breast.[4]

As discussed in Part I, Chap. 3, alcohol appears to act both as a direct carcinogen, entering and subverting cell machinery, and as a promoter, enhancing the progression of the cancer process.

Studies have not actually quantified a low-risk dose of alcohol. Recent research suggested that as little as one serving of alcohol per week may increase cancer risk,[11] but newer evidence disputes this.[12]

So...what's the best approach? For the "purist," the answer is to avoid alcohol entirely. From a health standpoint, this, unfortunately for social drinkers, appears to be the best approach. Alternatives—alcohol-free wine and beer—are becoming increasingly available and provide a convincing stand-in for their star-crossed counterparts. Cheers!

Other Factors. Besides the items discussed above, there may be other nutrition-related factors to consider in cancer development. Issues raised in Part I, Chaps. 1, 2, and 3 remain concerns for many scientists and consumers alike. But, of all the topics we've discussed, fat appears to be the overriding nutrition concern in the development of cancer. In fact, dietary fat is the most convincing and consistent nutrition link to cancer, and it should be of more concern to consumers than pesticides, additives, and natural toxins combined!

Nutrition as a Treatment for Cancer

Promising research is showing that women with breast cancer are somewhat protected from a relapse if they eat a low-fat diet.[13] Also interesting is the finding that breast cancer sufferers are likely to have small, curable tumors if they've followed a low-fat, high-fiber diet *before* the cancer developed,[13] which underscores the importance of a prevention-oriented diet.

However, a particularly disquieting development has been the emergence of self-styled experts who espouse extreme eating patterns, such as macrobiotics, as a *cure* for cancer. While it's too early to have a clear picture of the ways in which nutrition may help curb or reverse the growth of already-established cancer, it is not advisable for most cancer sufferers to embark on the extremely restrictive eating practices recommended by most such "experts."

Certainly, the testimonials of those helped by such changes in diet are convincing, and it's hard to ignore the fact that sometimes this approach seems to work, although such factors as changes in attitude and mere coincidence may be responsible for these seeming miracles. But the fear among most legitimate health professionals is that such practices may further weaken the body of the cancer patient, giving the cancer a chance to take over more rapidly. Another concern is that the cancer patient, convinced that this will work, may turn completely away from more traditional medical care, further endangering his or her health status by avoiding medical visits through which tumor growth and general health can be monitored.

Until research gives us a better picture of how it all works, it makes the most sense for cancer patients to focus on getting enough *calories* to maintain proper weight and immune function. Moderating fat and animal protein intake also makes sense, but if done in such a way that calorie needs are not met, it may be counter-productive.

Megavitamin therapy for cancer treatment is still considered dangerous and experimental. Excesses of some vitamins produce toxic symptoms that can compound the serious health problems of the cancer sufferer. In a carefully monitored environment under the direction of a competent medical researcher, this approach, while still experimental, is less risky. Perhaps this type of intervention will ultimately prove useful as a routine form of treatment in the future, and in some cancer treatment centers, it already is. However, it is not advisable to experiment with this approach on one's own.

Recommendations

Now that we've covered the high points, let's distill all of this down into some practical cancer-prevention guidelines:

1. *Eat more fruits and vegetables.* You may have noticed a surprising similarity in the foods recommended for each of the anticancer substances. For example, cruciferous vegetables contain vitamin C, fiber, as well as those unique substances called indoles, and many of them also contain beta-carotene. Vitamin C–containing foods all contain fiber, and some, such as cantaloupe, also contain beta-carotene. All of the foods that contain anticancer substances, except fish oils, are fat-free. What it all boils down to is that consumers should be eating lots of fruits and vegetables. The latest edition of the *Dietary Guidelines for Americans* recommends a total of 3 to 5 servings of vegetables and 2 to 4 servings of fruits per day.[14] To ensure adequate intake of anticancer substances, fo-

cus on cruciferous vegetables; orange, yellow, green, and red fruits and vegetables; citrus fruits; and juices made from any of these.

2. *Reduce fat intake.*   This is not a new guideline. In fact, you've probably heard this one more than any other, but most likely in reference to reducing heart-disease risk. The evidence is quite strong that fat increases cancer risk and enhances tumor growth. Reducing fat intake means focusing on lean and skinless meats and poultry (if meats are eaten); avoiding fried foods; using small amounts of oils, spreads (butter, margarine), fat-containing salad dressings, gravies and sauces (unless fat-free), nuts and nut butters, full-fat dairy products, baked goods (unless fat-free), chocolate candies—the list goes on. We've highlighted some of these foods in previous chapters, and we'll address this issue further in later chapters.

3. *Reduce smoked, salt-cured, and charbroiled foods.*   How much is too much? That's still unclear. But daily consumption of these types of foods is probably too much. Commercially smoked foods have less cancer-causing potential than home-smoked foods, and charbroiled foods prepared using the precautions outlined above and in Part I, Chap. 3, *Natural Toxins in Food,* present far less risk than those prepared without these precautions.

4. *Increase fiber.*   Cutting down on fat means smaller portions of foods such as meats and poultry, traditional centerpieces of the American dinner table. To fill the gaps, consumers should reach for more vegetables, whole grains (breads, brown rice, whole-wheat pasta, other grains), dried beans and peas (kidney beans, chickpeas, split peas, etc.), and fruits. High-fiber breakfast cereals are also a good idea. The goal—20 to 30 grams of fiber per day.

5. *Reduce alcohol consumption.*   The evidence is pretty convincing that certain cancers are linked to alcohol intake. A safe dose is probably none at all. Try alcohol-free versions of wine, beer, and champagne as substitutes.

References

1. American Cancer Society, *Cancer Facts & Figures—1990,* American Cancer Society, Atlanta, Georgia, 1990.

2. Burkitt, D. P., "Some Diseases Characteristic of Modern Western Civilization," *British Medical Journal* 1:274–278, 1973.

3. Poirier, L. A., P. M. Newberne, and M. W. Pariza, "Essential Nutrients in

Carcinogenesis," in *Advances in Experimental Medicine and Biology,* Vol. 206, Plenum, New York, 1987.

4. National Research Council, *Diet and Health: Implications for Reducing Chronic Disease,* National Academy Press, Washington, D.C., 1989.

5. Lanza, Elaine, Ph.D., and Ritva Butrum, Ph.D., "A Critical Review of Food Fiber Analysis and Data," *Journal of the American Dietetic Association* 86(6):732–743, 1986.

6. Koop, C. Everett, M.D., Sc.D., *The Surgeon General's Report on Nutrition and Health,* U.S. Department of Health and Human Services, Washington, D.C., 1988.

7. National Research Council, *Diet, Nutrition, and Cancer,* National Academy Press, Washington, D.C., 1982.

8. National Research Council, *Alternative Agriculture,* National Academy Press, Washington, D.C., 1989.

9. Kleijnen, J. et al., "Vitamin B_6 in the Treatment of Premenstrual Syndrome—A Review," *British Journal of Obstetrics and Gynaecology* 97(9):847–852, 1990.

10. Appel, M. J., et al., "Azaserine-Induced Pancreatic Carcinogenesis in Rats: Promotion by a Diet Rich in Saturated Fat and Inhibition by a Standard Laboratory Chow," *Cancer Letter* 55(3):239–248, December 17, 1990.

11. Schatzkin, A., et al., "Alcohol Consumption and Breast Cancer in the Epidemiologic Follow-Up Study of the First National Health and Nutrition Examination Survey," *New England Journal of Medicine* 316(19):1169–1173, 1987.

12. Howe, G., et al, "The Association between Alcohol and Breast Cancer Risk: Evidence from the Combined Analysis of Six Dietary Case-Control Studies," *International Journal of Cancer* 47(5):707–710, 1991.

13. Gershoff, Stanley N., Ph.D., ed., "Diet May Count Even after Breast Cancer Develops," *Tufts University Diet and Nutrition Letter* 7(11):1, January 1990.

14. USDA and USDHHS, *Nutrition and Your Health: Dietary Guidelines for Americans,* 3d ed., U.S. Department of Agriculture and U.S. Department of Health and Human Services, Hyattsville, Maryland, 1990.

CHAPTER 4

CALORIES &
YOUR WEIGHT

Americans are fixated on calories, and our food-labeling system feeds into our obsession. While there are definite advantages to knowing the calories in foods, calories aren't the whole story when it comes to healthy food choices. Still, they do provide the basis for the undeniable physics of energy production and storage in our bodies.

Pounds Away

Despite our fantasies, calories are still the reason for weight gain and loss. Indulging in extra calories will, over time, produce a gain in weight, while creating a calorie deficit will, over time, lead to weight loss. One hundred extra calories per day will fill you out by an extra ten pounds at the end of a year.

"Extra" calories are calories we don't use after they're consumed, digested, and absorbed. These "extras" are turned into fat, which slips quietly into our fat cells, unceremoniously adding excess poundage.

An extra 3500 calories results in a gain of one pound, more or less. If the excess calories are from fatty foods, the storage process is extremely efficient, and virtually "zero" calories are used in transforming them into body fat. If the excess calories are from carbohydrate or protein, the body is less efficient at storing them, exacting a caloric cost for their transformation into fat.

Excess calories are far easier to tuck away *into* fat tissue than to *retrieve*. Once our fat cells are puffed up with excess fat, they like to hold onto it. Unfortunately for people in food-abundant countries like the U.S., the human body is programmed to resist starvation by tenaciously gripping its extra poundage, making weight management a challenging endeavor indeed.

The Risks

Certainly, no one's pleased about a few extra pounds. Struggling into those once-perfect jeans or fretting about the next bathing suit can sprout many a gray hair.

But the really important consequences of excess weight—even as little as 5 percent over a desirable weight for one's height—are the health risks. Studies have shown that the number of deaths in a population is 25 percent higher than expected among those who are merely 5 to 15 percent overweight.[1] The death rate rises to more than *five times* the expected rate for people who are 25 percent or more overweight.[1]

Excess weight substantially increases chances of developing heart and blood-vessel diseases, particularly among women.[1] For both sexes, excess weight is linked with increased blood cholesterol, rising blood pressure, increased uric acid (related to gout), and increased blood sugar (related to diabetes).[1] Overweight is also linked to increased risk of sudden death.[1]

Overweight adults are more likely to develop diabetes, gallbladder disease, and a wide array of cancers. Compared to other adults, overweight women experience more cancers of the gallbladder, bile duct, uterus, ovaries, and cervix, while overweight men experience more cancers of the prostate and colon.[1]

Weight Standards

How much *should* you weigh?

The ideal weight for an individual is not easily defined. One can always consult the Metropolitan Life Insurance tables, but these tables have serious limitations of their own. For example, they don't consider the composition of the weight—that is, how much is muscle and how much is fat? And they don't acknowledge how weight is distributed on the body—is it centered in the abdomen or more widely distributed? (The latter question is a newer area of concern, as we'll explore below.)

The 1990 edition of the *Dietary Guidelines for Americans* has tackled this issue with a new table called "Suggested Weights for Adults."[2,3] While still somewhat controversial among health professionals, this table is based on a well-established index for determining health risks, called the BMI or *body mass index*. A desirable body mass index represents reduced risk of sudden death and of all the weight-related health risks described above. Using this concept, the Dietary Guidelines Committee took a table of BMIs that appeared in the National Research Council's 1989 report on chronic disease[1] and translated it into desirable weight ranges for adults from 5 ft. to 6 ft.-6 in. tall. Two age groups, 19 to 34 years and 35 years and over, were broken out, with no specific gender categories. And, for the first time, the table is based on nude weights and shoeless heights. (See Table 1.)

As you can see, this new set of weight standards allows for the natural tendency of humans to gain weight as they age. In fact, studies show that elderly people who are on the thinner side, thus having BMIs similar to those desirable for young adults, have higher death rates than those with higher BMIs.[1,4] This new table is based on BMIs associated with the lowest mortality, or death rate, for each age group.[1,4]

How do you measure up?

TABLE 1. Suggested Weights for Adults

Height (no shoes)	Weight without Clothes, pounds	
	19–34 years	35 years and over
5'0"	97–128*	108–138
5'1"	101–132	111–143
5'2"	104–137	115–148
5'3"	107–141	119–152
5'4"	111–146	122–157
5'5"	114–150	126–162
5'6"	118–155	130–167
5'7"	121–160	134–172
5'8"	125–164	138–178
5'9"	129–169	142–183
5'10"	132–174	146–188
5'11"	136–179	151–194
6'0"	140–184	155–199
6'1"	144–189	159–205
6'2"	148–195	164–210
6'3"	152–200	168–216
6'4"	156–205	173–222
6'5"	160–211	177–228
6'6"	164–216	182–234

*The higher weights in the ranges generally apply to men, who tend to have more muscle and bone; the lower weights more often apply to women, who have less muscle and bone.

SOURCE: Derived from National Research Council, 1989.[1]

Note: This table also appears in *Dietary Guidelines for Americans,* 3d ed., 1990, p. 9.[3] See information on ordering in Part V, *The Resource Corner.*

Apples versus Pears

Recent research also shows that the *location* of excess poundage is a critical predictor of illness, more critical to our health than the actual *number* of excess pounds. In fact, *distribution* of body fat is more important to health than *percent* body fat.[5] This finding is addressed in the 1990 *Dietary Guidelines for Americans,* where distribution of weight is recommended as another way of assessing the "healthiness" of your current weight.[3]

The term used to describe the distribution and size of fat stores is *adiposity.* Studies of adiposity have found that body fat located in the abdominal, or waist, region is far more dangerous to health than fat in the gluteal, or hip, region. Results of these studies have allowed researchers to define low-risk and high-risk distributions of fat, and they've come up with a useful tool called the *waist-to-hip ratio,* or WHR.

When the waist measurement is either similar to or larger than the hip measurement, the shape of the body is rounded at the midsection.

This body shape is called an "apple." Waist measurements that are sub-stantially smaller than hip measurements produce a "cinched" look at the waist, with fuller hips below. This body type is called a "pear." Which are you?

To find out, you need to determine your WHR. Here's how: Use a measuring tape to find your waist circumference, defined as the small-est circumference below the rib cage and above the navel, without clothing. Now, measure your hips, defined as the circumference at the greatest protrusion of the buttocks, without clothing.[1]

Divide your waist measurement by your hip measurement, and you'll get a a number somewhere between 0.6 and 1.2. For example, a waist measurement of 32 in. divided by a hip measurement of 41 in. equals 0.78.

To interpret your result, consult Table 2.

When it comes to fruit, apples and pears are equally nutritious. When it comes to body shapes, it's healthier to be a pear than an apple.

TABLE 2. Waist-to-Hip Ratios

Age range	Risk level	Men	Women
20–29	Very high risk	0.93 and above	0.81 and above
	High risk	0.89–0.92	0.77–0.81
	Moderate risk	0.82–0.88	0.71–0.77
	Low risk	Less than 0.82	Less than 0.71
30–39	Very high risk	0.95 and above	0.85 and above
	High risk	0.91–0.94	0.78–0.84
	Moderate risk	0.83–0.90	0.72–0.77
	Low risk	Less than 0.83	Less than 0.72
40–49	Very high risk	1.0 and above	0.87 and above
	High risk	0.95–0.99	0.80–0.86
	Moderate risk	0.87–0.94	0.73–0.79
	Low risk	Less than 0.87	Less than 0.73
50–59	Very high risk	1.02 and above	0.88 and above
	High risk	0.96–1.01	0.82–0.87
	Moderate risk	0.90–0.95	0.75–0.81
	Low risk	Less than 0.90	Less than 0.75
60–69	Very high risk	1.03 and above	0.91 and above
	High risk	0.98–1.02	0.85–0.90
	Moderate risk	0.91–0.97	0.77–0.84
	Low risk	Less than 0.91	Less than 0.77

Note: Table is based on data presented in "Percentiles of Fat Distribution" appearing in *Diet and Health: Implications for Reducing Chronic Disease Risk,* Na-tional Research Council, 1989, p. 566.[1] These data have been presented in sev-eral publications by Bray and Gray, including Ref. 6, p. 164.

Problems with the Genes

A 1990 study demonstrated the weighty effects of excess calories on identical twins[7]—and drew major media attention. After feeding 12 pairs of identical twins an excess of 1000 calories per day for 14 weeks, researchers made some startling discoveries. Despite the identicalness of the extra calories consumed, the various sets of twins gained a wide range of excess pounds—9.5 to 29.25. But, besides that, one unmistakable reality emerged—each twin within a pair gained a similar amount of weight. Twins within pairs also distributed excess pounds similarly. But these similarities did not extend outside each pair. For instance, Tim and Tom* gained 10 and 11 pounds, respectively, and distributed it evenly at the waist and hips, while Dan and Don* gained 20 and 22 pounds, respectively, and gained it mostly in the abdominal area. The upshot—genetics (heredity) played a major role in how much weight was gained, and where it settled.

The implications for the rest of us *seem* depressingly clear—our "weight fates" are programmed at birth. But let's examine this more closely.

Two details of the study escaped media fanfare. First, all of the twins were male. Because of this, we can't really know how relevant these results are for females, where hormonal factors may modify outcomes. Second, the subjects were all sedentary, which discounts the potent effects of exercise in determining body weight. Of course, the whole point of this research was to establish a link between genetics and body weight, and it certainly did that. But the outcome makes the entire matter seem so hopeless—and that really wasn't the point. Our *genes* may be programmed at birth, but our *weights* are the result of decisions we make, *not* mere matters of fate!

So regardless of the genetic hand we're dealt, we *can* take command of our weight. What this study has done is to remind us that everyone isn't going to look like a bathing-suit model, since we all deposit fat differently. It's also reminded us that everyone has different calorie-burning rates. What we *can* do is grab onto healthy techniques—including exercise—that will help us reach and maintain a healthy weight and produce a pleasing distribution of the weight we have. Let's address these healthy techniques, and a few myths, one by one.

Fat versus Carbohydrate

Many folks still believe that the way to lose weight is to "cut out the breads." If you're one of those folks, now hear this: Don't do it!

*Fictitious names used for illustrative purposes only.

Avalanches of research show that the most efficient—and generally safest—way to lose weight is to *cut out fat* and increase carbohydrates. On average, adults in the U.S. consume 37 percent of their calories from fat. That's far too much! More and more data keep convincing researchers that high-carbohydrate, low-fat, high-fiber diets are the way to go.

With high-fat diets, people tend to consume more total calories. Spoonful for spoonful, fat contains more than twice as many calories as carbohydrate or protein. Unfortunately, many popular high-protein American foods are also high in fat—many steaks, roasts, burgers, and chops; poultry with skin; fried meats and fish; cold cuts; cheese; and peanut butter, for instance. Translation: a high-protein diet in the U.S. often means a high-fat diet.

High-carbohydrate foods, on the other hand—breads, potatoes, corn, pasta, rice, whole grains, cereals, mature beans and peas—are virtually fat-free, unless prepared with fats or slathered with fatty condiments. High-fiber foods—fruits, vegetables (except avocado), mature beans and peas, whole grains—are also generally fat-free. So, a diet built on starches (complex carbohydrates) and high-fiber foods offers lots of bulk, large portions, and moderate calories.

Here's a knock-ya-over fact: a typical twelve-ounce steak has more calories than *seven* baked potatoes. That's right, seven. Now, which makes you feel fuller? Most people would beg for mercy after the second or third potato, but the typical restaurant patron would scarf down not only that whole twelve-ounce steak, but also a potato spilling over with butter and sour cream, a salad with ladles of dressing, and bread thick with butter. It's time to re-evaluate the way we look at portions!

Finally, as mentioned earlier, excess calories from dietary fat are stored more efficiently than carbohydrate or protein calories, which means that virtually every excess fat calorie ends up as body fat. Some excess carbohydrate calories, on the other hand, are used up in the process of transforming them into fat. The bottom line: Food fat is amazingly effective at filling up our fat cells—more incentive to shy away from it.

"Light" Foods

One of the most misused terms in food labeling today is the word *light*. At this writing, new regulations are being drafted that will limit the use of this term, and the final regulations should go into effect by mid-1993. But, at this moment, *light* is used to mean anything that a food manufacturer wants it to mean—from a light, crispy texture ("light" batter-dipped fish fillets) to a lighter flavor ("light" olive oil). Occasionally, *light* even means lower in calories—but don't count on it.

The only way to tell if a food proclaiming *light* or *lite* is actually lower

TABLE 3. Definitions—Calories on Food Labels

Low calorie	A serving of the food supplies no more than 40 calories; the food does not supply more than 0.4 calories per gram or is a sugar substitute.
A low calorie food or Low in calories	Same as for *Low calorie*.
Reduced calorie	Contains at least one-third fewer calories than the non-reduced-calorie version of the same food, and is not nutritionally inferior to the food for which it substitutes.
Diet, Dietetic, Artificially sweetened, Sweetened with nonnutritive sweetener	Must meet requirements for *Low calorie* or *Reduced calorie* and must bear those words, or else be clearly labeled in a manner that clearly shows *what* the food is helpful in regulating, if other than caloric intake, e.g., *For low-sodium diets*.
Sugar free, Sugarless, No Sugar	Must also meet requirements for *Low calorie* or *Reduced calorie,* unless accompanied by a statement such as *Not a reduced calorie food* or *Useful only in not promoting tooth decay.* These words may appear on foods sweetened with juices.

SOURCE: Code of Federal Regulations 21, Part 105.66, pp. 67–69, revised April 1, 1990.[8]

in calories is to look at the nutrition label. Simply blasting the word *light* on a label invokes the requirement for a nutrition label. Compare the calories for the same portion of the *regular* item versus the *light* version. If there's little or no difference, or if the light product is *higher* in calories, then don't kid yourself—there's no calorie savings to be found here.

See Table 3 for current definitions of food-label terms.

Weight-Loss Diets

The weight-loss industry coaxes billions of dollars out of the pockets of hopeful Americans each year. The sad fact is that many of these dollars will be wasted. What's worse, some of these dollars will buy massive health problems, booby prizes from unhealthy or improperly supervised reducing programs.

Let's not be too specific here. Investigative TV reports do a masterful job at blowing the whistle on "too good to be true" diet plans, and TV networks can handle the litigation they may inspire. Here, let's settle for a few general guidelines:

1. *Avoid plans that promise "quick" weight loss.* There's no question—speedy weight loss leads to equally speedy weight gain, even if the program is based on "real food" as opposed to a liquid meal replacement. Spare yourself the health risks of quick weight-loss plans. Recent guidelines encourage adopting a plan that allows a ½ to 1 pound per week loss.[3] Such plans are safe, easy to stick to, and encourage lifelong changes in eating habits.[2] Resist the urge to see weight loss as a short-term project. If it's going to work, it's going to *take* work—for more than a few weeks.

Recent headline-grabbing research has shown that "yo-yo" dieting—repeated weight loss followed by weight gain—is more dangerous than staying at a higher weight.[9] So if you can't handle the thought of a long-term project, do your body a favor and don't do it at all.

2. *Avoid plans that use liquid meal replacements in place of food.* What's the point of depriving yourself of food if the diet is doomed to failure? How can you establish new eating habits if you're not eating? The most dangerous meal-replacement diets are those under 500 calories per day, but any diet with fewer than 800 calories per day is classified as a very-low-calorie diet, or VLCD.[10] The medically supervised VLCDs are not risk-free, but risks are minimized by close monitoring. Still, the incidence of gallbladder attacks and other rapid-weight-loss health problems is high with any such diet. And don't kid yourself—getting the weight off is less than half the battle. The *real* work begins when the diet is over.

Liquid diets that replace only *two* meals per day, with the rest of the intake coming from a "sensible" meal, may be safer. But what has the dieter learned at the end of all this deprivation? Certainly not how to *keep* the weight off.

3. *Choose a balanced, rational weight-loss plan based on real foods.* The words *balanced* and *rational* may seem like a sales pitch, but they define a safe approach to weight control. Here, we're talking about a reasonable distribution of carbohydrate, protein, and fat, and a rational number of calories—generally, no fewer than 1200 calories for women and no fewer than 1600 to 1800 calories for men. To help you get a fix on a healthy plan for you, consider consulting a registered dietitian (R.D.). (See Part V, *The Resource Corner*, for information about finding an R.D.) An R.D. can help you individualize a weight-loss plan based on your health needs, food preferences, and lifestyle.

Grapefruit

The grapefruit myth has survived generations of dieters. But let's set the record straight: Grapefruit has no special fat-burning powers. The number of intelligent, well-educated people who still believe in the magic of grapefruit is compelling testimony to our irrationality about weight.

Grapefruit and grapefruit juice are both high in vitamin C and potassium, and they're relatively low in calories (½ grapefruit = 45 calories; 8 oz. grapefruit juice = 90 calories). But let's be real—grapefruit is just another fruit. If eating it before a meal helps you eat less, then go ahead. But eating it before a fat-laden feast will do nothing to wipe out the fat in the meal.

Weight-Loss Pills

You've probably tried them. They're available everywhere. Appetite suppressants are a popular over-the-counter drug. Do they work?

The over-the-counter types have limited effectiveness. The really effective ones are the prescription variety, and they have serious side effects. In addition, every study ever done on appetite suppressants shows that, if they work, they only work while they're being used. Graphs demonstrating their effects show a steady drop in weight—until the pills are stopped. Then, a perfectly symmetrical upward swing in weight takes place, with dieters ending up where they started. Why endure the side effects for such short-lived success?

Fiber supplements used as appetite regulators remain controversial. While not harmful if used as directed, such supplements are ineffective at reducing weight.[10]

The Seventeen-Meal-a-Day Plan

A study reported in the *New England Journal of Medicine* compared the effects of hourly mini-meals—seventeen "snacks"—with the three-meal-a-day approach.[11] The study revived the long-held belief that *several* daily meals are superior to a few caloric "binges" in promoting weight loss.

Unfortunately, researchers gave all participants the exact same number of calories, whether they were "nibbling" seventeen snacks or "gorging" on three large meals. Because of this, there were no weight differences between the "nibbling" phase and the "gorging" phase.

What researchers *did* find was a reduction in blood cholesterol and low-density lipoprotein (LDL) levels in the nibblers, as well as lower production of cortisol, a hormone released during stress. These findings imply that breaking up our daily calories into several small meals helps prevent heart disease—and lowers our body's stress level.

In general, eating several times a day *is* a good idea—if we control the size of our "nibbles." Previous studies concluded that the benefits of the nibbling approach are offset by the tendency of the nibbler to eat more total calories.

For many people, eating just *three* meals a day is an increase over their normal pattern. In an effort to lose weight, save time, or sleep later, many Americans skip breakfast. For some, this leads to a larger calorie intake later in the day, or the tendency to binge.

The best approach in terms of control, and in terms of increasing metabolic rate, appears to be a substantial breakfast, a moderate lunch, and a small dinner. You've heard the expression "Eat breakfast like a king (queen), lunch like a prince (princess), and dinner like a pauper." That's the idea.

A famous study continues to be trotted out at times like this. Researchers gave human subjects one huge meal per day, either in the morning or at night, with no other food or beverages for the rest of the day. The amazing result was this: *all* subjects lost weight when they ate all of their daily calories as breakfast, and many *gained* weight when consuming all of their day's calories as dinner, even when the number of calories was identical.[12]

The message here: Don't save all your eating for the end of the day. Typically, Americans eat a very substantial portion of the day's calories at the evening meal, and then continue an evening "eatathon" in front of the tube. This is the perfect recipe for corporal expansion.

The Exercise Connection

Our sedentary lifestyles make us forget that, in earlier times, people didn't worry about their weight. Since electricity had yet to be invented, people used their own energy to do everything. Daily calorie outputs were considerable, and overweight was not a national problem.

Today, machines do much of our work for us, and obesity is the most prevalent health problem in the nation. More and more tasks can be taken care of from our homes, via computers or telephones. Even grocery shopping can be done via computers and modems, resulting in home-delivered goodies. And delivery of take-out meals is a rapidly-growing phenomenon.

With current lifestyles, it takes conscious effort to burn calories. Finding ways to sneak exercise into our lives is critical. By increasing exercise, we not only burn extra calories *during* the exercise; we also accelerate our calorie-burning rate *at rest*. Now *there's* a payoff!

Exercise cajoles our bodies into producing more muscle and burning up fat. By increasing muscle, we increase the amount of tissue that burns calories at rest. Fat just sits there, a ready repository for excess calories, but nearly inert, burning no calories to exist. Muscle, on the other hand, burns calories just sitting there. So, increased muscle boosts our resting calorie-burning rate, or resting metabolic rate (RMR). And that means we burn more calories every day.

Most dieters focus on their *intake* of calories as the key to weight loss. But that's only half of the equation. To lose weight, we need only produce a calorie deficit. You can only go so low on the "input" side of the equation before you approach dangerously low calorie levels. By increasing calorie *output* through exercise, you can successfully produce a calorie deficit with minimal health risk.

The most successful approach to weight loss is a combination of reduced intake and increased output. The most effective exercises at burning fat are low- to moderate-intensity types, such as walking, slow jogging, low- to moderate-intensity aerobics, and low- to moderate-intensity biking. Intensive activities like sprinting, fast biking, rapid running, and high-intensity aerobics burn a high percentage of calories as glycogen, a stored form of carbohydrate, rather than fat. They're great activities, but they don't produce significant fat loss. It's the slow, steady activities that are the dieter's greatest ally; they're also the safest activities for the overweight and/or untrained body.

Swimming is a great activity, but some research shows that it causes the body to produce a layer of fat to protect itself from heat loss in the cooler-than-body-temperature water of swimming pools. Because of this, it is not the ideal exercise for weight loss. It *is* a great activity for aerobic benefit and all-around muscle use, especially *after* the weight is off.

Getting Fit, Losing Fat

So, where does all this take us?

The path to weight loss is multifaceted. First, there's calorie input control, designed to produce a steady weight loss of ½ to 1 pound per week. You may want to seek the assistance of a Registered Dietitian to help you with a plan.

Then there's exercise, designed to produce another fraction-of-a-pound loss per week, and aimed at increasing the calorie-burning rate and general fitness and reducing body fat. Stick with low- to moderate-intensity types of exercise to maximize fat burning.

Be realistic about your goal weight. If you have identified 120 pounds as your "perfect" weight, imagine yourself trying to maintain that weight. If you can't, then upgrade your goal to something more reasonable.

There's also food-behavior-pattern control, such as not eating in front of TV, sitting down rather than standing for each meal or snack, finding pleasurable alternatives to eating, and seeking outlets for negative emotions rather than drowning them with food. This sort of effort pays off quickly, and helps keep you from sliding back up the scale.

Also important is learning how to decode food labels which proclaim their "lightness." The proof is in the calorie listing.

Finally, there's resisting the temptation to dive into a widely-advertised quick-weight-loss program that will produce no permanent loss beyond the loss of your money.

See *The Resource Corner* section at the end of this book for recommended weight-control publications.

References

1. National Research Council, *Diet and Health: Implications for Reducing Chronic Disease Risk,* National Academy Press, Washington, D.C., 1989.

2. Dietary Guidelines Advisory Committee, USDA, *Report of the Dietary Guidelines Advisory Committee on the Dietary Guidelines for Americans, 1990,* U.S. Department of Agriculture, Hyattsville, Maryland, June 1990.

3. USDA and USDHHS, *Nutrition and Your Health: Dietary Guidelines for Americans,* 3d ed., U.S. Department of Agriculture and U.S. Department of Health and Human Services, Hyattsville, Maryland, 1990.

4. Andres, R., "Mortality and Obesity: The Rationale for Age-Specific Height-Weight Tables," in R. Andres et al. (eds.), *Principles of Geriatric Medicine,* McGraw-Hill, New York, 1985, pp. 311–318.

5. Gray, David S., "Diagnosis and Prevalence of Obesity," *Medical Clinics of North America* 73(1):1–13, 1989.

6. Bray, George A., M.D., "Classification and Evaluation of the Obesities," *Medical Clinics of North America* 73(1):161–184, 1989.

7. Bouchard, Claude, et al., "The Response to Long-Term Overfeeding in Identical Twins," *New England Journal of Medicine* 322:1477–1482, 1990.

8. Office of the Federal Register, *Code of Federal Regulations (CFR) 21,* Parts 100–169, National Archives and Records Administration, Washington, D.C., April 1, 1990.

9. Lissner, L. et al., "Variability of Body Weight and Health Outcomes in the

Framingham Population, *New England Journal of Medicine* 324(26):1887–1889, 1991.

10. Atkinson, Richard L., M.D., "Low and Very Low Calorie Diets," *Medical Clinics of North America* 73(1):203–215, 1989.

11. Jenkins, D. J. A., et al., "Nibbling versus Gorging: Metabolic Advantages of Increased Meal Frequency," *New England Journal of Medicine* 321(14):929–934, 1989.

12. Halberg, F., "Protection by Timing Treatment According to Bodily Rhythms—An Analogy to Protection by Scrubbing Before Surgery," *Chronobiologia 1* (Suppl. 1): 27–68, 1974.

PART 3
MAKING
FOOD
SELECTIONS
CHOICE CHOICES

Finally, it's time to put all the pieces together. At this point,
you're a veritable expert on food safety and disease prevention.
Now, fasten that seatbelt—there'll be a quiz: making food
selections, and seeing them through to the plate. This could be
the most important test of your life!

In this section, we'll check out the best ways to tackle the
supermarket, learn savvy tips for taking care of your food
purchases, and explore strategies for transforming those super
selections into safe health-promoters in your home.

C H A P T E R 1

SUPERMARKET TOUR

Here we are in your favorite supermarket. You're armed with your cou-
pons, a shopping cart, and your copy of *What's Left to Eat?* Now to
tackle this business of making healthy food choices!

Let's start with "The Aisle of Challenges"—the produce aisle.

Produce

There was a time when the produce aisle felt like the safest place to
make selections. All those bright and shiny fruits and vegetables
seemed to bespeak health.

But now we're in the 1990s, and shiny fruit and vegetables may ad-
vertise the presence of fungicide-containing wax, applied to keep items
like apples, tomatoes, and cucumbers looking fresh, and to prevent
spoilage. Some waxy coatings are simply vegetable oil mixtures applied
to prevent shriveling and flavor loss, and contain no pesticides.
Brightly-colored, flawless produce *may* signal the use of gases, growth
regulators, and pesticides to intensify brilliance—and consumer acceptance.

Your decisions regarding produce, from a chemical-safety standpoint, ultimately depend on how careful, how "purist," you want to
be. While intensive research is still underway, most experts agree that
the chemical residues remaining on harvested produce present little
danger to the average consumer.

If you choose the purist route, look for signs designating produce
that has been certified by an organization such as NutriClean (or one of
the other certifying organizations listed in *The Resource Corner,* at the
end of this book). Or look for the *organically grown* produce section, if
your store has one. You may choose to abandon the supermarket altogether for your produce purchases, and take your business instead to
an organic outlet, such as a food co-op or health-food-type store or
mail-order organic supplier. But be prepared to pay much higher prices
in these smaller outlets.

Another produce option is to buy foods that are locally grown. This
will limit your selection, but local small farmers use smaller amounts of
pesticides and apply them less often, leaving insignificant residues on
harvested produce. Also, *locally grown* means shorter traveling dis-
tances for your produce, eliminating the need for spoilage-delaying
fungicides and waxes.

An additional option is to look for signs announcing *low-spray* or *low-
pesticide* produce. Such signs are showing up in a growing number of

supermarkets and at many farmers' markets, and they generally designate integrated pest management (IPM) produce.

Yet another choice is to simply steer clear of wax-coated fruits and vegetables. This will protect you and your loved ones from the fungicides that may be trapped in the wax, but will not ensure that all your produce will be residue-free. Still, it's a beginning.

Finally, your path-of-least-resistance option is to buy produce without considering chemical residues. Ultimately, your health risks will probably not differ significantly from those of the purist, and you will be afforded the widest selection possible. Nevertheless, if you have a social conscience and are concerned about sustaining our planet, keep in mind that reduced use of pesticides affords environmental advantages. Consider keeping an eye out for low-spray and pesticide-free produce.

Natural Toxins

While most of us may get riled about agricultural chemicals, many of us never even consider the natural components of produce that present health risks. As we noted earlier, green-tinged potatoes contain a cancer-causing substance called solanine, produced by sun exposure. These greenish sections can simply be removed to eliminate risk. Still, when choosing potatoes, you can reduce waste by avoiding the green-tainted ones.

Aflatoxin is another natural cancer-causing substance. Peanuts may contain traces of this mold-produced chemical. How can you tell? You can't. Samples of aflatoxin-prone products are tested by government regulators to ensure that a safe level is maintained, and shipments are rejected if they exceed safe levels. Nevertheless, it may be wise to eat peanuts and products that contain them intermittently, reducing your frequency of exposure.

See Part I, Chapter 3, *Natural Toxins in Food,* for additional factors you may want to consider.

Okay, So What's in It for You?

Now let's focus on nutrition aspects of produce selection.

As you'll recall from Part II, fruits and vegetables are terrific sources of fiber and other disease-prevention factors. They're also low in fat (except for avocados), cholesterol-free and, in general, low in calories. Eaten raw or cooked, they fill you up, leaving less room for fatty, higher-calorie foods.

When you choose produce, aim for variety. Zero in on deep orange and bright or dark green vegetables. Excellent choices include carrots, kale, broccoli, spinach, red and green peppers, dark green lettuce (like Romaine), Brussels sprouts, sweet potatoes, winter squash (butternut, acorn, hubbard). All of these choices are high in beta-carotene, a cancer risk inhibitor. Many of these also contain vitamin C.

Also, don't forget the cruciferous (cabbage family) vegetables. Among those already mentioned are kale, broccoli, and Brussels sprouts. Other cruciferous vegetables include cabbage, turnip, turnip greens, mustard greens, collard greens, bok choy, Chinese cabbage, nappa, and Swiss chard. Never tried some of these? In Part IV, we'll show you some delectable ways to prepare each of these vegetables. Their claim to fame? Each of these vegetables contains special natural compounds that reduce cancer risk, in addition to fiber and vitamin C.

Among fruits, any choice is a good one. All fruits contain at least *some* fiber, all are virtually fat-free and completely cholesterol-free, and most contain vitamin C. Those highest in vitamin C include all citrus fruits and cantaloupe. Those highest in beta-carotene include apricots, cantaloupe, papaya, guava, mango, and persimmons.

Fruits and vegetables are also high in potassium, which we've already mentioned as being helpful in managing and, perhaps, preventing high blood pressure. The best sources include potatoes, oranges, bananas, prunes, raisins, kale, collard greens, turnip greens, and mustard greens. (Don't dismiss those greens yet! Just wait 'til you try the recipes!)

Tofu is also found in sealed plastic tubs in the produce aisle in most supermarkets. In some stores it's available in bulk in larger, water-filled vats into which one plunges tongs to fish out cakes of tofu. If it's in bulk, be aware that bulk tofu can become contaminated with bacteria if the water in the vat isn't changed every few days; check with the manager to be sure. If the tofu is pre-packaged, check the freshness date. Also, look for calcium sulfate listed on the label; some tofu makers use it as the coagulator to make tofu congeal, making such tofu a good source of calcium. Tofu can be whipped as a dip base, stirred into scrambled eggs, added to stir-fry dishes, and tossed into salads. It absorbs the flavors of seasonings used in preparation, so be generous with the seasonings when you prepare it!

We could spend all day in the produce section, but who has time? Let's move on to the meat section.

Meats

If you've already made a firm choice against meat and are content with your decision, you need not read this section. But if you are a frank meat enthusiast, or a closet meat-lover, or an uneasy vegetarian, or any other form of meat-eater, or simply curious, this section is for you.

Are there really meats worth eating? There's been so much bad news about meat, it's hard for most health-conscious people to buy even an occasional steak without feeling guilty.

There's no question that, for the average American, meat contributes a significant chunk of the annual intake of fat, saturated fat, and cholesterol. But that doesn't have to be the case. It's possible, through careful selection of meats, and judicious use of them, to stay healthy and meet nutritional guidelines while you occasionally indulge the meat-lover in you.

First, let's talk about *beef*. If you like beef, choose the cuts with the least fat, such as sirloin and round. Some beef displays its U.S. Department of Agriculture (USDA) grade—*select* grade has the least fat, followed by *choice*. Stick to small packages—a family of four doesn't need a 6-pound roast or four 1-lb steaks. Choose enough to provide a 3- to 4-oz serving for each diner, allowing for about 25 percent shrinkage. That's not enough to fill up most adults, but we all should be loading up on the healthier "carbos" and vegetables, not pounds of meat.

Ground beef is a confusing choice these days. *Lean, extra lean,* and *diet lean* have come to mean whatever the meat department at your store decides. Many packages tell you what percentage of fat is contained in the meat, so look for the numbers. Go for the lowest fat available, preferably 10 percent or less (90 percent fat-free).

Don't assume that *ground turkey* and *ground chicken* are better choices than ground beef—they often contain large amounts of ground up poultry fat, so check the label for a fat percentage. Good choices are 93 to 97 percent fat-free. You can't usually tell the fat content by the color when it comes to ground poultry, but you can often tell by the price. The lower the price, the higher the fat content, generally speaking. Play it safe and look for the percent-fat numbers, or go with a name brand you trust. (We'll return to poultry in a moment.)

Pork has gotten a bad rap over the years, mostly because many popular pork cuts *are* fatty. This has led to the assumption by many consumers that all pork is "bad." The truth is that some cuts of pork are extremely lean. Tenderloin is the leanest, followed by center loin. Well-trimmed center-cut pork chops are also a good choice. Again, stick with small packages. *Try to consider meat a condiment, rather than the central focus of the meal.* A single center-cut pork chop, thinly sliced, stir-fried with vegetables and served with rice, can generously feed two diners.

Ham is also a good choice from a fat standpoint. Extra-lean hams are available in most supermarkets, and they score well nutritionally. The major drawback of ham is the salt used in curing. Also, nitrites and smoking materials add a splash of danger to this product. Soaking or boiling hams to "remove the salt" doesn't work, so don't waste your time. Enjoy ham occasionally, if you like it, and look for low-salt ham if you're concerned about your blood pressure.

A general tidbit to keep in the back of your head as you choose meat—pesticides and other toxic substances that an animal may have eaten tend to be stored in the fat. So, meat fat, besides being "bad news" from a heart-disease, calorie, and cancer standpoint, may also carry some unsavory chemicals—another reason to avoid *fatty* meats.

Back to poultry. American consumers choose chicken more often than turkey, but, on average, *turkey* contains less fat. With the growing availability of turkey parts, it's no longer necessary to cook a whole bird every time you want turkey. Turkey light meat, without skin, has the lowest fat content, and a whole turkey breast can be roasted in a fraction of the time required to cook a whole turkey. Turkey wings, thighs, and drumsticks, without skin, also measure up well fat-wise.

Chicken has become "The Great American Diet Food." Many people tell me they've eaten so much chicken they could cluck. For the most part, chicken is an excellent choice. Eaten without the skin, it has slightly more fat, on average, than turkey, but it's still a low-fat food. As with turkey, skinless light meat is the best choice, followed by skinless dark meat.

With poultry, shrinkage and waste (bones, skin, fat) account for a larger percentage of the purchase weight, up to 50 percent for a whole chicken, so buy accordingly. Allow about ½ to ¾ pound per person when buying whole chickens and turkeys. As with other meats, keep the serving sizes modest.

Duck and *goose* are dripping with fat, so they're better left sitting in the store than taking off in your shopping cart. If you love either of these delicacies, eat them sparingly. (*Wild duck* is low in fat, so it's an acceptable choice.)

Organ meats are high in nutrients but are also concentrated sources of cholesterol. They may also contain traces of pesticide residues and growth stimulants. Use only occasionally.

Lamb is generally a high-fat choice, except for the shank, which is a good choice. Well-trimmed loin chops are also acceptable fatwise. Shrinkage is similar to that of beef, about 25 percent, so don't buy too much!

Veal is a good choice, except for the breast. Stick with arm steaks, blade steaks, rib roasts, or loin chops for the lowest-fat options. Allow for about 20 to 25 percent shrinkage, and keep the servings at 3 to 4 ounces after cooking.

Hot dogs, regardless of the type, are a high-fat food. Even turkey dogs and chicken dogs are anything but lean. But if you really love hot dogs, the turkey or chicken variety are the best choices. Look for 9 grams of fat or less per frankfurter. You'll notice that the sodium is often higher in poultry franks than in beef or pork-and-beef franks, so consider carefully and eat sparingly. Watch for *tuna dogs* in some stores—they're very low in fat, and they're worth a try. All types of dogs, even tofu-based hot dogs, are high in sodium.

Sausage remains a high-fat choice, but *turkey sausage* has emerged for the health-minded sausage enthusiast. Unless otherwise labeled, turkey sausage usually contains about 10 percent fat, like *diet lean* ground beef. The flavor of many of these newer options is quite good, and they're available both breakfast style and Italian style. Most contain about 3 to 4 grams of fat per Italian-style link, and that's a fat bargain for sausage! Keep an eye on the salt.

Turkey and chicken cold cuts can be a rip-off, so read the label carefully. *Chicken or turkey bologna,* even if 80 percent fat-free, is a high-fat food. Consider that 80 percent fat-free means that 20 percent represents the fat content—one-fifth of the weight of the contents. *Salami made from turkey* is also high in fat. These cold cuts require a certain amount of fat to provide the textures we associate with bologna and salami, so they're virtually always going to be high in fat. *Turkey ham* is usually no leaner than extra-lean ham, but it *is* cheaper and it *is* a good choice fat-wise. *Turkey pastrami* is another good choice. All cold cuts contain a fair amount of salt, and many contain nitrites to guard against botulism. Pay attention to the sodium numbers on the label.

When buying any cold cuts, look for labels declaring at least *95% fat-free.* You'll find such labels on many hams, some ham substitutes made from turkey or chicken, and turkey and chicken breast. Look for other 95%-fat-free cold cuts, too, since food companies keep coming up with new products.

Bacon is so low in protein, it's considered a fat. *Canadian bacon* is an exception—it resembles extra-lean ham nutritionally,[1] and is an acceptable choice from a fat standpoint. Again, salt and nitrites muddy the picture, so use sparingly.

Fish

Fresh fish is an excellent choice. Look for signs of freshness—flesh that springs back after a gentle poke, clear, bright eyes (if whole), no unpleasant odor. The more "fishy" fish smells, the older it is, and that detracts from flavor. Look for the freshness date on packaged fish to make sure it's not old.

Avoid breaded fish, whether chilled or frozen. Even "light" breaded fish may be a major source of fat. Stick with unembellished whole fish, filets, steaks, or chunks.

On to the "Inner Aisles!"

Canned, Jarred, and Bottled Goods

Vegetables in cans can be a good choice. Watch for brands with no added salt. If you like *baked beans,* stick to the vegetarian varieties to lower the fat content, and watch the sodium. Newer reduced-sodium vegetarian baked beans are available in many stores.

Canned fruits are now sold in various types of juices. Remember that *packed in juice* does not mean *packed in calorie-free fluid.* Most juices used as syrup replacements are concentrated, meaning the calories are concentrated, too. Fruits packed in water have the fewest calories, followed by those packed in juice. If you still want the kind packed in syrup, head for light syrup instead of heavy.

Canned soups are usually heavily salted, containing over a teaspoon of salt per can in many cases. Look for the *⅓ less salt* varieties. Use creamy soups only occasionally, since they're high in fat, and thin with skim (nonfat) milk.

Canned fish—tuna, sardines, mackerel, halibut steaks, herring, clams, shrimp, crab, and lobster—are available in most stores. Except for sardines and shrimp, which are considered high in cholesterol, all of these choices are good. If the type you like is available packed without oil, that's the best option. Most canned fish is high in salt, so use sparingly if you're worried about your blood pressure.

Canned stews, pasta, and casseroles are usually highly salted. However, they *are* quick and convenient, and they *can* make a lowfat meal. Look for choices with the least fat—shoot for less than 8 grams per serving. Avoid these entirely if you have high blood pressure.

When choosing canned foods, avoid dented, bulging, or leaking cans. Bulging or leaking cans are likely to contain food-poisoning bacteria, and dented cans *may* contain them, so leave these cans alone despite their attractive marked-down price.

With all canned goods, try to avoid lead-soldered cans. Imported foods are likely to be in lead-soldered cans. Lead usually leaves a bumpy seam, and the edges of the can will be lapped over at the seam. If the can is molded (bottom of can fits into top of same-size can, so they stack easily), no lead has been used. If the can has a smooth seam, which may only be detectable after removing the label or opening the can, or if the seam is a pencil-thin line, then it's unlikely that lead has been used.

Pasta sauces have exploded onto the scene, with a new variety seeming to appear every month. Watch the fat in these. Most are pretty low in fat, except the Alfredo types and other creamy sauces. Look for the ones lowest in fat—shoot for 5 grams or less per 4-ounce serving.

Canned and bottled juices offer more varieties than ever before. Select brands with no added sugar. Consider the calories—usually over 60 per 4-ounce serving—and keep the servings small. Put them on a diet by diluting them with seltzer or water. Remember—juice *drinks* and juice *cocktails* are not 100 percent juice. They may contain as little as 8 percent juice, along with lots of sugar. Check the labels for added water, along with sweeteners such as sugar, corn syrup, fructose, and others listed in Part I, Chapter 2, Table 1 (page 29).

Sodas are not nutrient-packed beverages. Consider the juice-plus-seltzer varieties. If you must have "real" soda, choose the caffeine-free types and check the ingredient label for what's inside. Watch out for brands with *seltzer* in the name—many have corn syrup or other sweeteners and are not, then, calorie-free. Plain or flavored seltzers with no sweetening are the best choices.

Bottled water may offer no insurance against contamination with natural toxins and chemicals, so don't be fooled. Generally, chlorine is the only chemical filtered out. If you prefer bottled water's flavor, check for filtered types that have some additional impurities screened out. Watch for freshness dates which are projected to appear on bottled water in the near future.

Alcohol-free wines and beers are now available in many supermarkets. If you like the taste of wine or beer but don't like the alcohol, or if you're trying to cut down on your alcohol intake (a good idea for everyone!), give them a try. They're lower in calories than their traditional counterparts, and many folks can't tell the difference flavor-wise.

Now for the packaged "dry goods."

"Dry Goods" and Nuts

Flour is now available in a variety of styles, including bleached, unbleached, whole wheat, and rye. Both bleached and unbleached flour have had the bran and germ removed, removing the vitamins, minerals, and fiber. By law, these types of flour must be *enriched,* so three vitamins and iron are returned to the flour at levels roughly equal to those in the unmilled grain. Bleached flour has undergone a chemical bleaching process to make it whiter, while unbleached flour has not. Nutritionally, bleached and unbleached flour are identical.

Whole wheat and rye flour contain the bran and germ of the whole grain, so several vitamins and minerals are naturally present in these flours—far more than in enriched flour. Whole-wheat flour makes great cookies, muffins, and dessert breads, and both rye and whole-wheat flours make delightful yeast breads.

Oat flour is also available. Look for labels telling you the whole grain has been used. The words *contains oat bran* are good clues.

Cold, ready-to-eat cereals now come in more varieties than ever before! But many of the healthy-sounding ones have more fat than you may realize. Keep the fat under 2 grams per serving. Check the ingredients, and steer clear of choices containing coconut oil, palm oil, or palm kernel oil. Look for fiber counts of 2 grams or more per serving. And check the number of times sugar in various forms appears on the ingredient label: three or more is often a bad sign. Watch the *sucrose and other sugars* section on the lower part of the nutrition label—aim for 9 grams or less (without milk).

New varieties of *hot cereals* have been springing up ever since oat bran hit the news. Pure oat bran is a good choice, as are whole-wheat-based hot cereals and old-fashioned or quick oats. Even the creamy "white" hot cereals are good choices—unless they've been flavored and sweetened. Instant hot cereals, including instant oatmeal, are always much higher in sodium than their regular-cook counterparts, so consider the price for convenience. And steer clear of the sweetened ones, unless your household won't eat the unflavored varieties.

Grains for use in soups or as side dishes are a great addition to your pantry shelf. Consider *barley, brown rice, kasha, quinoa,* and *bulgur* (toasted cracked wheat). Some stores also carry *whole-wheat berries,* which are simply kernels of whole wheat. Cornmeal is another versatile food. You can use it in cornbread, in cookies, as a hot cereal, or as an ethnic side dish (see the recipe section). Reach for *yellow cornmeal* for extra vitamin A.

Keep in mind that cornmeal and commercial products made from it may contain some aflatoxin if made from contaminated corn. Some corn chip manufacturers test their products to ensure low aflatoxin levels, and the Food and Drug Administration (FDA) routinely monitors grains to weed out contaminated lots. Milling and cooking destroy most aflatoxins, so undue concern is unwarranted.[2]

Rice is a popular food among American consumers. Try *brown rice* for extra nutrients and flavor. *White rice* is also a good food, high in "good" carbohydrates, virtually fat-free, and "enriched" with three vitamins and iron. *Rice side-dish mixes* that contain seasoning packets usually contain a lot of salt—and many pick up a great deal of fat in preparation. If you must have these, cut down on the fat called for in preparation, and try using less of the seasoning packet.

Pasta, whether whole wheat, vegetable, or regular, is a great food. Like rice, it's high in "good" carbohydrates and virtually fat-free. It's also easy to prepare, and can be served in a variety of low-fat ways. Most stores carry a wide variety of shapes and styles of pasta, so keep a variety on hand.

Dry beans and peas are a great overlooked food in most American kitchens. They're an easy nonfat way to add protein, minerals, and fiber to grain dishes, and they come in so many varieties that they're never boring. Try black beans, red lentils, small white beans, great northern beans, pinto beans, chickpeas, yellow or green split peas, dark or light red kidney beans—the list goes on. Toss them into salads, pasta dishes, rice dishes, chili, and soups, and puree them with garlic and spices for mexican-style dips.

Dinner mixes, such as macaroni and cheese dishes and hamburger stretchers, generally pack a whollop of sodium. Some also call for a load of fat, such as margarine or butter, in preparation. If you rely on them for an occasional boost in the kitchen, consider "diluting" them with extra pasta, and pare down the fat called for in preparation.

Instant noodles and "Oriental style" noodles (such as ramen) are a quick, hot side dish. But they're *very* high in sodium, so don't indulge too often. If you have high blood pressure, toss out the seasoning packet or use just a smidge of it.

Dry soups and *bouillon* are also sodium-packed. Some types of instant broth packets are low-sodium, so look for these. Dry soups and broths tend to be low in calories, and, if you don't have high blood pressure, they can be a satisfying snack or meal-starter for occasional use. If you have high blood pressure, stick to the low-sodium types, or forget them entirely.

Crackers have emerged in a constantly expanding range of types. Many brands now offer low-fat versions of their traditional counterparts. But don't confuse *low-salt* with *low-fat*. Some crackers are both, but look for both sets of words on the label—most low-salt versions are *not* also reduced-fat versions. Whole-wheat crackers also have the reputation of being low in fat, but the most popular brands of whole-wheat crackers are quite high in fat. Look for a fat content of 3 grams or less for a serving of crackers. If you must have the higher-fat varieties, keep the serving sizes small. Fat-free, or nearly-fat-free, crackers are crisp-breads, melba toast, packaged bread sticks, rusks, soda crackers, zwie-back, grahams, and matzah.

Cookies are generally no calorie bargain, so choose wisely. The creme-filled types are usually the highest in fat. Contrary to popular opinion, *sugar-free* cookies are not fat-free, and they're not always low in calories. The lowest-fat commercial cookies are gingersnaps, fig bars, animal crackers, vanilla wafers, and graham crackers. Others keep popping up, so look at the nutrition label. The goal is 3 grams of fat or less per serving. Chocolate cookies are not always high in fat, since cocoa pow-der is virtually fat-free. It's the fudge-covered or fudge-filled types that are likely to be high in fat. If you're diabetic, check with your healthcare provider before adding *any* cookies to your meal plan.

Dessert mixes—cakes, puddings, brownies, cookies—offer an advan-tage over prepared desserts because *you* can control the amount of fat- and cholesterol-containing ingredients used in preparation. Cakes, brownies, and cookies can be made with egg whites instead of whole eggs, and you can use less oil than called for. Puddings can be made with skim milk. Unless sugar-free varieties are purchased, they *all* con-tain a fair amount of sugar, a problem for people with blood-sugar dis-orders such as diabetes.

Packaged pie crust, whether in sticks or preformed in a pie plate, is usually a high-fat proposition. Consider one-crust pies with graham cracker crust for a little nutrition along with the fat.

Frosting is a nutritional nightmare, high in both fat and sugar. Believe it or not, whipped cream is a better choice, nutritionally. Other health-ier options for cake toppings are meringue (fat-free, moderate in sugar), fruit pie filling (try the reduced-sugar types), pudding (use skim milk), and fresh or frozen fruit. Packaged whipped topping (powdered vari-ety) is another low-fat choice. Make it with skim milk.

Nuts are high in fat, ranging from 12 to 16 grams per ounce regardless of the roasting method. They *do* contain a wide variety of nutrients, so don't write them off. The best choices are the dry-roasted unsalted types. Snack on a handful, not the whole jar.

Peanut butter is another high-fat, high-nutrient food. As previously mentioned, peanut butter is likely to contain a small amount of aflatoxin. Stick to the pre-ground, factory-packed stuff in jars, and go for the sugar-free old-fashioned types. Avoid "make your own" ma-chines, which are likely to be clogged with rancid fat and to produce a peanut butter higher in aflatoxin than the jarred varieties. If you want that make-your-own taste, buy roasted, unsalted peanuts in jars or cans and take them home to your blender, food processor, grinder, or home peanut-butter machine. Remember that peanut butter contains about 8 grams of fat per tablespoon and over 100 milligrams of sodium (unless unsalted).[1] *All* peanut butter is cholesterol-free, so don't let the labels fool you.

Coffee and tea contain a few toxins that we've discussed earlier, caffeine being just one of them. If you're hooked, consider cutting down. Herbal and decaffeinated types still cannot assure freedom from some natural toxins, so consider other beverages (water, seltzer, juice) as alternatives.

Candies and Snacks

Candy bars are high-fat snacks, but sales are brisk. As an occasional treat, or for the adolescent or athlete with extraordinary calorie needs, they do have a place. Those containing nuts or peanut butter offer a better nutrition profile than others, but they're all high in fat and sugar. Avoid them entirely if you have a blood-sugar disorder.

Dried fruit is a nutrient-packed alternative to candy. Eating dried fruit with nuts is a way to reduce the tendency for the natural sugar to stick to the teeth, paving the way for dental cavities. Also, the natural sugar in dried fruit can be a problem if you have diabetes, so keep the portions small.

Fruit bits and fruit rolls, candylike snacks sold in pouches and boxes, often contain sweeteners besides fruit. They also, like dried fruit, tend to stick to the teeth, promoting cavities. If followed by nuts, crackers, or toothbrushing, they may present less cavity risk.

Snack chips are usually high in fat. If you love them, check the labels and choose the ones lowest in fat. Remember—*cholesterol free* chips are *not* "diet" chips! It's the *fat* that really matters. Consider the *low-salt* or *no-salt* varieties. Forget the fatty dips and nacho cheese. Serve them instead with salsa or yogurt-based dips. Also, remember the aflatoxin discussion related to cornmeal, above. The risk of contamination is low, but it's worth considering.

Popcorn can be a great choice. Skip the cheese-flavored ones unless you can afford the fat and calories. Notice that the serving sizes on many bags of popcorn are ridiculously small—who's going to get eight servings out of one medium-sized bag of popped popcorn? Consider how much of the bag *you'll* eat, and figure the fat from there. For example, if the bag supposedly makes eight servings, and each serving contains 5 grams of fat, and you usually eat half the bag, you'll eat four servings. Multiply the fat by 4 to figure out *your* actual intake, in this case 20 grams—too much. Consider buying unpopped popcorn and air-popping it at home. Watch out for *microwave popcorn*: its labels also suf-

fer from the small-portion charade. Choose the "light" varieties of microwave popcorn, and be sure the label verifies that it's really lower in
fat. Remember that "light" doesn't mean "fat-free"—search for the
lowest-fat brand of "light." Try the single-serving pouches of microwave light popcorn to limit your intake.

Pretzels are nearly fat-free. Nevertheless, they are high in salt. If
you're concerned about your blood pressure, look for unsalted pretzels.

Oil, Dressings, and Condiments

Vegetable oil may confuse you. Ignore the labels that say *cholesterol-free.*
Remember—*ALL* OILS ARE CHOLESTEROL-FREE! If you remember
nothing else when you close this book, remember this. The big concern
with oils is the amount of saturated fat and unsaturated fat. Corn, saf-
flower, sunflower, peanut, olive, canola, and soy varieties are all acceptable oils. Research seems to keep pointing to olive oil as a particularly good choice, due to its high monounsaturated fat content that
helps reduce heart disease risk. Remember: all oils are 100 percent fat,
containing over 120 calories per tablespoon, so don't use them too liberally.

Pick up some *nonstick spray* to use in place of other fats applied to
cookware to reduce sticking. Nonstick spray is made with oil, but it
contains special dispersants and other ingredients that allow a very thin
layer to do the job, saving fat and calories.

Mayonnaise comes in a wide array of calorie and cholesterol contents.
Don't be fooled by *cholesterol-free* labels—"cholesterol-free" does not
mean "fat-free" or "low-calorie." Some brands of cholesterol-free mayo
are low-fat or fat-free *and* "low-calorie"—check the nutrition label. Aim
for no more than 50 calories per tablespoon and no more than 5 grams
of fat.

Salad dressings also come in many breeds. More and more companies
are introducing fat-free dressings. These types usually contain a small
amount of oil, but it's so little that the amount in each tablespoon adds
up to less than 1 gram of fat. These are generally a good choice. The
word *light* may appear on a dressing that's as little as ⅓ lower in calories than the regular version of the same brand, and that's not always a
calorie or fat bargain. Shoot for 3 grams of fat or less per tablespoon. If
you buy packets of mix-your-own dressing, you can control the fat by
reducing the amount of oil or mayonnaise used in preparation and sub-
stituting water, low-fat or fat-free mayo, yogurt, or skim milk.

Ketchup, mustard, relish, and pickles are low-calorie, fat-free choices, but they're usually high in salt. Pick the lower-salt versions if you're concerned about your blood pressure, or use the regular ones sparingly.

Frozen Foods

Frozen dinners are now available for the health-conscious consumer. While many of the "diet" types are high in salt and fat, newer versions have emerged that offer both low-sodium and low-fat fare. Check the labels for a maximum of 10 grams of fat and 600 milligrams of sodium per dinner.

Pot pies are high in both fat and sodium, containing up to 24 grams of fat and 1300 milligrams of sodium per small round pie.[1] They *are* quick and filling, and, if balanced with low-fat, moderate-sodium fare for the rest of the day, they can be an occasional indulgence. Stick to *one* small pie, and fill up on veggies or starches if you're tempted to go for another.

Frozen vegetables without sauces are great food. Stick to the unadulterated versions. They're perfect for the microwave and they won't spoil like fresh ones, if you tend to eat at home sporadically. Keep in mind that frozen peas and limas may have been sorted by soaking them in brine, so they may be higher in sodium than other frozen vegetables.

Frozen desserts—frozen yogurt, ice cream, ice milk, and fat-free ice cream substitutes—tease even the most committed health nut. Shoot for 4 grams of fat or less per half-cup. If you must have the ultra-rich ice creams, consider them a rare indulgence, not the norm. Other frozen dessert items, such as cheesecake and "diet" cake, may pack more of a calorie and fat whollop than you realize, even the light versions. Check them out and set your goal at 5 grams of fat or less per serving. If you have diabetes, check with your doctor and, if it's okay, stick with occasional half-cup servings of ice milk or frozen yogurt, or try the sugar-free frozen desserts.

Frozen whipped toppings usually come emblazoned with *no cholesterol* labels, but they are nutritionally inferior to real whipped cream. The total fat content is usually the same in frozen toppings as in real whipped cream, but the frozen toppings contain *more* saturated fat than whipped cream, and less (or no) vitamin A. Frozen toppings also boast a wide array of additives to make them creamlike. Who needs 'em? Stick with real whipped cream, and use sparingly.

Frozen juices are a great choice nutritionally. Concentrated juices can be used straight from the can as toppings for waffles, pancakes, and yogurt. Look for added sugars, and avoid juices that contain them.

Dairy Case

Milk is a great source of calcium, riboflavin, and protein. Unless someone in your household is under age 2 or needs to gain weight, it's usually best to head for low-fat or nonfat (skim) milk. Consider the needs
of those at home (including you!) and buy as many varieties as you
need to keep everyone happy. Whole milk contains 3.25 percent fat by
weight, while 2% milk contains 2 percent fat by weight, and 1% milk
contains 1 percent fat by weight. Skim or nonfat milk contains almost
no fat at all, less than half a gram per cup. Keep an eye on the freshness
date, and don't buy it if it's expired.

If you or someone in your household doesn't tolerate milk due to a
sensitivity to lactose (milk sugar), try low-lactose milk. This type now
comes in both 1% and nonfat versions.

Sour cream isn't the "bad guy" that many folks believe. One level tablespoon of regular sour cream contains 26 calories and about 2.5 grams
of fat[1]—hardly a nutritional nightmare. The quantity, of course, becomes the issue. The average well-dressed baked potato probably
sports a full quarter cup, over 100 calories. If you like sour cream, stick
to small portions. Try light versions—they're usually lower in fat, but
the fat contents vary enormously, so read the nutrition label.
Remember: if it's not lower than 2.5 grams of fat per tablespoon, it's no
better than the original. Leave the imitation sour cream on the shelf—
despite its "cholesterol-free" label, it's higher in saturated fat than the real
thing.

Whipped cream is a product that most health-minded consumers feel
they should give up. Not so! As with sour cream, the quantity is the
issue. Avoid heavy cream—it's too decadent, and, when it's whipped,
it doesn't lighten up. The pressurized whipped cream in a can is the
lowest-calorie choice among whipped creams, because lots of air gets
mixed in, making it very light. It averages 8 calories per tablespoon,
with less than 1 gram of fat. Among fluid creams, reach for the type
labeled *whipping cream* instead of heavy cream. With all whipped
creams, watch the freshness date, and keep the portion size modest.

Coffee lighteners are a rapidly-growing product line, and many still
contain tropical oils, high in saturated fat. Half and half has the same
calories (20) and slightly more fat per tablespoon than most of the
"nondairy" coffee lighteners.[1] Consider using evaporated skim milk or
skim milk powder as fat-free coffee lighteners. Powdered (*not* reconsti-
tuted) skim milk has only 15 calories per tablespoon, and provides calcium and other nutrients. Cream and nondairy coffee lighteners contain
virtually no calcium.

Yogurt is a high-calcium, high-protein food, and, if chosen properly, it's also low in fat. If the nonfat versions leave you flat, try low-fat varieties. Aim for 3 grams of fat or less per cup. If you're restricting your sugar intake, reach for yogurts sweetened with NutraSweet® that are available in many brands. Watch the freshness dates, and re-refrigerate immediately to avoid escalating tartness.

Cheese is traditionally high-fat fare. Among the natural cheeses, skim-milk mozzarella is the lowest in fat, at 5 grams or less per ounce. Feta is also lower in fat than other cheeses, with only 6 grams of fat per ounce. An ounce of feta also boasts 316 milligrams of sodium, higher than many other cheeses. Other natural cheeses run from 7 to 11 grams of fat per ounce.

Low-fat cheese has been springing up in new varieties. Look for 5 grams of fat or less per ounce, and sample them until you find one you like. *Cream cheese* is high in fat, with 10 grams of fat per ounce (2 tablespoons). Use it sparingly, or try low-fat cream cheese. *Whipped cream cheese* is easier to spread than the block type, so you may find it useful for paring down serving sizes. *Cottage cheese* is a good source of protein. Pick up one with 2 grams of fat or less per half-cup.

Eggs continue to be the subject of vigorous controversy. If your cholesterol is high, consider low-fat egg substitutes, and keep your egg intake at 2 to 3 yolks per week from all sources (including muffins, custard, etc.). If your cholesterol is normal or low, enjoy a few eggs per week. They're an inexpensive source of high-quality protein, and they're quick and easy to prepare.

Now for *butter, margarines, and spreads.* Consumer confusion is rampant here. Manufacturers' claims compound the confusion, having you believe that every new product is better than the last.

The key to understanding spreads is reading the nutrition label. The first order of business is checking the portion size. Until new labeling regulations go into effect in 1992 and 1993, manufacturers are not required to use a common portion size for all butter-type spreads. Most packages list one *tablespoon* as the portion size, but if yours lists one *teaspoon,* multiply the numbers by 3 to compare your brand to the others.

A good spread contains 6 grams or less of fat per tablespoon. If yours contains more, you can whip it to reduce the fat per tablespoon, or you might consider buying the whipped version of your brand to get closer to the 6-gram target.

The big nutritional differences between butter and margarine are the amount of saturated fat (more in butter) and the presence of cholesterol in butter (none in margarine). If you love butter, check out the butter-margarine blends, especially those marked *light.*

Regardless of the type you choose, all spreads should be used with a light touch. Even those proclaiming *highest in unsaturates* and *no choles-*

terol are pure fat, through and through. And newer research casts some doubt on the nutritional superiority of hydrogenated or hardened fat over butter. Hydrogenated fat does not translate into saturated fat on the margarine label, because, chemically, it is largely a form of mono-unsaturated fat. However, our bodies appear to use hydrogenated fats differently from naturally-occurring monounsaturates, such as those in olive oil. So, stick with small amounts, go for the ones with the lowest fat, and try to choose those with the smallest numbers for saturated fat. Soft margarines in tubs are usually the best way to go.

Consider trying *butter-flavored sprinkles* as a substitute for butter or margarine to season cooked foods.

Tortillas are often in the dairy case. Both corn and flour tortillas are low in fat, unless you fry them! Look for those with 2 grams of fat or less per tortilla.

Our shopping trip is almost over! Let's finish up with baked goods.

Breads and Baked Goods

Breads present more options than ever. Most breads are good choices when you focus on fat. Look for pita, French, Italian, rye, and pumpernickel varieties.

Whole-grain breads are the best nutritionally. Check the ingredients and weed out those with *wheat flour* as opposed to *whole-wheat flour*. Look for *100% Whole Wheat* on the label. Bran breads and breads containing bits of whole grain usually have gluten flour added to keep them from being too heavy; these are good choices. Look for fiber on the nutrition label—it's not always listed. If it is, aim for 1 gram or more per slice, and keep the fat at 1 gram or less.

Muffins often sound healthier than doughnuts, but the store-made types are usually high in fat and calories. Don't be fooled by the *oat bran* label on store muffins—they're not the cholesterol-lowering kind. Most store muffins run about 80–100 calories per *ounce,* with medium-sized muffins ranging from 1.5 to 3 ounces, or 120 to 300 calories. Giant muffins (about 4–5 ounces) average 400 calories apiece, with about 11 grams of fat—and that's *without* a smear of margarine. Better to make them at home and control the fat. *English muffins* are just like bread nutritionally—low in fat and good sources of iron and some B vitamins. Go for whole-grain varieties.

Doughnuts sometimes look better nutritionally when you compare them with muffins. Here, size is important, too. A small, 1-ounce cake-type donut has just over 100 calories and 7 grams of fat. Typical doughnuts weigh 2 to 3 ounces and range from 230 to 330 calories, with 12 to 19 grams of fat apiece[1]—pretty hefty, eh?

Bagels are a healthy choice. The problem comes in when they get buried under cream cheese. Consider melting low-fat cheese over a toasted bagel, or try low-fat cottage cheese or skim-milk ricotta cheese as a spread.

Cakes usually get ruined by frosting. If you want a store-baked treat, try mini-muffins or dessert breads like banana. Angel food cake is another excellent choice; it's great brightened with fresh fruit and crowned with a dollop of frozen yogurt.

Cookies made in store bakeries are often large, and they're almost never low in fat. A rare treat, perhaps.

Checking Out

Okay, you've done it all. Be sure to make a beeline for the cash registers—you don't want any of that great food to start sprouting bacteria! Next chapter—keeping it fresh.

References

1. Pennington, Jean A. T., *Bowes and Church's Food Values of Portions Commonly Used,* 15th ed., J. B. Lippincott, New York, 1989.

2. Webb, Densie, ed., "Q & A," *Environmental Nutrition,* June 1989, p. 3.

CHAPTER 2

FOOD HANDLING: KEEPING IT SAFE

I have met the enemy, and he is us.   POGO

When it comes to food-poisoning and food-borne illness, the enemy *is* us. And, though caution is wise while dining at restaurants and buffet tables, you may be surprised to learn that most food-borne illness happens at home, by one's own hand.

High-Risk Behavior

The riskiest practices from a food-safety perspective begin at the store.

It's no accident that the layout of U.S. grocery stores offers a measure of protection for most shoppers. Perishable items are generally positioned toward the end of the shopping excursion. And it's the rare one-stop shopping trip that stretches beyond 2 hours, the critical "window" for safety.

But such advantages don't wipe out the risk of food-borne illness for the inveterate shopper who takes the "long way" home. It's hard to resist the urge to snap up the best buys at a cartful of stores. The problem, of course, is not the yen for a bargain. It's the growing expanse of time without refrigeration. Those glorious chicken breasts bought on sale could be salmonella cutlets after a long trip in a hot car, *before* they're returned to the cool waves of a refrigerator.

Our track record doesn't look good. Only 7 percent of shoppers in a recent poll said they *avoid* leaving meat out (at room temperature) as a way of ensuring its safety.[1] Pretty poor performance for a savvy population.

While some shoppers stash the bulk of their perishables in the refrigerator, a growing segment of consumers freeze them.

Contrary to popular belief, freezing *does not* kill bacteria—it just temporarily halts their growth. So, those salmonella cutlets going into the freezer will *still* be salmonella cutlets when they come out. And if you thaw them on the counter...look out! Those crafty bacteria feverishly resume growth the moment they're treated to the balminess of room temperature.

Four Essentials

In order to multiply, bacteria need four things: moisture, proper temperature, a low-acid environment, and something to eat.

High-risk foods like meat, fish, poultry, milk products, deli foods, and gourmet take-out selections act as natural breeding grounds for bacteria. When such foods are allowed to stay in the 40 to 140 degree Fahrenheit (°F) range longer than two hours, bacterial growth can be astounding. Room temperature—roughly 70°F—is the perfect temperature for most food-poisoning bacteria to flourish.

Foods that make the trip in and out of the refrigerator several times in their natural lives—like leftover holiday turkey—present greater risk. Each time that turkey spends an hour or more at room temperature, bacterial growth has a chance to get going again. And, unless the turkey is heated thoroughly, those bacteria go with it back into the refrigerator.

But how does bacteria get into food, anyway? Isn't the government making sure that food doesn't carry bacteria in the first place?

The Government's Role

A branch of the government called the Food Safety and Inspection Service (FSIS) takes the lead in inspecting meat and poultry and setting industry standards for their safety. The Food and Drug Administration (FDA) sets the standards for safety of foods *other than* meat and poultry, monitors for unsafe pesticide levels in food, and shares responsibility with the Agricultural Marketing Service (AMS) for egg safety. The National Marine Fisheries Service, part of the U.S. Department of Commerce, provides a voluntary, fee-for-service inspection program for fish and fish products. Finally, the Environmental Protection Agency (EPA) sets limits for pesticide residues in foods sold in the U.S.

The efforts of both government agencies and the food industry combine to ensure a high degree of safety for our food. New methods of checking for bacteria at packing plants are emerging, making the whole process easier and more accurate. One such method uses a biosensor system called Microfresh™ to pinpoint, in mere minutes, the degree of deterioration of both meat and fish.[2] This system, originated in Canada, is being adopted in many progressive manufacturing and packing plants in the U.S.

Fish inspection remains a controversial area. Because the government's current fish inspection program is voluntary, most fish is never inspected. New proposals being considered at this writing would strengthen regulatory control over fish safety in the U.S. And that's good news for consumers.

At Home

Okay, so now, after taking the precautions we've discussed, you're reasonably certain that the food you brought home is safe. But remember—food that's safe right now may contain small numbers of bacteria, and it can easily become a *breeding ground* for those bacteria if handled improperly. Let's explore ways of making sure it *stays* wholesome.

Produce should be kept at room temperature if unripe, then refrigerated to retard spoilage. Remove outer leaves of leafy vegetables, such as cabbage, to eliminate concentrated pesticide residues. Use all fresh produce within 7 days.

Tofu should be refrigerated immediately. Change the water every 2 days until you use it, to discard food-spoilage bacteria and keep bacteria from multiplying. Use within one week of purchase.

Meats require special care. Meat should *never* stay at room temperature longer than 2 hours, not to mention in a hot car! In warm weather, bacteria multiply with breathtaking speed—don't give 'em a chance! Get home with that food immediately.

Most meats keep well in the refrigerator for 3 to 5 days. If you plan to use them more than 5 days from date of purchase, freeze them as soon as possible after you buy them. If you wait until 5 days to freeze meat, it may be too late. Chances are good that bacteria are already threatening to spoil your expensive roast or chops, and freezing will just slow the process, not destroy the bacteria.

Hamburger, ground chicken and turkey, and *poultry* present greater risk of spoilage. Ground meat has been handled extensively before packaging, increasing the chances of contamination. Poultry is likely to become contaminated at some point during the packing process. Both ground meat and poultry should be used within 1 to 2 days of purchase, or frozen if to be used later than that.

Consult Table 1 for safe refrigerating and freezing time limits.

Once you decide to use meats, remember the important food-safety tips we discussed earlier: (1) thoroughly clean all surfaces and equipment, including hands, before they come in contact with raw meat; (2) thoroughly clean, with warm soapy water, all surfaces and equipment, including hands, *after* they come in contact with raw meat; (3) clean cutting surfaces and knives *during* the preparation process, between types of meat and before chopping other foods, such as vegetables. It's usually best to reserve one cutting board for meats, fish, and poultry, and one for other foods.

Never thaw protein foods at room temperature. Plan ahead and let them thaw in the refrigerator, or use a microwave to defrost frozen meat, fish, and poultry. A last resort is to thaw frozen meats, fish, and poultry in a cold water "bath," changing the water frequently.

Fish should be treated with particular respect. It, too, presents special food-safety risks. Check the flesh of the fish for worms: many parasites bury themselves in fish. Remove skin and inner organs—these may

TABLE 1. Storage Limits for Meat and Poultry*

Product	Refrigerator (days at 40°F)	Freezer (months at 0°F)
Fresh Meats		
Roasts (beef)	3–5	6–12
Roasts (lamb)	3–5	6–9
Roasts (pork, veal)	3–5	4–8
Steaks (beef)	3–5	6–12
Chops (lamb)	3–5	6–9
Chops (pork)	3–5	3–4
Hamburger, ground and stew meat	1–2	3–4
Organ meats (tongue, brain, liver, kidney, heart)	1–2	3–4
Sausage (pork)	1–2	1–2
Cooked Meats		
Cooked meat and meat dishes	3–4	2–3
Gravy and meat broth	1–2	2–3
Processed Meats		
(frozen, cured meat loses quality rapidly and should be used as soon as possible)		
Bacon	7	1
Frankfurters	7[†]	1–2
Ham (whole)	7	1–2
Ham (half)	3–5	1–2
Ham (slices)	3–4	1–2
Luncheon meats	3–5[†]	1–2
Sausage (smoked)	7	1–2
Sausage (dry, semidry)	14–21	1–2
Fresh Poultry		
Chicken and turkey (whole)	1–2	12
Chicken pieces	1–2	9
Turkey pieces	1–2	6
Duck and goose (whole)	1–2	6
Giblets	1–2	3–4
Cooked Poultry		
Covered with broth, gravy	1–2	6
Pieces not in broth or gravy	3–4	1
Cooked poultry dishes	3–4	4–6
Fried chicken	3–4	4
Game		
Deer	3–5	6–12
Rabbit	1–2	12
Duck and goose (whole, wild)	1–2	6

*This chart gives short, conservative storage times. You may be used to keeping food longer, but following the chart will help protect you from food spoilage (what you risk with long refrigeration) and from taste loss (what happens when food is left too long in the freezer).

†Once a vacuum-sealed package is opened. Unopened vacuum-sealed packages can be stored in the refrigerator for 2 weeks.

SOURCE: USDA FSIS, *The Safe Food Book,* 1988, p. 14.[3]

contain concentrated residues of pesticides and industrial wastes. Refrigerate immediately, and use within 1 to 2 days of purchase. To keep fresh fish freshest, loosely wrap in plastic wrap or waxed paper and place on a bed of ice in a plastic or glass container in your refrigerator. This will retard spoilage and keep that nice, fresh fish smell. Fish that smells of ammonia or has a strongly "fishy" smell is old and has deteriorated.

Shellfish should be alive until cooked or opened (as with clams, oysters). Mollusks should be tightly closed—if not, they're dead, so toss 'em.

Canned foods should be checked carefully for bulges, dents that penetrate the can, and leaks. If any of these appear, take them back to the store, or save the can and contents and report this possibly-contaminated food to your local health department. *Jars* with loose or bulging lids or cracks should also be returned or reported. If cans or jars do not make a "pop" or "gasp" when opened the first time, this means that the vacuum seal has already been broken. Don't use the contents.

Rotate your supplies of canned and jarred foods—that is, move the ones in the back of the cupboard up front, and put new supplies in back. Keep them in a cool, dry place. *Don't* store canned foods near an oven or over your refrigerator—these spots get too hot. Temperatures over 100°F accelerate spoilage of canned goods. Check for *use by* dates, if displayed, and keep watching for leaks and bulges. Low-acid canned goods keep longer than high-acid canned products, about 2 to 5 years versus 12 to 18 months. Higher acidity may eat away at the can's seal and may corrode the can itself, reducing its shelf-life. High-acid products include citrus juices, tomato juice, tomatoes, grapefruit, pineapple, apples and apple products, mixed fruit, berries, peaches, pears, plums, pickles, sauerkraut, and foods containing mayonnaise or vinegar.[3]

Canned ham must be refrigerated in its can until used, and must be used within 6 to 9 months to ensure its safety.

Dry, packaged goods include a wide variety of foods, with some differing storage needs:

Flour should be checked for bugs. Keeping white or unbleached flour at room temperature accelerates the hatching of tiny insect eggs present in all flour, resulting in the tiny black bugs often found in older flour. For best quality, store white and unbleached flour in the refrigerator or freezer, perhaps keeping just a small amount on the counter if frequently used.

Whole-grain flour, including oat flour and oat-flour blends, should also be refrigerated to prevent rancidity. Natural oils in the bran and germ of whole grains easily become rancid at room temperature. Freezing extends shelf-life even further, particularly if you tend to use flour sporadically.

Cold cereals should be stored in a cool, dry place, unless they're used rapidly. If you buy several boxes at once, make sure you keep rotating your stock and watch the *use by* dates. Rancidity can occur in whole-grain cereals, particularly those containing no preservatives. If cereals are rarely used, keep them in the refrigerator or freezer to extend shelf-life. Discard cereals that emit an "off" odor—rancidity has struck!

Hot cereals made of refined grains, such as creamy white cereals, can be kept at room temperature. *Whole-grain-containing cereals,* including oatmeal and cornmeal, can become rancid unless packaged in individual packets, so refrigeration is best. If hot cereals are not refrigerated, watch for bugs.

White rice is pretty resistant to spoilage, so room-temperature storage is fine. *Brown rice,* because of the bran and germ, can become rancid, even before opening, so keep in the fridge from time of purchase. If it starts to smell rancid, toss it.

Pasta gets "buggy" if kept too long at room temperature or if stored in a warm place, such as an attic. The bugs result from hatching of tiny insect eggs present in the grain used to make the pasta. Dry pasta is best kept in a cool dry place, and used within a year of purchase. *Whole-grain pasta* easily becomes rancid, so refrigerate from time of purchase. *Fresh pasta* must be refrigerated—it usually contains fresh eggs.

Dry beans and peas should be kept in a cool, dry place. Watch for stones and other foreign matter.

Crackers and *chips* should be used before their *use by* date. Rotate stock if you keep several boxes or bags on hand. Keep in a cool, dry place. Once opened, keep tightly closed to reduce contact with air, which accelerates rancidity. Toss them out when they develop an "off" odor or a rancid flavor.

Cookies should also be used before their *use by* date. Refrigerate if they contain no preservatives. Keep soft cookies, such as fig bars and hermits, in the refrigerator to keep soft and mold-free, unless they're used quickly. As with other grain-based products, keep in a cool, dry place.

Nuts should be kept in tightly-covered jars or cans, or sealed plastic bags, and used within a few weeks of opening. If you have large supplies of nuts, or don't use them quickly, keep refrigerated or frozen to ward off rancidity. Discard if they become rancid.

Peanut butter can be kept at room temperature, but not in a "hot spot." *Old-fashioned peanut butter* should be refrigerated after opening—rancidity strikes surprisingly quickly.

Dried fruit keeps best if refrigerated after opening. Tightly secure the inner lining, if present, or roll the top of the box over and secure with a rubber band to eliminate air. If purchased in a canister, cover tightly before refrigerating. If dried fruit hardens, consider stewing rather than discarding.

Popcorn, if fresh and unpopped, keeps for months in a refrigerator or freezer. If kept at room temperature, it may become rancid and should then be thrown out.

Vegetable oils generally keep well at room temperature, since the natural vitamin E in them protects against rancidity. Most oils do not contain preservatives. If you tend to use oil extremely slowly, buy in small bottles to reduce risk of rancidity. Refrigerating oils may help improve keeping quality, but oils often congeal in the refrigerator, making it nearly impossible to use them. Keep out of "hot spots," which accelerate deterioration.

Nonstick sprays keep well at room temperature. If in an aerosol can, keep away from heat sources to prevent bursting.

Mayonnaise, although it contains eggs, is more resistant to spoilage than most consumers believe. This is due to its high acidity, contributed by lemon juice, vinegar, or some other acid-containing flavoring agent, which keeps bacteria at bay. Salt in mayo also helps increase resistance to bacterial growth. Of course, mayonnaise must be refrigerated after opening, and can be kept in the fridge for 2 months. Don't freeze mayonnaise or foods that contain mayonnaise—the mayo separates, creating an oily mess.[3]

Salad dressings must be refrigerated after opening, particularly the creamy types. Keep checking for off odors, and discard if they occur.

Condiments, such as relish, mustard, and pickles, should be refrigerated after opening. They keep for several months.

Frozen dinners and *pot pies* should be returned to the freezer as soon as you walk in the door with them. If allowed to thaw, they become breeding grounds for bacteria, and the texture of many ingredients will change. Check for *use by* dates.

Frozen vegetables should be kept solidly frozen until use. Avoid thawing and refreezing—this affects texture.

Frozen confections, such as ice milk and frozen yogurt, should also be kept solidly frozen. Slip them into a freezer bag to reduce risk of freezer burn. Don't keep forever—these products tend to shrivel and become chewy if kept for exceptionally long periods. If allowed to soften due to suboptimal freezing conditions, they will become icy when refrozen.

Milk products from the dairy case should be rushed to the refrigerator when you return home from your shopping trip. Strictly abide by the *use by* date. Toss out if off odors appear, or if containers bulge. *Powdered milk* can be stored at room temperature, and should be used within 3 months.

Hard cheese, if tightly wrapped and refrigerated, keeps as long as 6 months. Cheese can also be frozen, although the texture often becomes crumbly. *Soft cheeses,* including cream cheese, are more perishable. Keep these tightly wrapped and use within a week or two. *Prewrapped processed cheese slices* keep for several months in the refrigerator—check the freshness date.

Eggs keep well under refrigeration. Use raw shell eggs within 5 weeks of purchase (within *one* week for highest quality).[4] Don't wash eggs—they've already been washed by the packers. Avoid eating raw eggs or foods containing raw eggs, such as homemade versions of egg nog, Caesar salad, hollandaise sauce, ice cream, and mayonnaise. Commercial versions of these products use pasteurized eggs, which eliminates risk of *Salmonella*. Use leftover egg yolks or whites within 2 days of opening egg, and cover leftover yolks with cold water to prevent their drying out. If eggs are soiled or cracked, use only in foods where they will be fully cooked, such as cakes, casseroles, or hard-boiled. Never use soiled or cracked eggs for soft-cooked, poached, or soft-scrambled eggs. People with serious illnesses and suppressed immune systems are at greatest risk from undercooked eggs.

Hard-cooked eggs should *never* be left out of the refrigerator for more than 2 hours. If they are, such as for an Easter-egg hunt, they should not be eaten. Hard-boiled eggs can be kept fresh under refrigeration for up to 7 days.

Butter, margarines, and spreads must be refrigerated. Observe the *use by* dates, unless you freeze these items. Freezing allows you to extend freshness for several months, and these products thaw quickly in the refrigerator.

Tortillas should be refrigerated and used by the freshness date. *Taco shells* and *corn tortillas*, if kept at room temperature, become rancid, affecting both safety and flavor. Use taco shells by the date on the package, or keep refrigerated or frozen.

Breads and baked goods should be refrigerated if they contain no preservatives or if made with whole grains. Mold grows rather quickly on whole-grain and unpreserved baked goods. All bread stays fresher in the refrigerator.

Summing Up

Foods stay healthful and safe if you care for them properly. Think of them as an investment in your health. Next, *preparing* foods to minimize risk, and maximize health!

References

1. Opinion Research Corporation, *Trends: Consumer Attitudes and the Supermarket 1990,* Food Marketing Institute, Washington, D.C., 1990, p. 61.

2. Microfresh℠ information available through Pegasus Biotechnology, P.O. Box

319, Agincourt, Ontario, Canada M1S 3B9. For validation of this testing procedure in its newer application to fish, see J. H. T. Luong et al. National Research Council, Canada, "Development of a Fish Freshness Sensor," *American Biotechnology Laboratory,* November 1988.

3. U.S. Department of Agriculture Food Safety and Inspection Service, *The Safe Food Book: Your Kitchen Guide,* Home and Garden Bulletin Number 241, U.S. Department of Agriculture, Washington, D.C., 1988.

4. FDA and USDA, *Consumer Bulletin: Handling Eggs Safely at Home,* Food and Drug Administration and U.S. Department of Agriculture, Washington, D.C., September 1988.

CHAPTER 3

FOOD PREPARATION: ON THE PLATE

Okay. You've purchased great food, kept it properly refrigerated, and you're ready to cook. Now's your chance to "fine tune" your purchases and reduce your health risks even further.

Cooking Equipment

First off, let's consider cooking equipment, since much of your food preparation will involve cooking.

Avoid *ceramic* cookware and servingware, unless labeled *lead-free*. Many ceramic products are glazed with coatings that contain lead. Lead, which can cause lead poisoning, is most likely to leach out if wet or acidic foods are served from improperly glazed ceramicware. The Food and Drug Administration (FDA) routinely tests pottery for unsafe glazes, but gifts and souvenirs brought into the U.S. by tourists or via mail generally are not tested. Home lead-testing kits are available, if you have any doubts (see Part V, *The Resource Corner*, at the end of the book). Ceramic pieces intended for decoration are usually not screened for lead, and often contain high levels of lead in the paints used to decorate them.[1]

Excellent cookware for both the microwave and conventional ovens and stoves is manufactured by Corning. *Corningware*® and *Visions*® cookware are composed of special types of glass that withstand high temperatures. This type of cookware does not leach toxic materials into food.

Aluminum cookware has continued to be rejected by many consumers ever since fear of Alzheimer's disease has grabbed the public. A discovery in the 1970s of high levels of aluminum in the brains of many Alzheimer's victims has led some consumers to trade in their aluminum pots and pans. Continuing research has not yet produced convincing scientific evidence that aluminum *causes* Alzheimer's disease, but the jury's still out on this. Even if aluminum *is* implicated in this disease, aluminum cookware is only a minor source of aluminum for consumers. Certain medications, such as antacids and buffered aspirin, contain up to thousands of times more aluminum than foods cooked in aluminum pots and pans. Even fruits, vegetables, grains, and meats contain aluminum, since aluminum is the third most common element in soil. In addition, most aluminum cookware has undergone special treatment to reduce the chances of aluminum leaching into foods.[1]

Stainless-steel cookware is noncontroversial and appears to provide a completely safe cooking surface. Often, stainless steel is used as the inner surface of pots and pans that contain copper and/or aluminum layers to enhance heat conduction.

Copper, like lead, is toxic if consumed in significant quantities. Copper cookware is safe if prepared with an inner surface of stainless steel or tin, as most new copper cookware is.[1]

Microwave Ovens

Many consumers refer jokingly to *microwaving* as "nuking," but some consumers truly believe that microwaves are like x-rays or other dangerous radiation. Microwaves are short radio waves, similar to those used to send radio signals. They target items in the microwave oven, focusing on the area approximately 1 inch in from the outer circumference of the food. Unless someone in the household has a pacemaker or a copper-7 IUD (intrauterine device), microwaves appear to be safe. It's best not to stand too close while the oven is operating—18 inches away is a good limit, just in case the oven leaks.

How do microwaves affect nutritional value of foods? The results of extensive research are quite favorable. Most foods retain the same, or more, nutrient value after microwaving as compared with conventional cooking.[2] One reason is that microwaves are fast, so the food is subjected to heat for a shorter time, preserving heat-sensitive nutrients like vitamin C and folate. Reheating foods by microwaving also helps retain more nutrients than does reheating by conventional methods.[2]

Some research has suggested that microwave heating of infant formula produces potentially-hazardous by-products that allegedly damage nerve cells.[3] This view, however, has been challenged,[4] and no convincing evidence exits that any chemical hazards are produced by microwaving formula.[5] However, several authorities discourage the practice of heating infant formula in a microwave oven because of the creation of "hot spots" in the milk that can *easily* burn an infant's mouth or skin. Also, plastic bottle liners may explode after microwaving, spilling hot formula over the baby's body.[5]

In addition to infant safety, a major public health concern with microwaving is meat and poultry safety. Because foods are cooked so quickly by microwaves, bacteria that could cause food poisoning may not be killed. To keep your microwave oven an ally in your fight against food poisoning, follow these tips.[6]

Defrosting

1. *Remove food from its wrappings before thawing.* Some plastic wraps and foam trays may melt or migrate into the food.

2. *Don't let food defrost or stand for over 2 hours.* This is the critical window for bacterial growth.

3. *Finish cooking defrosted foods immediately after thawing.* This will prevent a potentially lengthy, and unneccessary, trip through the food-safety "danger zone" of 40 to 140 degrees Fahrenheit (°F).

Cooking

1. *Remove bones from large pieces of meat.* Bones can shield meat from microwaves, preventing cooking.

2. *Place foods uniformly in a covered dish, and add a bit of liquid.* Steam produced under the cover can kill bacteria. You may want to vent a small area to allow steam to escape. Avoid letting plastic wrap touch the food.

3. *Large pieces of meat cook more thoroughly if cooked longer at 50 percent power ("medium" on most ovens).* This allows inner areas to cook, without overcooking surface areas. Try oven cooking bags to increase tenderness. Also, try the newer microwave roasters that are available, and follow directions carefully.

4. *Move food around several times during cooking.* Stirring food and re-arranging pieces of food helps prevent cold spots, where bacteria will not be subjected to heat. Turn the entire dish around, too, if you don't have a turntable, to help distribute the heating.

5. *Don't cook whole, stuffed poultry in microwave.* Microwaves can't penetrate the center of the bird, and bones shield some meat from cooking.

6. *Don't partially cook food unless used immediately.* Prolonging the length of time that meat is warm and undercooked produces an ideal breeding ground for bacteria.

7. *Use a meat thermometer or temperature probe to ensure proper heating.* Red meats should reach 160°F, poultry 180°F.

8. *Consider variations in oven wattage.* If a recipe was written for a higher-powered oven than yours, cook longer and rely on the thermometer to ensure safety.

9. *Don't shorten the "stand" times.* Standing times are necessary to achieve proper internal temperatures.

Reheating

1. *Cover foods with microwave-safe plastic, waxed paper, or a glass lid.* This prevents drying and helps achieve proper temperature.

2. *Make sure warmed food is steaming when uncovered.* Check with probe or thermometer for 160°F.

3. *Watch out when warming baby bottles and baby food.* Hot spots in bottles and food can burn sensitive little mouths. In fact the tendency to overheat is so prevalent and dangerous that the *best* advice is to warm bottles the old-fashioned way—in a warm-water bath. If you *must* microwave, shake bottles and stir dishes of food; TEST before giving to baby.

What's Safe to Use Inside?

Don't use margarine tubs, whipped topping containers, and other plastic tubs unless approved for use in microwave ovens; when heated, chemicals may migrate into food.

Don't use brown grocery bags or newspapers; they may contain recycled materials, such as metals, which aren't safe in the microwave oven.

Don't reuse cooking containers (plates, trays, baking "pans," browners) provided with convenience foods; materials in these products are approved for one-time use, and further use may allow chemicals to migrate into food.

Don't eat foods prepared in a browning package or on a browning surface that has become charred.

Don't let plastic wrap touch food—it may melt when food gets hot.

Do use waxed paper, oven cooking bags, and microwave-safe plastic wrap.

Most paper plates, paper towels, and napkins have not yet been tested for safety in the microwave oven. If you use them, use plain white products to avoid transfer of color to food,[6] or look for the newer "microwave safe" types.

Fruits and Vegetables

If you've purchased truly *organic* produce—that is, grown without *any* pesticides—the key issue is reducing your potential exposure to natural toxins present in the food. Here, we're talking about aflatoxin, glycoalkaloids, nitrites, and nitrates.

If produce is not organically grown or has not been certified as *residue-free,* wash it carefully before using. Make sure all dirt has been removed. Scrubbing with a vegetable brush helps get rid of many pesticide residues. Remove outer leaves of leafy vegetables such as cabbage. Peeling fruits and vegetables also removes pesticide residues, but some fiber is lost along with them. Peeling might be something you reserve for waxed produce.

Remember our earlier discussion about cantaloupes—wash the rinds with water, scrub, and rinse thoroughly before cutting melons. This minimizes the chances of spreading *Salmonella* bacteria from the rind to the flesh. New FDA recommendations suggest that this might be a good approach for *all* fresh produce served raw, particularly if the produce will not be eaten immediately.

Potatoes should be checked for bruises, green-tinged areas, and insect infestation. Remove these undesirable sections. When eating potatoes, pay attention if you feel a burning sensation (not caused by the temperature of the potato) or a bitter taste in your mouth, and discard the rest of the potato.

If you like mushrooms, consider serving them cooked more often to destroy the hydrazines in them, but occasional consumption of raw mushrooms certainly seems to be safe. Again, it's a personal decision—how many risks do you want to control? How careful do you want to be?

Vegetables are great raw, but they can also be enjoyed cooked. Try these low-fat preparation methods: grilling, microwaving, stir-frying with broth or water instead of oil, and steaming.

Meats and Poultry

Meats need special care to prevent food poisoning. Thoroughly clean all surfaces, including hands and utensils, before tackling raw meat and poultry and between cooking steps. Never thaw meat or poultry at room temperature. Always cook meat and poultry within 2 hours of removing from refrigeration. If defrosted in the microwave, cook immediately.

Removing fat and skin eliminates both a nutritional risk factor and a food-safety risk factor—pesticide residues, hormones, and drugs tend to concentrate in animal fat.

Remember to watch the portion sizes—plan for shrinkage of 25 percent for boneless meat and poultry, and cook enough to produce 3-ounce portions for each diner. If you're used to serving larger meat portions, better double your regular recipe for rice, potatoes, or pasta to fill 'em up.

Stick with low-fat preparation methods. Grill occasionally, avoiding fatty marinades or basting sauces. Wrap meats or grilling surface in foil before grilling or put meat in a pan on the grill to eliminate some grilling hazards. Removing all fat from foods before grilling also reduces formation of cancer-causing substances in grilled foods.

Microwave meats according to the rules detailed above. Broil occasionally, keeping in mind that burned and browned material contains some carcinogens. Roast, stew, or stir-fry with broth instead of oil.

Fish

Remove inner organs and skin to eliminate chemical residues. Make sure the fish smells and looks fresh. Keep it chilled until just before cooking.

Try low-fat preparation methods, such as grilling without fatty basting sauces or poaching. Try fish in soup or stew, using evaporated skim milk instead of cream.

Grains

With rice, remove foreign material before cooking. If it's brown rice, make sure there's no rancid smell. Cook without fat, using directions on the bag, but leave out the butter or margarine. Season with onions, garlic, or low-fat broth.

Breads spread with butter or margarine lose some of their nutritional excellence. Try alternatives to high-fat spreads, such as skim-milk ricotta, pure-fruit spreads, apple butter, and low-fat cottage cheese. Warm bread in the oven to fill your kitchen with a homey fragrance and to crisp the outside of the loaf. Try squeezing a clove of roasted garlic on a slice of fresh French bread—heaven!

Don't turn plastic bread bags inside out and then reuse them for food—the lead paint used on the outside can rub off on your food.

Try pasta with low-fat sauces, such as tomato sauce, or toss with lightly-stir-fried vegetables.

Watch the portion size on cold cereals, especially granola types. Stick with the low-fat ones described in an earlier chapter. Consider using hot cereals more often, cooked with dried fruit and/or cinnamon.

Eggs

Watch the frequency of egg consumption, aiming for no more than 4 per week if your cholesterol's okay, fewer if it's not. Forget the four-egg breakfast—stick with one or two.

Prepare eggs by poaching, poach-frying using a dab of margarine along with the poaching water, or boiling.

Avoid raw eggs. Make sure cracked eggs are used immediately in dishes where they'll be fully cooked.

Make sure you thoroughly wash all surfaces that have been in contact with raw eggs.

Crackers

Rotate supplies of crackers to prevent rancidity. Use low-fat spreads and dips, such as cottage cheese, pure-fruit spreads, Mexican salsa, and yogurt-based dips.

Other Snacks

Make sure peanuts contain no mold, are not oil roasted, and are not rancid. Watch the portion size for fat and calories.

Check other nuts for rancidity, and keep the portion size modest.

Rotate supplies of peanut butter to prevent rancidity. Refrigerate if "old-fashioned." Watch the portion size—peanut butter packs a whollop of fat.

Rotate supplies of cookies to ward off rancidity. Serve with skim or 1% milk.

Use chips only occasionally, serving with salsa or other low-fat dips.

Dairy Foods

Keep dairy foods refrigerated until used, and re-refrigerate immediately. Watch the dates and keep track of "off" odors.

If you love chocolate milk, use skim or 1% milk and add powdered chocolate beverage mix (virtually fat-free) or powdered cocoa plus an artificial sweetener if sugar is a problem.

Summing Up

Making sure food stays safe and healthy is just a matter of priorities. Keeping in mind that food poisoning remains a serious threat to the public health and that heart and blood-vessel diseases are the number one causes of death in the U.S. may help you keep all the pesticide and additive scares in perspective!

Next, let's rustle up some healthy menus and recipes!

References

1. Broihier, Catherine, M.S., R.D., "Answers to Cookware Safety Questions," *Environmental Nutrition,* February 1991, p. 2.

2. Klein, Barbara P., Ph.D., "Retention of Nutrients in Microwave-Cooked Foods," *Contemporary Nutrition* 14(2):1–2, 1989.

3. Lubec, G. et al., "Aminoacid Isomerisation and Microwave Exposure," *Lancet* 2(8676):1392–1393, 1989.

4. Wolfe, S., "Microwave Heating of Milk," *Lancet* 335(8687):470, 1990.

5. Nemethy, Margaret et al., "Microwave Heating of Infant Formula and Breast Milk," *Journal of Pediatric Health Care* 4(3):131–135, 1990.

6. Templin, Susan, CiCi Williamson, and Marilyn Johnston, "A Microwave Handbook," *Food News for Consumers (USDA)* 7(1):14–15, Spring 1990.

PART 4
SAFE & HEALTHY MENUS & RECIPES

Okay, it's time to prepare the ultimate healthy meal. Having expertly managed your food-shopping excursion, followed the rules of proper food handling, and taken proper measures to reduce additional food-safety hazards, you're now ready to put all this healthy stuff into delightful concoctions.

Our plan, of course, is to prevent disease—both the short-range kind (like food poisoning) and the long-range kind (like heart disease and cancer).

Now watch what we can do to make this an incredible dining experience! The only requirements are some cooking facilities, an open mind, an adventurous spirit, and a commitment to health!

CHAPTER 1

MENUS

Finally, a sampling of low-fat, high-fiber menus designed to provide less than 30 percent calories from fat and more than 100 percent great taste! They're spiked with all the good things we've talked about—beta-carotene, potassium, calcium, vitamin C, fruits, vegetables, and complex carbohydrates. When menu items appear with an asterisk (*), you'll find them in the recipe section that follows. (In addition to the recipes used in these menus, a variety of other yummy recipes also appear in the recipe section.)

Special Note: Using seasonal fruits and vegetables should be a high priority for all of us, since produce provides the best value and highest quality when it's in season. These menus focus on seasonal produce items and are accompanied by lists of produce bargains for each season.

Winter Teasers

BREAKFAST MENU IDEAS

Sliced kiwifruit
Whole-grain pancakes
Citrus Yogurt Topping*

🐦 🐦 🐦 🐦 🐦 🐦 🐦 🐦

Orange slices
Hot oatmeal or oat bran with cinnamon
and grated orange peel
Nonfat or 1% milk

🐦 🐦 🐦 🐦 🐦 🐦 🐦 🐦

LUNCH OR LIGHT SUPPER MENU IDEAS

Tomato-Vegetable Barley Soup*
Whole-grain bread
Banana
Nonfat or 1% Milk

🐦 🐦 🐦 🐦 🐦 🐦 🐦 🐦

Risotto with Grated Cheese*
Raw vegetable sticks
Grapefruit wedges
Nonfat or 1% milk

🐦 🐦 🐦 🐦 🐦 🐦 🐦 🐦

DINNER MENU IDEAS

Zingy Baked Chicken*
Slim Potato Wreath*
Steam-Fried Cabbage with·Carrots*
Bananarama*

🐦 🐦 🐦 🐦 🐦 🐦 🐦 🐦

Oriental Salmon*
Steamed Quinoa* or brown rice
Stir-Fried Broccoli*
Papaya and kiwifruit slices

Brazilian Black Beans*
Brown rice
Steamed Brussels sprouts
Raw vegetable sticks
Fresh tangerines

WINTER PRODUCE BEST BUYS

Vegetables	**Fruits**
Winter squash	Tangerines
(acorn, butternut,	Oranges
hubbard)	Lemons
Parsnips	Grapefruit
Broccoli	Kiwifruit
Turnips	Papayas
Brussels sprouts	Bananas
Potatoes	
Cabbage	

Spring Delights

BREAKFAST MENU IDEAS

Sliced strawberries with
Ready-to-eat whole-grain cereal
Nonfat or 1% milk
Whole-grain toast with low-fat margarine

❧ ❧ ❧ ❧ ❧ ❧ ❧ ❧

Orange wedges
Whole-wheat English muffins
Poach-Fried Egg*
Nonfat or 1% milk

❧ ❧ ❧ ❧ ❧ ❧ ❧ ❧

LUNCH OR LIGHT SUPPER MENU IDEAS

Not-Egg-Salad* sandwich with alfalfa sprouts and
Romaine lettuce on whole-wheat pita
Carrot sticks
Banana
Nonfat or 1% milk

❧ ❧ ❧ ❧ ❧ ❧ ❧ ❧

Low-fat cottage cheese with chives
Low-fat whole-rye crackers or crispbread
Raw vegetables (jicama sticks, broccoli
florets, carrot sticks)
Fresh strawberries and fresh banana
Nonfat or 1% milk

❧ ❧ ❧ ❧ ❧ ❧ ❧ ❧

DINNER MENU IDEAS

*Chicken Breasts Veronique**
Steamed rice (white or brown)
Steamed asparagus
Mixed green salad with spinach
Spring Green Dressing or*
*Creamy Salsa Dressing**
Sliced guava

Stir-Fried Vegetables (bok choy, kohlrabi, garlic,*
green onion)
Steamed rice, bulgur, or quinoa
*Seasoned Pork Loin Roast**
Sliced fresh pineapple

❖   ❖   ❖   ❖   ❖

SPRING PRODUCE BEST BUYS

Vegetables	**Fruits**
Asparagus	Strawberries
Artichokes	Pineapple
Bok choy	Bananas
Chinese cabbage	Guava
Onions	
Broccoli	
Kohlrabi	
Okra	
Chives	
Green Onions	
Garlic	
Jicama	
Mushrooms	
Spinach	

Summer Flavors

BREAKFAST MENU IDEAS

Blueberries with nonfat yogurt
Whole-wheat toast with
low-fat margarine

🐦 🐦 🐦 🐦 🐦 🐦 🐦 🐦

Crenshaw melon cubes, balls, or wedges
Healthy Omelet with Cheese*
Whole-grain English muffin

🐦 🐦 🐦 🐦 🐦 🐦 🐦 🐦

LUNCH OR LIGHT SUPPER MENU IDEAS

Curried Rice–Bean Salad*
Tangy Cucumbers*
Crunchy Chilled Green Beans*
Peaches and plums
Nonfat or 1% milk

🐦 🐦 🐦 🐦 🐦 🐦 🐦 🐦

Sliced turkey breast in pita with Romaine lettuce and
low-fat mayonnaise
Zucchini and carrot sticks
Nectarine or Bartlett pear
Nonfat or 1% milk

🐦 🐦 🐦 🐦 🐦 🐦 🐦 🐦

DINNER MENU IDEAS

Pasta with Ernie's Amazing Fresh Tomato Sauce*
Steamed zucchini with onions
Grated Parmesan or Romano cheese
Crusty French or Italian bread
Green salad with snow peas
Melon wedges with frozen low-fat yogurt

🐦 🐦 🐦 🐦 🐦 🐦 🐦 🐦

Bean-Stuffed Peppers*
Garden Vegetable Platter*
Corn on the cob
Berries and peaches with
frozen low-fat yogurt

🐦 🐦 🐦 🐦 🐦 🐦 🐦 🐦

SPECIAL EVENT

Honey Dew and cantaloupe cubes on skewers
Grilled swordfish and Grilled Chicken*
Grilled Vegetables*
Grilled Potatoes*
Crusty French Bread with Roasted Garlic*
Green salad with low-fat dressing
Angel food cake with fresh fruit or
Tangy Apricot Ice*

❖   ❖   ❖   ❖   ❖

SUMMER PRODUCE BEST BUYS

Vegetables	Fruits
Tomatoes	Pears (Bartlett)
Summer Squash	Apricots
(zucchini, yellow	Cherries
crookneck)	Honey Dew
Green beans	Crenshaw melon
Corn	Nectarines
Cucumbers	Plums
Green peppers	Peaches
Loose leaf lettuce	Cantaloupe
Radishes	Blueberries
Snow peas	Watermelon
Herbs	
Onions	
Carrots	

Autumn Pleasers

BREAKFAST MENU IDEAS

*Microwave-Baked Apple Slices**
with nonfat yogurt (plain)
Whole-grain English muffin
Low-fat margarine

❧ ❧ ❧ ❧ ❧ ❧ ❧ ❧

Hot cereal with dates
Walnuts (topping)
Nonfat or 1% milk

❧ ❧ ❧ ❧ ❧ ❧ ❧ ❧

LUNCH OR LIGHT SUPPER MENU IDEAS

*Creamy Carrot Soup** *or Sweet Potato Soup**
Low-fat cheese
Whole-grain bread
Nonfat or 1% milk
Pear

❧ ❧ ❧ ❧ ❧ ❧ ❧ ❧

*Special Tuna Salad**
Whole-wheat pita
Vegetable sticks
Nonfat or 1% milk
Apple

❧ ❧ ❧ ❧ ❧ ❧ ❧ ❧

DINNER MENU IDEAS

Raw vegetable sticks with
*Spring Green Dip** *or Creamy Salsa Dip**
*Tomato-y Cabbage with Garden Vegetables**
Grated Parmesan or Romano cheese
Steamed rice (white or brown)
*Sliced Pears with Yogurt Sauce**

❧ ❧ ❧ ❧ ❧ ❧ ❧ ❧

Eggplant Medley* over whole-wheat pasta
Part-skim or skim-milk mozzarella sticks
Steam-Fried Kale or Collards*
Green Salad with Special Dressing*
Sliced seasonal fruit

AUTUMN PRODUCE BEST BUYS

Vegetables	Fruits and Nuts
Carrots	Cranberries
Cabbage	Dates
Eggplant	Apples
Kale	Pears (d'Anjou, Bosc, Pomice)
Collards	Pomegranates
Leeks	
Cauliflower	
Pumpkin	
Sweet potatoes	
Swiss chard	
Beets	

RESOURCES

Produce best buys listings were adapted from information compiled by Produce Marketing Association, 1500 Casho Mill Road, P.O. Box 6036, Newark, Delaware 19714-6036 and by United Fresh Fruit and Vegetable Association, Washington, D.C.

CHAPTER 2

RECIPES

Dips and Dressings

Great with low-fat crackers, matzoh, or raw
vegetables!

MEXICAN SALSA

Ingredients

1 28-oz. can crushed tomatoes (*without* puree
or Italian seasonings)
1 small onion, finely chopped
2 cloves garlic, finely minced
1 small can chopped chili or
jalapeno peppers
½ tsp. hot pepper sauce

Directions

1. Combine all ingredients.
2. Chill at least 2 hours before
serving, to let flavors blend.
Makes 4 cups.
Per ¼ cup:
Calories 14
Fat (g) 00
Cholesterol (mg) 0
Sodium (mg) 82
Fiber (g) 1

◆ ◆ ◆ ◆ ◆ ◆ ◆ ◆

CREAMY SALSA DIP AND
SALAD DRESSING

Ingredients

1 cup nonfat yogurt
1 cup sour cream
½ cup mexican salsa

Directions

1. Combine all ingredients.
2. Chill or serve immediately.

Makes 2½ cups (40 Tbsp.)
Per tablespoon:
Calories 16
Fat (g) 1.2
Cholesterol (mg) 3
Sodium (mg) 12
Fiber (g) 0

◆ ◆ ◆ ◆ ◆ ◆ ◆ ◆

ZINGY DIP AND SALAD DRESSING

Ingredients

1 cup nonfat yogurt
1 cup sour cream
3 green onions (scallions)
1 tsp. salt-free herb seasoning
½ tsp. low-sodium soy sauce
Carrot sticks and other raw veggies
or salad

Directions

1. Chop scallions finely.
2. Combine all ingredients, except raw vegetables.
3. Chill at least 2 hours to let flavors blend.
4. Serve with raw vegetables or salad.

Makes 2¼ cups (36 Tbsp.).
Per tablespoon:
Calories 17
Fat (g) 1.4
Cholesterol (g) 3
Sodium (mg) 11
Fiber (g) 0

◆ ◆ ◆ ◆ ◆ ◆ ◆ ◆

SPRING GREEN
DRESSING OR DIP

Reproduced with permission. Contributed by
Nancy Kelley Crevier, Natural Foods Consultant.

Ingredients

8 oz. firm tofu
1 cup tofu mayonnaise or lowfat
mayonnaise
2 Tbsp. Dijon-style mustard
1 cup fresh chives (1½ oz.)
2 whole scallions (1 oz.)
1 clove garlic
2 large sprigs parsley
½ Tbsp. soy sauce or tamari
1 Tbsp. fresh lemon juice
2 tsp. cider vinegar
¼ cup water

Directions

1. Process tofu and mayo in food
processor with steel blade until
smooth.
2. Add remaining ingredients,
except water, and process several
minutes until very smooth and
green in color.
3. Add water to thin for salad
dressing, or omit water and use
chilled as vegetable or shrimp dip.
4. Will stay fresh in refrigerator
for 7 to 10 days.
Makes 3 cups (48 Tbsp.) salad
dressing, 2 ¾ cups (44 Tbsp.) dip.

Per tablespoon (made with cholesterol-free mayo):

	Salad dressing	Dip
Calories	22	23
Fat (g)	1.8	2.0
Cholesterol (mg)	0	0
Sodium (mg)	20	22
Fiber (g)	0	0

◆ ◆ ◆ ◆ ◆ ◆ ◆ ◆

SPECIAL DRESSING

This is not a lowfat dressing, but it's extremely delicious and the fat is monounsaturated. Use it when the rest of your meal is very low in fat.

Ingredients

3 Tbsp. extra virgin olive oil
1 Tbsp. red wine vinegar
⅛ tsp. garlic powder
½ tsp. sugar
1 tsp. soy sauce
Fresh ground black pepper to taste

Directions

1. The best method of applying this dressing is to first distribute the oil over the salad greens. Toss.
2. Add rest of ingredients and toss. Serve immediately.
Makes enough dressing for a salad for 4.
Per ¼ recipe:
Calories 93
Fat (g) 10.1
Cholesterol (mg) 0
Sodium (mg) 86
Fiber (g) 0

Salads

TANGY CUCUMBERS:
TWO WAYS

Ingredients

¾ cup unseasoned rice wine vinegar
or cider vinegar
¼ cup sugar
¼ cup chopped fresh parsley
4 green onions (scallions), sliced
3 medium cucumbers
Sauce:
½ cup yogurt
1 tsp. sugar
½ tsp. dry mustard

Directions

1. In a medium bowl, combine vinegar, sugar,
parsley and onions. Stir to dissolve sugar.
2. Refrigerate until cool.
3. Peel cucumbers if desired, or if
skin is thick or tough. Cut in
half lengthwise and scrape out
seeds with a spoon.
4. Cut the cucumbers crosswise into
thin, half-moon slices. Put into bowl
with vinegar mixture and marinate
in refrigerator for 1 to 2 hours.
5. Cucumbers can be served with
the marinade, or they can be
drained and tossed with sauce.
Makes 4 to 5 servings.

Per ¼ recipe:		
	Without sauce	**With sauce**
Calories	77	92
Fat (g)	0.3	0.4
Cholesterol (g)	0	0.5
Sodium (mg)	7	29
Fiber (g)	3.5	3.5

Note: This zesty, refreshing salad is a good accompaniment to highly seasoned or spicy foods. It goes especially well with fish or chicken and makes a delicious picnic salad.

Author's note: Even if you avoid cucumbers because they "repeat," you'll enjoy this salad because the cucumber seeds, the culprits in "repeating" cucumbers, have been removed.

CURRIED RICE—BEAN SALAD

Reproduced with permission. Copyright
Culinary Hearts Kitchen Course, 1984. Copyright
American Heart Association.

Ingredients

3 cups cooked, long-grain rice, white or brown
1½ cups unsalted cooked white or
red kidney beans
4 green onions (scallions),
thinly sliced
½ green pepper, diced
2 stalks celery, diced
¼ cup chopped fresh parsley
½ cup mayonnaise
1 Tbsp. of lemon juice
¾ tsp. curry powder
Black pepper to taste

Directions

1. Combine rice, beans, onions, green pepper, celery, and parsley. Toss to mix.
2. Combine remaining ingredients and blend thoroughly with rice mixture. This mixture can be served loose in a lettuce-lined bowl. Or it can be pressed into a 5-cup ring mold, chilled, unmolded and brought back to room temperature just before serving. Fill center of ring with cherry tomatoes or watercress.

Makes 6 servings.

Per ⅙ recipe:

	White rice, reg. mayo	Brown rice, low-fat, cholesterol-free mayo
Calories	*291*	*221*
Fat (g)	*14.8*	*6.0*
Cholesterol (mg)	*11*	*0*
Sodium (mg)	*129*	*116*
Fiber (g)	*3.9*	*4.8*

Notes: Rice will have more flavor if you cook 1 cup raw rice in 2½ cups boiling, salt-free chicken stock *or* 2½ cups boiling water to which ½ tsp. basil and ½ tsp. oil have been added.

Brown rice can be substituted for white rice to increase the fiber content of the dish. The amounts and cooking time will be different. Follow the directions on the package of brown rice. Cook in (fat-free) homemade chicken stock or water.

If you use dried beans, place beans and water in a saucepan. (Dry beans double in size when cooked so use ¾ cup dried beans to equal 1½ cups cooked beans.) Bring to a boil and cook 2 minutes. Do not drain. Set aside for 1 hour.

Return beans to heat, adding water to cover if necessary. Simmer for 1 hour or until beans are tender. Drain and set aside.

If you use canned beans, check labels for the low-sodium varieties. You can also rinse canned beans to remove much of the added sodium if you cannot locate low-sodium varieties in your grocery store.

Serve with slices of lemon so each person can squeeze a bit of lemon over the salad. Some may want a stronger lemon flavor.

Author's note: Substitute low-fat mayonnaise, if desired.

GARDEN VEGETABLE PLATTER

Contributed by Ernie Gebo.

Ingredients

3 fresh garden tomatoes
1 green pepper
1 small onion or 2 scallions
Fresh-ground black pepper
1 large cucumber
1 Tbsp. chopped fresh basil
1 Tbsp. olive oil
2 tsp. red wine vinegar

Directions

1. Slice all vegetables. Arrange on platter.
2. Scatter chopped basil on top.
3. Drizzle oil and vinegar over all. Sprinkle with black pepper.

Serves 4.
Per ¼ recipe:
Calories 64
Fat (g) 3.8
Cholesterol 0
Sodium (mg) 10
Fiber (g) 2.9

◆ ◆ ◆ ◆ ◆ ◆ ◆ ◆

NOT-EGG-SALAD

Reproduced by permission. Contributed by
Nancy Kelley Crevier, Natural Foods Consultant.

Ingredients

1 lb. firm or extra-firm tofu, in small dice
⅓ cup celery, minced
¼ cup scallion, minced
¾ cup tofu mayonnaise or low-fat
mayonnaise
1 Tbsp. soy sauce or tamari
1 Tbsp. Dijon-style mustard
Black pepper
½ tsp. turmeric

Directions

1. Combine tofu, celery, and scallion in bowl.
2. In another bowl, whisk rest of
ingredients.
3. Add mayo mixture to tofu,
mashing slightly.
4. Adjust seasonings. Serve on
whole-grain bread with sprouts and
lettuce.
Makes 3½ cups (7 half-cup
servings).
Per ½ cup (made with low-fat,
cholesterol-free mayo):
Calories 168
Fat (g) 12.9
Cholesterol 0
Sodium (mg) 316
Fiber (g) 0.7

◆ ◆ ◆ ◆ ◆ ◆ ◆ ◆

SPECIAL TUNA SALAD

Ingredients

1 6½-oz. can tuna in water, drained and rinsed
⅛ tsp. onion powder
1 medium carrot, grated finely
2 Tbsp. nonfat yogurt
2 Tbsp. low-fat mayo
Pinch of sugar
Dash black pepper

Directions

Combine all ingredients. Chill. Serve as salad
or sandwich filling.
Makes 2 servings.
Per ½ recipe (made with low-fat,
cholesterol-free mayo):
Calories 185
Fat (g) 4.7
Cholesterol (mg) 59
Sodium (mg) 435
Fiber (g) 1.2

Vegetables

BRAISED CABBAGE WITH CARROTS

Ingredients

½ medium head green cabbage, cut in
medium chunks
2 medium carrots, thinly sliced
2 cloves garlic, minced
2 tsp. olive oil
1 Tbsp. dry sherry

Directions

1. Heat oil in large saucepan on high heat until fragrant.
2. Add other ingredients, stirring briskly until garlic starts to brown.
3. Add 1 to 2 Tbsp. water. Cover tightly and lower heat to medium.
4. Cook, stirring occasionally, until cabbage is crunchy-tender, about 5 to 10 minutes.
5. Add sherry. Cook, without cover, 1 minute.
6. Serve with low-sodium soy sauce.

Makes 2 generous servings.

Per ½ recipe:

	Without soy sauce	**With ½ tsp. low-sodium soy sauce**
Calories	132	132
Fat (g)	5.0	5.0
Cholesterol (mg)	0	0
Sodium (mg)	65	151
Fiber (g)	10.1	10.1

◆ ◆ ◆ ◆ ◆ ◆ ◆ ◆

TOMATO-Y CABBAGE WITH GARDEN VEGETABLES

Ingredients

1 Tbsp. olive oil
1 large onion, coarsely chopped
1 large head green cabbage, cut in large chunks

1 large (28 oz.) can crushed
tomatoes or 4 to 5 large garden
tomatoes, peeled and chunked,
retaining all juice
1 large green pepper, in medium
chunks
Black pepper to taste
Grated Parmesan or Romano cheese
(optional)

Directions

1. Heat oil in large cast iron skillet or
Dutch oven.
2. Add onion; sauté until
transparent, but not brown.
3. Add remaining ingredients,
including juice from tomatoes.
4. Reduce heat; cover, simmer,
stirring occasionally, until cabbage
is soft (20 minutes).
5. Serve with grated cheese,
if desired.

Makes 4 generous servings.

Per ¼ recipe:

	Without cheese, with fresh tomatoes	With 2 tsp. Parm., canned tomatoes	Canned tomatoes, no cheese
Calories	145	162	143
Fat (g)	4.5	5.8	4.5
Cholesterol (mg)	0	3	0
Sodium (mg)	58	441	363
Fiber (g)	12.2	11.6	11.6

◆ ◆ ◆ ◆ ◆ ◆ ◆ ◆

STEAM-FRIED KALE OR COLLARDS

Ingredients

1¼ lb. fresh kale or collards
1 medium onion, chopped
1 Tbsp. olive oil
Salt and pepper to taste

Directions

1. Carefully clean greens in several cold water baths, making sure to remove all dirt and sand. Shake to remove excess water.
2. Chop off and discard tough ends on stems of all leaves.
3. Coarsely chop stems of all leaves. Set aside.
4. Layer several leaves on top of one another and slice crosswise into 1-inch slices.
5. Place oil in bottom of large pan. Add chopped onion, then chopped stems.
6. Turn heat to high and heat until onions and stems are sputtering. Stir.
7. Add sliced leaves and 3 Tbsp. water to pot. Cover tightly and turn heat to medium.
8. Cook until leaves and stems are crunchy-tender, about 15 to 20 minutes. Season to taste.
Makes 4 servings.
Note: Other greens—turnip, mustard—may be substituted.

Per ¼ recipe:	Collards	Kale
Calories	62	72
Fat (g)	3.7	3.9
Cholesterol	0	0
Sodium (mg)	28	23
Fiber (g)	2.0	3.7

EGGPLANT MEDLEY

(Great on pasta!)

Ingredients

1 large eggplant (2 lb.)
1 clove garlic, minced
1 large onion, chopped
Fresh-ground black pepper
1 can (28 oz.) crushed tomatoes
1 Tbsp. chopped fresh parsley

Directions

1. Leaving skin on eggplant, cube into 1-inch cubes.
2. Combine all ingredients, except parsley, in large saucepan. Heat on high until boiling; stir; reduce heat to medium or low.
3. Continue simmering until eggplant is tender, about 20 minutes. Stir in parsley just before serving.

Makes 4 large servings.

Per ¼ recipe:
Calories 79
Fat (g) 0.8
Cholesterol 0
Sodium (mg) 327
Fiber (g) 6.0

◆ ◆ ◆ ◆ ◆ ◆ ◆ ◆

CRUNCHY CHILLED GREEN BEANS

These are a great lunch-box treat. They make yummy finger foods to replace french fries or chips with sandwiches and other cold meals.

Ingredient

1 lb. whole fresh green beans

Directions

1. Wash green beans; remove stems and tips.
2. Plunge into boiling water, or steam in steamer basket, for 3 to 4 minutes, or until crunchy-tender. Remove and toss into cold water until beans cool to room temperature.
3. Chill. Serve whole.
Makes 4 servings.
Per ¼ recipe:
Calories 35
Fat (g) 0.3
Cholesterol 0
Sodium (mg) 3
Fiber (g) 2.4

◆ ◆ ◆ ◆ ◆ ◆ ◆ ◆ ◆

STIR-FRIED BROCCOLI

Ingredients

1 bunch broccoli
1½ Tbsp. olive oil
3 cloves garlic, minced
1 Tbsp. soy sauce

Directions

1. Chop off tough ends of broccoli stalks; discard.
2. Wash broccoli thoroughly. Peel tough outer layer of stems, if necessary. Slice stalks into ¼-inch slices. Set aside.
3. Separate flower end of broccoli stalks into small florets.
4. Heat oil in large pot or wok until fragrant. Add garlic and sliced broccoli stalks, reserving florets. Stir-fry until softened.
5. Add florets; stir-fry until crunchy-tender. *Carefully* add water in small amounts, not more oil, if broccoli begins to stick.
6. Toss with soy sauce just before serving.

Makes 6 servings.
Per ¼ recipe:
Calories 65
Fat (g) 3.8
Cholesterol 0
Sodium (mg) 204
Fiber (g) 4.5

◆ ◆ ◆ ◆ ◆ ◆ ◆ ◆

STIR-FRIED VEGETABLES

The above directions for stir-fried broccoli are the basic directions for all stir-frying. For any vegetable you stir-fry, use just enough oil to make a thin coating on the bottom of the pan or wok. If this seems to be too little, *carefully* add water, a tablespoon at a time, to vegetables in pan or wok to keep them from sticking.

◆ ◆ ◆ ◆ ◆ ◆ ◆ ◆

SLIM POTATO WREATH
(Microwave or conventional oven)

Ingredients
4 medium potatoes (1½ lb.)
3 tsp. olive oil
1 medium onion
Salt and pepper to taste

Directions
1. Scrub potatoes and remove bruised, green-tinged, and damaged sections. Do not peel. Slice into thin slices.
2. Thinly slice onion; separate into rings.
3. Coat bottom of microwave- or oven-safe pieplate (or dinnerplate) with nonstick spray.
4. Arrange potato slices in wreathlike fashion around outer edges of plate, covering the area from outer edge to 4 inches from outer edge. Scatter onion rings over potato slices.
5. Drizzle olive oil over "wreath," distributing evenly. Do not salt at this stage.

6. *For microwave oven:* Cover with waxed paper. Cook on high for 15 minutes (10 minutes per pound of potatoes). Let stand 5 minutes.

7. *For conventional oven:* Bake, uncovered, at 350°F for 45 to 55 minutes, or until potatoes are tender.

8. After cooking by either method, you may crisp potatoes by broiling about 10 inches from broiler for 5 minutes. Make sure plate is broiler-safe before doing this.

9. Season with salt and pepper *immediately* before serving, or let diners season their own at the table. (Salt will make potatoes soggy.)

Makes 4 servings.

Per ¼ recipe (before salting):
Calories 227
Fat (g) 3.6
Cholesterol 0
Sodium (mg) 14
Fiber (g) 3.9

◆ ◆ ◆ ◆ ◆ ◆ ◆ ◆

SKINNY MASHED POTATOES
(Microwave oven)

Ingredients

4 medium potatoes (1½ lb.)
2 green onions, chopped, *or* 1 small onion, chopped
2 Tbsp. sour cream *or* 1 Tbsp. low-fat margarine
⅓ cup powdered nonfat milk
2 tsp. butter-flavored sprinkles
Black pepper to taste

Directions

1. Scrub potatoes and remove bruised, green-tinged, and damaged sections. Do not peel. Cut into chunks.

2. Place potatoes in microwave-safe baking dish. Add 3 Tbsp. water. Cover with microwave-safe cover.

3. Cook on high for 15 to 20 minutes, or until potatoes are almost tender. Let stand, covered, 10 minutes. If potatoes are not tender, return to microwave oven and cook on high for another 3 to 5 minutes.

4. In a food processor with steel blade, process potatoes with peels on, adding potato water from microwave dish to keep machine from laboring.

5. Mix powdered milk with ¼ cup hot tap water. Add to potatoes as they are processed.

6. Add other ingredients while processing. Add more hot water if too thick. Continue to process until desired consistency is reached. Turn off machine and taste. Adjust seasonings.

Makes 4 servings.

Per ¼ recipe:

Calories 221

Fat (g) 1.7

Cholesterol (mg) 4

Sodium (mg) 136

Fiber (g) 3.5

Note: These potatoes are creamier than traditional mashed potatoes. They do not hold their shape on a plate.

♦ ♦ ♦ ♦ ♦ ♦ ♦ ♦

GRILLED VEGETABLES AND GRILLED POTATOES

Ingredients

Scallions, trimmed
Carrots, scrubbed
Whole small zucchini
Green and red peppers, seeded,
halved
Potatoes, scrubbed, cut in ½-inch
slices
Onions, peeled, halved
Olive oil

Directions

1. Arrange vegetables on preheated grill sprayed with nonstick spray. Brush each vegetable *lightly* with oil or a mixture of oil and water to keep from drying out.

2. Grill, turning frequently, until crunchy-tender. Cooking time varies with each vegetable, depending on size and density. Brush with water if surface dries out. Keep checking for doneness and remove quickly to avoid mushiness. Remove from grill before heavily blackened.

3. Keep grilled potatoes in a separate serving dish from other vegetables, or they'll lose their crispy outsides in vegetable juices.

4. Serves as many diners as you prepare for! Allow several pieces of each vegetable per diner—they're scrumptious this way, and even vegetable snubbers will be back for more! Fat content depends on the amount of oil you use, so use a light touch.

◆ ◆ ◆ ◆ ◆ ◆ ◆ ◆

GRILLED OR ROASTED GARLIC

An amazingly easy but luscious bread spread.
Just pick off a roasted clove and squeeze it onto
bread!

Ingredients

1–2 bulbs garlic
1 tsp. olive oil per bulb
Sprinkling of dried herbs (optional)

Directions

1. Peel off several papery layers of garlic peel,
leaving cloves covered and attached to bulb.
2. Place garlic bulb in custard cup
(for oven), or small "pan" shaped
from aluminum foil (for oven
or grill).
3. Drizzle ½ tsp. oil over each bulb,
making sure it works its way into
spaces between cloves. Sprinkle
with herbs, such as rosemary or
thyme, if desired.
4. *For oven:* Roast along with other
foods being baked. Add another
½ tsp. oil per bulb if garlic appears
dry. Roast at least 30 minutes at
375°F, or until garlic inside each
clove feels squishy.
5. *For grill:* Roast with top of grill
down while other foods are being
grilled. Cook for at least 20 minutes,
or until garlic inside each clove feels squishy.
Drizzle with another
½ tsp. oil per bulb if it starts to
dry out.

6. Serve as a butter substitute with warm, crusty bread or as a table seasoning for vegetables, potatoes, rice, or pasta. Instruct guests to pluck off a clove and squeeze the contents onto a slice of bread or other food to be seasoned.

One bulb serves 4 people. If you or your guests are real garlic aficionados, roast up to one bulb per person.

Per ¼ bulb (3 cloves):
Calories 22
Fat (g) 1.2
Cholesterol 0
Sodium (mg) 3
Fiber (g) 0.2

Grains

STEAMED QUINOA

Quinoa is a whole grain available at many health-food stores.

Ingredients

1 cup raw quinoa
1 cup hot water

Directions

1. Heat nonstick pan and add quinoa. Toast, stirring, for about 3 minutes.
2. Add hot water; bring to a boil.
3. Remove from heat and cover. Let stand until water is absorbed, about 15 minutes.

Makes 6 half-cup or 3 one-cup servings.

Per serving:

	½ cup	1 cup
Calories	105	210
Fat (g)	0.4	0.8
Cholesterol	0	0
Sodium (mg)	0	0
Fiber (g)	2.7	5.4

♦ ♦ ♦ ♦ ♦ ♦ ♦ ♦

ITALIAN POLENTA

Ingredients

1 cup yellow cornmeal
¼ tsp. salt

Directions

1. Combine cornmeal with ½ cup cool tap water.
2. Bring 3½ cups water to a boil. Carefully stir in cornmeal–water mixture.
3. Cook, stirring, over medium heat until cornmeal is softened and mixture is very thick, about 20 to 30 minutes. Add salt to taste.
4. Spoon onto individual dinner plates and let it comingle with sauce from entree. This dish is very bland, but is a great accompaniment to stews and cacciatores and highly seasoned foods.

Serves 4.
Per ¼ recipe:
Calories 109
Fat (g) 1.3
Cholesterol 0
Sodium (mg) 122
Fiber (g) 1.3

♦ ♦ ♦ ♦ ♦ ♦ ♦ ♦

RISOTTO WITH GRATED CHEESE

Ingredients

1 Tbsp. low-fat margarine
1 tsp. olive oil
1 medium onion, chopped finely
1 cup white or brown rice
4 cups hot chicken broth *or*
1 10½-oz. can of condensed chicken
broth with 2½ cups hot water
1 small envelope ground saffron
2 Tbsp. grated Parmesan or Romano
cheese

Directions

1. Melt margarine in large pan. Add oil.
2. Add onion and raw rice; sauté until rice begins to brown.
3. Add chicken broth in half-cup additions, stirring after each addition until broth is absorbed. Continue adding broth and stirring until all broth is used.
4. Just before serving, dissolve saffron in 2 Tbsp. warm water. Stir into rice.
5. Serve with grated cheese.

Serves 2 as a main course.

Per ½ recipe:

	White rice, canned broth	Brown rice, salt-free broth
Calories	483	496
Fat (g)	9.5	10.8
Cholesterol (mg)	6.3	6.3
Sodium (mg)	1213	289
Fiber (g)	1.9	4.1

Soups

CABBAGE APPLE SOUP

Reproduced by permission. Contributed by Nancy Kelley Crevier, Natural Foods Consultant.

This recipe uses miso, a soybean paste available in health-food stores. Miso lends rich, meatlike flavor without adding meat. If you wish to use a substitute, see the note at end of recipe.

Ingredients

3 cups green cabbage, finely chopped
1 cup red cabbage, finely chopped
2 tart apples, peeled and diced
2 large tomatoes, seeded and diced
2 red potatoes, scrubbed and diced
1 medium onion, diced
1 clove garlic, minced
1 cup carrots, small dice
½ cup celery, small dice
2 Tbsp. olive oil
1 Tbsp. balsamic vinegar
½ cup fresh minced parsley
1 Tbsp. dill weed
¼ cup miso, dissolved in hot water
Salt and pepper to taste

Directions

1. Heat oil in large pot until fragrant; add cabbage, apples, tomatoes, potatoes, onion, garlic, carrots, and celery. Stir over medium heat for 5 minutes.
2. Cover pot and cook on very low heat, stirring often, until onions and cabbage begin to turn translucent.
3. Add 3 quarts of water or vegetable stock and remaining

ingredients, except miso. Cover pot
and simmer for 1½ hours on very low heat.
4. Remove 3 cups soup and puree
in a blender or food processor with
miso. Return to pot and adjust
seasonings.
5. Serve hot, garnished with a sprig
of parsley and a dollop of low-fat
sour cream or yogurt, if desired.
Serve with crusty bread.
Makes about 4 quarts (16 one-cup
servings).
Per cup:
Calories 63
Fat (g) 2.2
Cholesterol 0
Sodium (mg) 170
Fiber (g) 2.3
Note: If desired, substitute miso with 2 Tbsp. Ve-Con,
also available in health-food stores. Flavor and
nutritional value will change somewhat.

◆ ◆ ◆ ◆ ◆ ◆ ◆ ◆

TOMATO-VEGETABLE
BARLEY SOUP

Reproduced by permission. Contributed by
Nancy Kelley Crevier, Natural Foods Consultant.

Ingredients

2 cups diced onion
2 cups diced carrots
1 cup diced celery
2 cloves garlic, crushed
5 cups chopped cabbage
½ cup raw barley
2 cups crushed tomatoes
2 tsp. dried basil

1 tsp. minced fresh parsley
¼ cup miso, dissolved in ¼ cup hot
water

Directions

1. Place all ingredients, except miso, in pot. Cover with 2 quarts water and bring to a boil.
2. Cover; simmer 2 hours, stirring often. Add more water if necessary.
3. Just before serving, add miso to soup. Adjust seasonings.

Makes 3 quarts (12 one-cup servings).

Per cup:
Calories 78
Fat (g) 0.7
Cholesterol 0
Sodium (g) 297
Fiber (g) 3.2

Note: If desired, substitute miso with 2 Tbsp. Ve-Con, also available in health-food stores. Flavor and nutritional value will change somewhat.

◆ ◆ ◆ ◆ ◆ ◆ ◆ ◆

SWEET POTATO SOUP

Reproduced by permission. Contributed by Nancy Kelley Crevier, Natural Foods Consultant.

Ingredients

4 medium sweet potatoes, cubed
3 medium potatoes, cubed
3 ribs celery, diced
3 cups onion, diced
1 Tbsp. salt
1 tsp. black pepper
1 Tbsp. caraway
1 tsp. thyme

2 Tbsp. fresh parsley, minced
3 Tbsp. miso, dissolved in ¼ cup
hot water

Directions

1. Place sweet potatoes, potatoes, celery, and onion in large pot. Add 2 quarts cold water and bring to a boil. Cover and simmer until potatoes are tender.
2. Add remaining ingredients.
3. Puree two-thirds of the soup and return to pot. Reheat over low heat.
Makes 4 quarts (16 one-cup servings).

Per cup:

	With skin on potatoes	Without potato skins
Calories	102	95
Fat (g)	0.4	0.4
Cholesterol	0	0
Sodium (mg)	499	496
Fiber (g)	1.9	1.5

Note: If desired, substitute miso with 2 Tbsp. Ve-Con, also available in health-food stores. Flavor and nutritional value will change somewhat.

CREAMY CARROT SOUP

Reproduced by permission. Contributed by Nancy Kelley Crevier, Natural Foods Consultant.

Ingredients

4 lbs. carrots, diced
1 lb. onion, diced
½ lb. celery, diced
⅔ cup rolled oats

¼ cup miso, dissolved in ¼ cup
hot water
1 tsp. fresh grated ginger
3 Tbsp. fresh minced parsley
½ Tbsp. ground nutmeg
1 tsp. ground cinnamon

Directions

1. Place carrots, onion, celery, and oats in large
pot. Cover with 6 inches of water.
2. Bring to a boil; cover and simmer
until carrots are tender.
3. Remove from heat and puree.
Return to pot.
4. Add rest of ingredients and stir
well. Reheat slowly and adjust
seasonings.
Makes about 5 quarts (20 one-cup
servings).
Per cup:
Calories 67
Fat (g) 0.7
Cholesterol 0
Sodium (mg) 168
Fiber (g) 4.1
Note: If desired, substitute miso with 2 Tbsp. Ve-Con,
also available in health-food stores. Flavor and
nutritional value will change somewhat.

Entrees

"TACO THING"
(MICROWAVE)

Ingredients

6 oz. 90% fat-free hamburger or 93%
fat-free ground turkey

1 medium onion, chopped
2 8-oz. cans tomato sauce
1 cup water
1 cup frozen peas and carrots
1 cup uncooked small macaroni
¼ tsp. hot pepper sauce

Directions

1. Combine ground meat and onion in 2-quart microwave-safe casserole.
2. Cook on high 3 minutes; stir; cook another 3 minutes. Stir and drain off fat.
3. Combine with rest of ingredients; cover; cook 8 minutes on high; stir; cook 6 minutes on medium to low; stir; cook 6 more minutes on medium to low.
4. Let stand, covered, 10 minutes before serving.

Makes 4 servings.

Per ¼ recipe:

	With ground turkey, reg. tomato sauce	**With ground beef, low-salt tomato sauce**
Calories	250	274
Fat (g)	5.1	6.2
Cholesterol (mg)	27	27
Sodium (mg)	752	87
Fiber (g)	6.6	6.6

◆ ◆ ◆ ◆ ◆ ◆ ◆ ◆

ERNIE'S AMAZING FRESH TOMATO SAUCE

Contributed by Ernie Gebo.

Ingredients

4 Tbsp. olive oil
9 cups fresh tomatoes, peeled and
cut into chunks
1 stalk celery, chopped coarsely
4 cloves garlic, minced
2 medium onions, chopped or sliced
1½ tsp. salt
1½ Tbsp. sugar (if needed)
½ tsp. black pepper
3–4 Tbsp. fresh basil, coarsely
chopped, or 1 tsp. dried basil
2 Tbsp. chopped fresh parsley or
½ tsp. dried parsley
¼ tsp. dried oregano

Directions

1. Heat oil in large pan until fragrant.
2. Add garlic; cook, stirring until light brown.
3. Add rest of ingredients except oregano.
4. Bring to a boil; lower heat; do not cover.
5. Simmer uncovered, until reduced to 1½ quarts (about 5 hours).
6. Add oregano; cook 15 minutes.
7. If serving immediately, add 2 cups water and heat to simmering before serving.
8. If freezing, leave in condensed form (don't add water). Freezes well.

9. When heating after removing from freezer, add 2 cups water.

Makes 8 cups (16 half-cup servings).

Per ½ cup:
Calories 76
Fat (g) 3.8
Cholesterol (mg) 0
Sodium (mg) 201
Fiber (g) 1.4

◆ ◆ ◆ ◆ ◆ ◆ ◆ ◆

WORLD'S BEST, EASIEST LASAGNA

Contributed by Cindi Cooper.

Ingredients

Nonstick cooking spray
½ lb. dry lasagna noodles
½ bunch broccoli, chopped
8 oz. part-skim mozzarella, shredded
1½ 26-oz. jars spaghetti sauce or equivalent homemade low-fat sauce

Directions

1. In bowl or pan, combine sauce with 2 cups water.
2. Coat bottom of 9 × 13-inch ovenproof baking dish with nonstick spray.
3. Preheat oven to 250°F.
4. Cover bottom of baking dish with layer of sauce.
5. Arrange layer of three lasagna noodles over sauce.
6. Place layer of chopped broccoli on noodles.

7. Scatter half of the shredded cheese over broccoli.
8. Cover with sauce.
9. Repeat with noodles, broccoli, cheese, sauce.
10. Arrange last three noodles on top of second layer.
11. Pour rest of sauce over top of dish.
12. Bake at 250°F for 2 hours.

Makes 8 servings.

Per ⅛ of recipe:

Calories 275

Fat (g) 8.9

Cholesterol (mg) 16

Sodium (mg) 771

Fiber (g) 7.3

♦ ♦ ♦ ♦ ♦ ♦ ♦ ♦

CHICKEN BREASTS VERONIQUE

Reproduced with permission. Copyright Culinary Hearts Kitchen Course, 1984. Copyright American Heart Association.

Ingredients

4 whole chicken breasts

1 cup cracker crumbs

½ tsp. salt

¼ tsp. freshly ground black pepper

½ tsp. dried tarragon

Pinch of nutmeg

3 Tbsp. margarine*

¼ cup chopped onion

½ cup chicken broth

½ cup dry white wine or vermouth

*The amount of margarine can be reduced here by using skillets with nonstick surfaces.

2 cups sliced fresh mushrooms
2 Tbsp. margarine
2 cups seedless or seeded green
grapes

Directions

1. Remove skin from chicken breasts and cut them in half. Combine cracker crumbs, salt, pepper, tarragon, and nutmeg. Coat chicken with this mixture.

2. Melt margarine in a skillet, preferably one with a nonstick surface. Brown chicken on both sides. Remove chicken and place in a single layer in a shallow baking pan. Preheat oven to 375°F.

3. Add onions to the margarine remaining in the skillet, and sauté until transparent. Drain off any excess oil. Pour on the broth and wine; bring to a boil. Pour around the chicken.* Bake, uncovered, for 30 minutes.

4. While chicken is baking, melt 2 Tbsp. margarine in a skillet. Sauté mushrooms until tender. Arrange mushrooms and grapes around chicken. Bake 8 to 10 minutes longer or until chicken is tender.
Makes 8 servings.

*The recipe can be prepared ahead of time, up to this point. Cover and refrigerate. Bring to room temperature and finish off just before serving.

Note: You may have trouble finding cracker crumbs that are low in fat. Matzo (matzoh) meal, available in the Kosher section in some supermarkets, can be substituted for the cracker crumbs. Another option is to purchase crackers low in saturated fats and pulverize them yourself.

Per ⅛ recipe (½ chicken breast):
Calories 291
Fat (g) 11.1
Cholesterol (mg) 59
Sodium (mg) 253
Fiber (g) 1.0

♦ ♦ ♦ ♦ ♦ ♦ ♦ ♦

ZINGY BAKED CHICKEN

Ingredients

2½ lb. chicken, cut up
2 cloves garlic, minced
2 Tbsp. lemon juice
1 tsp. salt-free herb seasoning

Directions

1. Remove skin and visible fat from chicken.
2. Spray bottom of baking dish with nonstick spray. Arrange chicken pieces in dish.
3. Sprinkle seasonings and lemon juice over chicken.
4. Bake at 350°F for 40 minutes. Check for doneness by cutting into area near bone. Bake longer if juices run pink.
Serves 4.

Per ¼ recipe:
Calories 261
Fat (g) 10.9
Cholesterol (mg) 118
Sodium (mg) 111
Fiber (g) 0

◆ ◆ ◆ ◆ ◆ ◆ ◆ ◆

ORIENTAL SALMON

Reproduced by permission. Contributed by
Nancy Kelley Crevier, Natural Foods Consultant.

Ingredients

2 cups water
4 Tbsp. soy sauce or tamari
2 Tbsp. toasted sesame oil
4 tsp. fresh grated ginger
2 Tbsp. minced scallion
2 large cloves garlic, crushed
4 Tbsp. dry sherry
1½ lb. salmon (6 oz. per person,
before boning)

Directions

1. In sauté pan, combine all ingredients except
salmon. Whisk.
2. Place salmon in pan with sauce
and simmer, covered, about 10
minutes per inch of thickness.
3. Remove salmon from pan and
place on plate. Debone if
using steak.
4. Increase heat under sauce to
high; boil liquid until reduced to
about ⅔ cup.

5. Blot any cooking liquid off of plate under salmon and drizzle with half of sauce.
Serves 4.
Per ¼ recipe:
Calories 265
Fat (g) 12.0
Cholesterol (mg) 56
Sodium (mg) 323
Fiber (g) 0.1

◆ ◆ ◆ ◆ ◆ ◆ ◆ ◆

BRAZILIAN BLACK BEANS

Reproduced by permission. Contributed by Nancy Kelley Crevier, Natural Foods Consultant.

Ingredients
1 lb. dried black beans
1 large onion, diced
1 green bell pepper, diced
4 large cloves garlic, crushed
2 Tbsp. lemon juice
½ tsp. cayenne pepper
2 Tbsp. ground cumin
¼ cup fresh minced cilantro
2 Tbsp. virgin olive oil

Directions
1. Pick through and rinse beans thoroughly. Cover with 2 quarts cold water and soak overnight.
2. Drain; place in large pot and cover with 2 quarts fresh, cold water. Bring to a boil.
3. Reduce heat to a simmer and cook about 20 to 30 minutes, covered, until tender. Drain, reserving cooking liquid.

4. Heat olive oil until hot. Add onion, peppers, and garlic; sauté, stirring often, until onions are transparent.

5. Add lemon juice, cayenne, and cumin and stir. Add beans and 1½ cups reserved cooking liquid.

6. Stir in cilantro and salt to taste. Adjust seasonings and serve over brown rice or quinoa. Top with parsley and chunks of low-fat cheese, if desired.

Makes 6 servings.

Per ⅙ recipe (without rice or cheese):

Calories 296
Fat (g) 6.1
Cholesterol 0
Sodium (mg) 8
Fiber (g) 8.0

◆ ◆ ◆ ◆ ◆ ◆ ◆ ◆

SEASONED PORK LOIN ROAST

Ingredients

2½ lb. pork tenderloin roast
3 cloves garlic, minced
1 tsp. dried rosemary or 3 tsp. fresh rosemary

Directions

1. Trim any fat from roast.

2. Poke small holes with knife around roast; insert garlic and rosemary leaves into holes.

3. Roast at 325°F for 1¼ to 1½ hours, or until meat thermometer registers at least 160°F.

4. Remove from oven; let stand 20 minutes
before carving. Slice into thin slices.
Makes about eight 3-ounce servings.
Per 3 oz.:
Calories 220.3
Fat (g) 13.1
Cholesterol (mg) 81
Sodium (mg) 64
Fiber (g) 0

♦ ♦ ♦ ♦ ♦ ♦ ♦ ♦

BEAN-STUFFED PEPPERS

Reproduced by permission. Adapted from recipe
by American Dry Bean Board.

Ingredients

5 medium green peppers
2 cups cooked red kidney beans
1 10-oz. package frozen chopped
broccoli, thawed
1 cup cooked brown rice
5 oz. part-skim or skim-milk
mozzarella, shredded
1 8-oz. can tomato sauce
½ cup skim milk

Directions

1. Cut each green pepper lengthwise in half;
remove seeds.
2. Chop one pepper half; set aside.
3. In 12-inch skillet in ½ inch
water, place pepper halves cut side
up over high heat; heat to boiling.
4. Reduce heat to low. Cover and
simmer 5 minutes or until peppers
are tender-crisp.

5. Meanwhile, in medium bowl
combine kidney beans, broccoli, rice, cheese, and
chopped pepper. Toss to mix well.
6. Remove peppers from skillet and
discard water in skillet; drain
peppers. Fill each pepper half with
some bean mixture.
7. Stir tomato sauce and skim milk
in same skillet. Carefully place
peppers in tomato sauce mixture.
8. Over high heat, heat to boiling.
Reduce heat to low; cover and
simmer 10 to 15 minutes until
vegetable mixture is heated through
and cheese is melted.
Makes 9 halves.
Per pepper half:
Calories 140
Fat (g) 2.9
Cholesterol (mg) 9
Sodium (mg) 246
Fiber (g) 5.9

♦ ♦ ♦ ♦ ♦ ♦ ♦ ♦

GRILLED CHICKEN

Ingredient

4 small chicken leg quarters

Directions

1. Remove all skin and fat from leg quarters.
Place on microwave-safe plate and microwave on
high for 4 minutes.
2. Place on preheated grill coated
with nonstick spray. Cook at
medium setting 15 to 20 minutes.
Remove to clean, microwave-safe
plate.

3. Finish cooking, covered with
waxed paper, in microwave oven on high. Pierce
area near bone with knife to check doneness.
Chicken is done when juices run clear, not pink.
Makes 4 servings.
Per leg quarter (3½ oz. meat after
boning):
Calories 182
Fat (g) 80
Cholesterol (mg) 89
Sodium (mg) 87
Fiber (g) 0

Breakfast

POACH-FRIED EGG

Ingredients

1 egg
2 Tbsp. water
½ tsp. low-fat margarine

Directions

1. In nonstick skillet, bring water to a boil. Add
margarine; melt.
2. Drop in egg. Cover and cook
until of desired doneness.
Serves 1.
Per recipe:
Calories 87
Fat (g) 6.5
Cholesterol (mg) 230
Sodium (mg) 92
Fiber (g) 0

♦ ♦ ♦ ♦ ♦ ♦ ♦ ♦ ♦

HEALTHY OMELET WITH CHEESE

Ingredients

1 whole egg or ¼ cup egg substitute
1 egg white
1 tsp. low-fat margarine
1 oz. low-fat cheese, in small pieces
Sprinkling of Italian seasoning

Directions

1. Melt margarine in nonstick pan. Beat egg and egg white; add to pan.
2. Lift edges of omelet as they coagulate, allowing uncooked egg to run into spaces. When almost firm, sprinkle with seasoning and pieces of cheese.
3. Fold omelet and cook until cheese is melted.

Serves 1.

Per recipe:

	With whole egg	With egg substitute
Calories	184	157
Fat (g)	12.0	8.5
Cholesterol (mg)	246	16.8
Sodium (mg)	297	339
Fiber (g)	0	0

Fruit and Desserts

CITRUS YOGURT TOPPING

Ingredients

½ cup plain low-fat yogurt
1 Tbsp. orange juice concentrate,
thawed
Sprinkling of cinnamon (optional)

Directions

Combine ingredients. Chill. Serve in place of
butter and syrup over pancakes and waffles.
Serves 1.
Per recipe:
Calories 100
Fat (g) 1.8
Cholesterol (mg) 7
Sodium (mg) 80
Fiber (mg) 0

♦ ♦ ♦ ♦ ♦ ♦ ♦ ♦

MICROWAVE-BAKED
APPLE SLICES

Ingredients

1 medium apple
1 Tbsp. raisins
¼ tsp. cinnamon
1 Tbsp. water

Directions

1. Wash and slice apple, removing pieces of
core. Do not peel.
2. Place in microwave-safe dish
with raisins, cinnamon, and water.
Cover.

3. Cook 3 to 4 minutes on high,
until apple is tender.
Serves 1.
Per recipe:
Calories 110
Fat (g) 0.5
Cholesterol (mg) 0
Sodium (mg) 3
Fiber (g) 4.2

◆ ◆ ◆ ◆ ◆ ◆ ◆ ◆

BANANARAMA

Ingredients

2 medium bananas
2 3-oz. packages vanilla pudding
(instant or cook'n'serve; sugar-
sweetened or with NutraSweet)
4 cups nonfat (skim) milk or Lactaid
6 whole graham crackers

Directions

1. In an 8 × 8-inch glass dish, place three
graham crackers in a single layer, breaking up
third cracker to fit.
2. Peel one banana and slice into
thin slices. Place in a single layer
over graham crackers in dish.
3. Prepare pudding according to
package directions, using the nonfat
milk or Lactaid. Pour one-half of
pudding over the graham cracker
and banana layers in dish,
smoothing to create a level surface.

4. Arrange the last three graham crackers over
pudding in dish,
again breaking up third cracker to
fit.
5. Peel the second banana and slice
thinly. Arrange slices in a single
layer over the graham crackers.
6. Pour remaining pudding over the
banana layer. Smooth top.
7. Chill 2 hours. If using cooked
pudding, chill 4 hours.
8. Cut into squares to serve.
Makes 9 servings.
Per ⅑ recipe, using skim milk and
cooked pudding (with sugar):
Calories 174
Fat (g) 1.0
Cholesterol (mg) 1.8
Sodium (mg) 200
Fiber (g) 0.7

◆ ◆ ◆ ◆ ◆ ◆ ◆ ◆

TANGY APRICOT ICE

Reproduced by permission. Copyright
Culinary Hearts Kitchen Course, 1984. Copyright
American Heart Association.

Ingredients

1½ cups dried apricots
2 Tbsp. lemon juice
⅓ cup sugar

Directions

1. Combine apricots with enough water to cover
in saucepan. Bring to boil over medium heat.

2. Reduce heat, cover, and simmer until fruit
is soft (about 20 minutes).
3. Drain. Reserve ¾ cup of fruit
liquid. Cool.
4. Puree fruit in a processor or
blender with reserved fruit liquid.
5. Add lemon juice and sugar to
fruit, and puree an additional 30
seconds.
6. Pour into 8-inch square pan
(or glass dish), and place in freezer,
stirring every 15 minutes until
creamy. Cover and freeze until
semihard.
Makes 4 servings.
Per ¼ recipe:
Calories 169
Fat (g) 0
Cholesterol (mg) 0
Sodium (mg) 5
Fiber (g) 4.5

Note: Just about any pureed fruit may be used to make
this refreshing dessert: strawberries, pears, Honey
Dew, pineapple, mango, and papaya, to name a few. If
fresh fruits are used, the proportion is 2 cups of pureed
fruit to ½ cup water (no cooking necessary). Make sure
the sugar is completely dissolved in the puree.

♦ ♦ ♦ ♦ ♦ ♦ ♦ ♦

SLICED PEARS WITH YOGURT SAUCE

Ingredients

1 ripe pear
½ cup plain nonfat yogurt
1 Tbsp. orange juice concentrate,
thawed

Directions

1. Slice pear vertically into thin slices. Arrange slices on dish or in bowl.
2. Stir together remaining ingredients. Pour over pear slices.
Serves 1 for breakfast or 2 for dessert.

Per serving:

	Entire recipe	½ recipe
Calories	210	105
Fat (g)	1.0	0.5
Cholesterol (mg)	2	1
Sodium (mg)	89	44
Fiber (g)	5.9	3.0

PART 5
RESOURCE
CORNER

There's nothing better than a good book—or newsletter, or cookbook, or magazine, or mail-order center. Here, we've collected the "Best of the Best"—truly fine publications and other resources you can trust.

Codes: CHD = Heart disease; WC = Weight control; CA = Cancer; HBP = High blood pressure; DM = Diabetes

Books

Many of the following books are available in softcover. Check your local bookstore.

CHD

Controlling Cholesterol: Dr. Kenneth H. Cooper's Preventive Medicine Program, Kenneth H. Cooper, M.D., M.P.H., Bantam Books, New York, 1988.

Count Out Cholesterol, Art Ulene, M.D., Random House, New York, 1989.

The Living Heart Diet. Michael E. DeBakey, M.D., Antonio M. Gotto, M.D., D. Phil., Lynne Scott, M.A., R.D., and John Foreyt, Ph.D., Raven Press–Simon and Schuster, New York, 1984.

Eater's Choice: A Food Lover's Guide to Lower Cholesterol, Dr. Ronald S. Goor and Nancy Goor, Houghton-Mifflin, Philadelphia, 1989.

General Nutrition

Eating on the Run. Evelyn Tribole, M.S., R.D., Humankinetics, Chicago, 1987.

WC

The Callaway Diet: Successful Permanent Weight Control for Starvers, Stuffers, and Skippers, C. Wayne Callaway, M.D. with Catherine Whitney, Bantam Books, New York, 1990.

Habits Not Diets, James M. Ferguson, M.D., Bull Publishing Company, Palo Alto, California, 1988.

WC, CHD, General

The Fat Attack Plan, Annette B. Natow, Ph.D., R.D., and JoAnn Heslin, M.A., R.D., Simon and Schuster, Inc., New York, 1990.

WC—Children

BIG KIDS: A Parents Guide to Weight Control for Children, Dr. Gregory Archer, New Harbinger, Oakland, California, 1989.

How to Get Your Kids to Eat...But Not Too Much, Ellyn Satter, R.D., M.S., Bull Publishing Company, Palo Alto, California, 1987.

HBP, CA, CHD, DM, General

The New American Diet, Sonja L. Connor, M.S., R.D., and William E. Connor, M.D., Simon and Schuster, New York, 1986.

CHD, HBP, CA, WC, General

The Restaurant Companion, Hope Warshaw, M.S., R.D., Surrey Books, Chicago, 1990. Available from Surrey Books, Inc., 101 East Erie Street, Suite 900, Chicago, Illinois 60611—write for free catalog.

Vitamin and Mineral Supplements

Complete Guide to Vitamins: Vitamins and Supplements, H. Winter Griffith, M.D., Fisher Books, Tucson, Arizona, 1988.

Cookbooks

CA, CHD, General

The Low Cholesterol Olive Oil Cookbook, Sarah Schlesinger and Barbara Earnest, Villard Books, New York, 1990.

CA, CHD, DM, HBP, WC, General

The Guiltless Gourmet: Low in Fat, Cholesterol, Salt, Sugar, Calories, Judy Gilliard and Joy Kirkpatrick, R.D., Diabetics Center, Inc., Minnetonka, Minnesota, 1987.

CA, CHD, WC, General

Jane Brody's Good Food Book: Living the High Carbohydrate Way, Jane Brody, W. W. Norton, New York, 1985.

Jane Brody's Good Food Gourmet: Recipes and Menus for Delicious and Healthful Entertaining, Jane Brody, W. W. Norton, New York, 1990.

A Lowfat Lifeline for the 90's, Valerie Parker, M.S., 1990. Available from Lowfat Lifeline, 52 Condolea Court, Lake Oswego, Oregon, 97035— (503) 636-1559.

Lowfat Microwave Meals, Barbara Methven, Cy DeCosse, Minnetonka, Minnesota, 1989. Available from Cy DeCosse Inc., 5900 Green Oak Drive, Minnetonka, Minnsota 55343.

Microwaving Light & Healthy, Barbara Methven, Cy DeCosse, Minnetonka, Minnesota, 1989. Available from Cy DeCosse Inc., 5900 Green Oak Drive, Minnetonka, Minnesota 55343.

CHD

American Heart Association Low-Fat, Low-Cholesterol Cookbook—An Essential Guide for Those Concerned About Their Cholesterol Levels, Scott Grundy, M.D., Ph.D., and Mary Winston, Ed. D., R.D., eds., Times Books–Random House, New York, 1989.

Count Out Cholesterol Cookbook, Mary Ward, Random House, New York, 1989.

CHD, HBP

American Heart Association Low-Salt Cookbook—A Complete Guide to Reducing Sodium and Fat in the Diet, Rodman D. Starke, M.D., and Mary Winston, Ed.D., R.D. Times Books–Random House, New York, 1990.

CHD, WC, General

Cooking Light Cookbooks, Oxmoor House, Birmingham, Alabama, (annual). Available from Cooking Light Books, P.O. Box 2463, Birmingham, Alabama 35201.

HBP

Recipes for the Heart: A Nutrition Guide for People with High Blood Pressure, Lucy M. Williams, M.S., R.D., Sandridge Publishing, Bowling Green, 1988.

WC

Microwaving on a Diet, Barbara Methven, Cy DeCosse, Minnetonka, Minnesota, 1989. Available from Cy DeCosse Inc., 5900 Green Oak Drive, Minnetonka, Minnesota 55343.

Newsletters

Environmental Nutrition (monthly) from Environmental Nutrition, 2112 Broadway, Suite 200, New York, NY 10023—(212) 362-0424.

Tufts University Diet & Nutrition Letter (monthly) from Tufts University Diet and Nutrition Letter, P.O. Box 57857, Boulder, Colorado 80322-7857—(800) 274-7881.

Harvard Heart Letter (monthly) from Harvard Heart Letter, P.O. Box 420234, Palm Coast, Florida 32142-0234.

University of California, Berkeley Wellness Letter (monthly) from University of California, Berkeley Wellness Letter, P.O. Box 359148, Palm Coast, Florida 32035.

Magazines

Cooking Light: The Magazine of Food and Fitness (bimonthly) from Cooking Light, P.O. Box 830549, Birmingham, Alabama 35282-9810—(800) 336-0125.

FDA Consumer from Food and Drug Administration, Office of Consumer Affairs, HFE-88, 5600 Fishers Lane, Rockville, Maryland 20857.

In Health (bimonthly) from In Health, P.O. Box 56963, Boulder, Colorado 80322-6863—(800) 274-2522.

Mail-Order Publication Centers

Lowfat Lifeline, 52 Condolea Court, Lake Oswego, Oregon, 97035—(503) 636-1559—write or call for free catalog.

Cooking Light Books, P.O. Box 2463, Birmingham, Alabama, 35201—write for free catalog.

Computer Software

USDA Dietary Analysis Program (reliable software you can access by modem for the cost of the phone call!)—contact David B. Haytowitz, Human Nutrition Information Service, U.S. Department of Agriculture, 6505 Belcrest Road, Room 315, Hyattsville, Maryland 20782—(301) 436-5194.

Food Poisoning and Food Safety

USDA's Meat and Poultry Hotline—1-800-535-4555 (in Washington, D.C. area, call 447-3333).
  Publications available through the Meat and Poultry Hotline:
- *The Safe Food Book: Your Kitchen Guide* (1988).
- *Safe Food to Go—A Guide to Packing Lunches, Picnicking & Camping Out* (1986).
- *Talking About Turkey: How to Buy, Store, Thaw, Stuff, and Prepare Your Holiday Bird* (1987).

Food News for Consumers (4 issues per year)—published by the USDA Food Safety and Inspection Service. Order from Superintendent of Documents, U.S. Government Printing Office, Washington, D.C. 20402.

Other USDA Publications

For a listing of "Publications for Sale," and for a free copy of *Nutrition and Your Health: Dietary Guidelines for Americans* (1990), contact Human Nutrition Information Service, USDA, 6505 Belcrest Road, Hyattsville, Maryland 20782—(301) 436-7725.

Locally-Available Publicly-Funded Nutrition Professionals

For a listing of *Cooperative Extension Service Home Economists*, check in your phone book for the nearest Cooperative Extension Office. Cooperative Extension may be listed under USDA (in the blue pages) or as part of your state's land-grant university (also in the blue pages), and is usually cross-referenced in the white pages under "Cooperative Extension."

For *State and Local Health Department Nutrition Specialists*, check with your phone book in the blue pages for listings under your state and local health departments.

Color Additives

Division of Colors and Cosmetics, FDA (HFF-442), 200 C Street, S.W., Washington, D.C. 20204—write for information regarding the names of color additives used and the types of products in which they're used.

Consulting Nutritionists

For *Registered Dietitians* available for consultation in your area, send your request plus a stamped, self-addressed business-size envelope to: American Dietetic Association, 216 West Jackson Boulevard, Suite 800, Chicago, Illinois 60606.

Special Resources

Nancy Crevier, Natural Foods Consultant, 10 Bausola Road, Andover, Connecticut 06232.

American Dry Bean Board (great bean recipes!), 4502 Avenue I, Scottsbluff, Nebraska 69361—(308) 632-1258.

Lead-Testing Kit

Frandon Enterprises, Inc., P.O. Box 300231, 511 North 48th Street, Seattle, Washington, 98103—(800) 359-9000—Kits available for testing water and for testing surfaces, such as ceramicware.

Mail-Order Organic Food Suppliers

For a list of mail-order organic food suppliers, contact Americans for Safe Food, Center for Science in the Public Interest, 1501 Sixteenth Street, N.W., Washington, D.C. 20036—(202) 332-9110.

Organic-Food-Certifying Agencies

More than 40 certifying agencies are active in the U.S. An organization that keeps track of these groups is Americans for Safe Food, Center for Science in the Public Interest, 1501 Sixteenth Street, N.W., Washington, D.C. 20036—(202) 332-9110.

A sampling of organizations follows:

- Organic Foods Production Association of North America (OFPANA), P.O. Box 31, Belchertown, Massachusetts 01007—(413) 323-4531—This is a trade association that "certifies the certifiers," but does not certify foods.
- Natural Organic Farmers Association (NOFA)—several chapters are active in New England. For general information, contact: Julie Rawson, RFD #2, Barre, Massachusetts 01005—(617) 355-2853.

- California Certified Organic Farmers (CCOF), P.O. Box 8136, Santa Cruz, California 95061—(408) 423-2263.
- Organic Crop Improvement Association Inc. (OCIA), P.O. Box 819, Kearney, Nebraska 68848—(308) 234-2645.
- Organic Growers and Buyers Association, P.O. Box 9747, Minneapolis, Minnesota 55440—(612) 378-8335.
- Bio-Dynamic Farming and Gardening Association, Inc., P.O. Box 550, Kimberton, Pennsylvania 19442—(215) 327-2420.

Index

Recipe
Index

ABOUT THE AUTHOR

Sue Gebo, MPH, RD, registered dietitian and consulting nutritionist, received her degrees in nutrition from Cornell University and the University of Michigan. She is currently a consultant for such academic institutions as Wesleyan University and the University of Connecticut Medical School, and has provided consulting services for many corporations, including ITT Hartford Insurance Group, Phoenix Mutual, Pfizer, Honeywell, and United Technologies. She has appeared on numerous TV and radio programs dealing with diet and health issues, and is a sought-after speaker on nutrition topics.